MANX ELECTRIC

MIKE GOODWYN

Published by Platform 5 Publishing Ltd., Wyvern House, Sark Road, Sheffield S2 4HG, England.

Printed in England by Alden Press, Osney Mead, Oxford OX2 0EF and BDC Printing Services Ltd., Slack Lane, Derby, DE3 3FL.

ISBN 1 872524 52 4

CONTENTS

1. An Outline History of the Manx Electric Railway 3
2. Traffic 20
3. Tickets 31
4. Rolling Stock 36
5. Overhead Equipment 68
6. Buildings and Premises 78
7. Training of Motormen 84
8. The Snaefell Mountain Railway 91

BIBLIOGRAPHY:

Pearson, F.K.: Isle of Man Tramways; David & Charles, 1968. THE ENGINEER; ENGINEERING; ELECTRICAL REVIEW; MODERN TRAMWAY; RAILWAY MAGAZINE; MANX TRANSPORT REVIEW; TRAMWAY & RAILWAY WORLD; MANX ELECTRIC RAILWAY SOCIETY.

Below: Opening day on the new Douglas – Laxey Electric Tramway with Car No. 7 and trailer 15 at the present Port Jack Crossing with the now demolished Douglas Bay Hotel in the background. The steam roller was being used in roadway construction work. Both motor car and trailer are still in regular service. *Manx Electric Railway*

ACKNOWLEDGEMENTS

The generous help and assistance of the following in the preparation of this booklet is most gratefully acknowledged with very sincere thanks: Mr. Robert Smith, Transport Executive, IoM Government Department of Tourism and Transport; Mr. John R. Gordon, Traffic Superintendent, and Mr. M. Graham Warhurst, Assistant Operations Superintendent; Mr. J. Maurice Faragher, Engineering Superintendent, and Mr. George Lawson, Assistant Engineering Superintendent; Mr. J.R. Oates, formerly General Manager, IoM National Transport Ltd, now General Manager, IoM Passenger Transport Board; Mr. Darryl Gribbin, Rolling Stock Superintendent; Mr. Harry L. Jones, Station Master, Douglas, Derby Castle and Mr. Alan Corlett, central administrative staff; Mr. Harold Gilmore, formerly General Manager & Engineer, MER Board, who has borne the brunt of technical and administrative queries over many years; Mr. George Lawson, formerly Hotels & Catering Manager, MER Board; the late Mr. Alan McMullen of Laxey and the late Lewis Gale, both formerly Rolling Stock Superintendents, MER Board; Mr. Tom Beckett, Kearsley, near Bolton; Mr. J.G. Fenton, Manchester; Mr. Ian L. Cormack, Cambuslang, Scotland; Mr. William P. Cubbon; Mr. Richard Dodge; Mr. A.H. Stewart, formerly General Manager, IoM Railway Company; the late Ambrose Hampton, formerly General Manager, Douglas Corporation Transport Department; Mr. Alan Kelly of Douglas; Miss Anne Harrison and her staff of the Manx Museum Library & Archives Department, Douglas; Mr. Olaf Laursen of Denmark; Mr. Harley McKnight of Ramsey; Dr C.C. Thornburn, Birmingham and Mr. Andrew D. Young of Missouri, USA; Mr. Jim Kennedy and Mr. Graham McFarlane, IoM Department of Tourism & Transport; Mr. Tony Gillett, IoM Department of Transport. Last but by no means least, Mr. Alex Townsend of Douglas, whose constant assistance, especially in the production stages, has been invaluable; and to all who have in any way assisted.

Mike Goodwyn
Douglas, July 1993

Front Cover: Winter saloon No. 19 and crossbench trailer No. 43 pass the cliffs at Howstrake on 29th May 1979. *M.R. Taplin*

CHAPTER ONE

AN OUTLINE HISTORY OF THE MANX ELECTRIC RAILWAY

Through inception, bankruptcy, two world wars, nationalisation, partial closure and the reigns of six monarchs, what is nowadays known as the Manx Electric Railway has provided a vital and quite unique link for the Island's northeastern seaboard. As a technological marvel born into an age of gaslamps and horse-drawn carriages, this remarkable inheritance prospered and continued to survive as a means of communication and as an increasingly vital adjunct to Island tourism. It was and is the only American-style electric interurban railway in the British Isles.

Prior to the coming of the Manx Electric, any communication between Douglas and Ramsey was dependent upon either a difficult and mountainous road via Laxey or a far longer and more circuitous route via St. John's and Kirk Michael. The other option was to use the coastal steamers and by the late 1870s, when investment in Manx tourist development was rising to its zenith, there were regular steamer services from Douglas to Laxey, Dhoon and Ramsey. The Manx Northern steam railway was opened in 1879 from Ramsey to St John's (where it connected with the Isle of Man Railway's Douglas–Peel line, opened in 1873) but this still left the entire north-eastern coast of the Island devoid of any direct rail link.

EARLY SCHEMES

That the surveyors of the Manx Northern drove their line to Ramsey along the western shore is scarcely surprising in view of the more difficult terrain elsewhere, but even by 1874, when the Isle of Man Railway was busy building its southern line to Castletown and Port Erin, the construction was proposed of a line from the Peel route near Quarter Bridge towards Hillberry and the back of Onchan and on down the south side of Groudle Glen, to the then-defunct Port Groudle. The real purpose of this terminal site is in some doubt, for the Groudle area was still an area of rough scrubland which was not developed until two decades later. Nothing further was heard of this scheme but on 1st March 1882, the Douglas, Laxey & Ramsey Railway Co. Ltd. was formed and a line surveyed from the Quarter Bridge via Ballameanagh and Glen Gawne, to Laxey. Despite a Prospectus, issued in August 1885, the scheme failed to attract support. Mr. George Noble Fell surveyed another northern route in 1887–8 for the section between Douglas and Laxey but construction never began. In September 1890 the Douglas, Laxey & Maughold Head Marine Drive & Tramway Co. Ltd. was registered in Douglas with a capital of £100,000, but no progress was made by this undertaking either. In 1891 an earlier Douglas, Laxey & Snaefell Railway scheme was revived and reappeared as Manx East Coast Railways, which planned a line, again leaving the IMR's Peel line at Quarter Bridge, via Tromode, Onchan and Groudle, to a point close to the Queen's Hotel in Laxey. Once again the project was stillborn and was duly followed by yet another proposal, this time for a "Douglas, Laxey & Dhoon Railway" which was to have begun from its own terminal in Douglas, in close proximity to the extant IMR Station at the top of the Harbour, then tunnelling through Bank Hill and out to the north of Douglas, eventually to reach the southern flank of Ballaragh at Bulgham Bay, at a mean height of 442 feet above sea level. Part of Fell's survey for this line was later to be utilised for the electric tramway scheme of 1893–4. Even after this electric line was in being, a rival plan for a railway between Laxey and Ramsey was proposed by an independent party and indeed sought to introduce a Bill in Tynwald, and which was actually granted on 9th April 1896. By October of the same year, the Isle of Man Tramways & Electric Power Co. Ltd. had also petitioned the Court for permission to introduce their own Bill for the construction of what is now termed "the Northern Line" of the Manx Electric, from Laxey to Ramsey and the opposition scheme was dropped.

DOUGLAS–GROUDLE

In 1892 Frederick Saunderson, backed by Alexander Bruce and A.J. Lusty, sought and obtained powers from Tynwald to develop part of the Howstrake Estates by driving a new roadway through from the north end of Douglas promenade, via Port Jack and Onchan Harbour to Groudle, and to construct a 3' 0" gauge railway or tramway along the route. The powers were transferred to Douglas Bay Estates Ltd., and in the spring of 1893 construction got under way of the first part of what was eventually to become the Manx Electric Railway. By May, rails and equipment were arriving by steamer and the erection of a Power House and car sheds was in hand at Port-e-Vada Creek, which was reclaimed from the sea and filled in for the purpose. A small jetty was built out into the Bay to receive shipments of rails and other constructional materials. The new line and its accompanying roadway necessitated the removal of over 100,000 tons of stone and soil. The Line's promoters had been keenly interested in the advantages of electric traction, then in its infancy, but considered that the Line's steep gradients and tight curves were unsuited to any form of conventional steam traction. Electrification of the Line was placed in the hands of Dr. Edward Hopkinson of Mather & Platt Ltd. electrical engineers and manufacturers of Salford Ironworks, Manchester, and 500 volts d.c. was chosen as the electrical pressure.

The first electric tramcars, numbered 1–3, together with six open trailer cars, were delivered by steamer in July and early August from their builders, G.F. Milnes & Co., of Birkenhead. Construction work was well on the way to completion and the cars and equipment were ready for use by 8th August. However, rather than use the already-proven under-running trolley for current collection from the overhead conductor wire, Hopkinson produced instead a patent bow collector, the unsatisfactory performance of which caused substantial and costly delays to the opening of the line. Not until 26th August did a car manage to get through to Groudle, where a new Hotel had been erected, and indeed licensed to sell alcohol from early in July, whilst the Glen itself was being developed as a scenic attraction. Two days after the first successful test car ran to Groudle and back, some sort of dress rehearsal service was operated, with members of the public being carried but not apparently paying for the ride, and it was not until 7th September 1893, that the line was officially opened for traffic and regular electric tramway services begun.

EXTENSION TO LAXEY

The new services operated with great success carrying over 20,000 passengers until the end of the season on 28th September, when operations were suspended to allow the contractors to take possession of the line in order to begin work on a new extension to Laxey, which was authorised on 17th November 1893, under the Douglas & Laxey Electric Tramway Act, 1893. This legislation also included incidental powers for the government to have a statutory inspection carried out prior to opening. The impressive Groudle Viaduct was built, the line doubled throughout its length through to Laxey, where it terminated close to the existing Car Depot near Rencell Road. The main contractor for the Laxey line was Brabner of Edinburgh whose resident representative was a Mr. Farquharson. The major civil engineering works including the three arch viaduct at Groudle, 130 ft in length,

were carried out by a notable local contractor Mr. Mark Carine, who was later to build the original Noble's Hospital in Douglas. The electrical work both in respect of supply and distribution, power stations and battery house, poles and wires and the equipment of the cars themselves, was superintended by Dr. Edward Hopkinson, by now managing director of Mather & Platt. He was assisted by Messrs. Ramage, later W. Wood (resident electrical engineer) Hewitt (resident mechanical engineer) and Josua Shaw as his assistant and with Mr. Barnard as the representative of sub contractor Callender & Co. who supplied the underground feeders. The line was laid in 56 lbs/yard flat bottomed rail rolled by Charles Cammell & Company Ltd and was inspected by Messrs. Rich and Cardew of the Board of Trade's Railway Inspectorate on 27th July 1894, although Major Cardew the electrical expert was somewhat aghast at the use of 500 volts, although he claimed to be aware that this was regarded as entirely standard in the USA and elsewhere. The line's official opening took place on the following afternoon and whilst the original introduction of the Groudle section in 1893 may have been a relatively low-key affair this time the stage was set for celebration. To supply additional traction current, a new power station was built at Laxey, some distance downstream and nearer the shore from the Car Depot, suitable for both feed and cooling water supply and in closer proximity to Laxey Harbour, where coal stocks were delivered by steamer.

To accommodate the increased traffic and length of line, the company purchased additional rolling stock, consisting of Cars Nos. 4–9 with another batch of trailer cars. The trailers, however, whilst of open crossbench design, were also equipped with clerestory roofs and bulkheads, unlike the original open toastrack trailers.

THE ISLE OF MAN TRAMWAYS & ELECTRIC POWER Co. Ltd.

All of the rolling stock now bore the title 'Douglas & Laxey Electric Tramway' on the rocker or dash panels, since the line's legal ownership had passed to the new Douglas & Laxey Electric Tramway Co. Ltd. in March 1894. This concern, after buying the horse tramway along Douglas promenade, changed its title to the "Isle of Man Tramways & Electric Power Co. Ltd." on 30th April 1894, and ncreased its authorised capital to £150,000. The Douglas horse tramway (opened in 1876) was handed over to its new owners on 1st May, and the two lines thereafter operated as a combined undertaking, with Mr. J. Aldworth as Manager.

The main objective in taking over the Douglas horse tramway was to provide the means towards its eventual electrification and the running of Manx Electric cars right down to the Victoria Pier. Negotiations for this project began shortly after, and continued fruitlessly for many years. The failure of the line to reach its obvious terminal in Douglas was to cost some millions of passengers in the years that followed. As part of the price of acquiring a lease of the horse tramway route, the Isle of Man Tramways Co. was obliged to agree to build a new tramway to serve Upper Douglas, and this materialised as the Upper

Right: Car No. I, built by G.F. Milnes & Co., Birkenhead, in 1893, and re-equipped with Brush Type D trucks in 1903, seen here at Laxey in 1979, is now one of the two oldest electric tramcars in the world, still at work on its original line.
W P Cubbon

Left: The first passenger service from Douglas to Laxey, posed on Groudle south curve, 28th July 1894.
Mather & Platt

Right: Car No. 2 of 1893 and a lightweight crossbench trailer, at the temporary Laxey terminus in July, 1894. The fence in the background bordered Rencell Road.
Mather & Platt

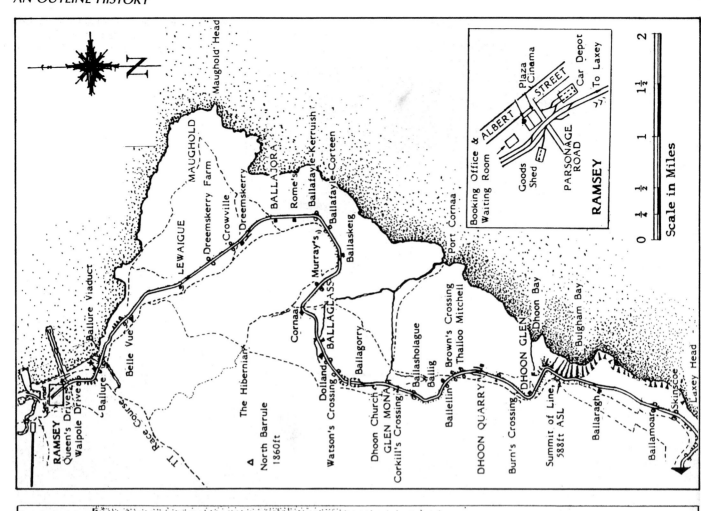

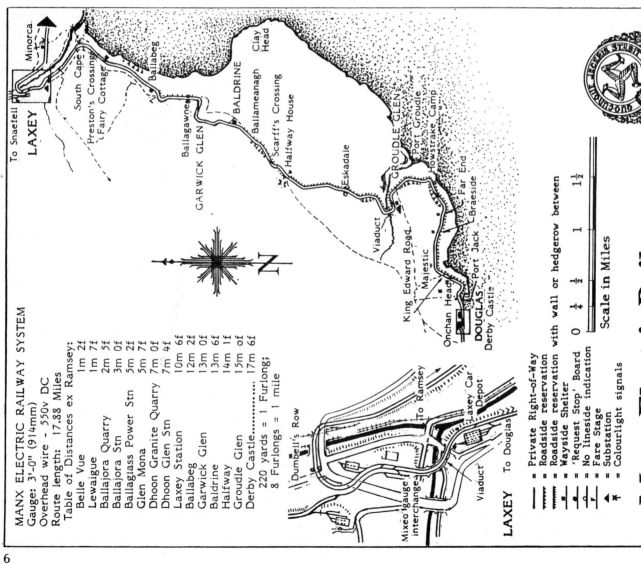

MANX ELECTRIC RAILWAY SYSTEM

Gauge: 3'-0" (914mm)
Overhead wire - 550v DC
Route length: 17.88 Miles

Table of Distances ex Ramsey:

Belle Vue	1m 2f
Lewaigue	1m 7f
Ballajora Quarry	2m 5f
Ballajora Stn	3m 0f
Ballaglass Power Stn	5m 2f
Glen Mona	5m 7f
Dhoon Granite Quarry	7m 0f
Dhoon Glen Stn	7m 4f
Laxey Station	10m 6f
Ballabeg	12m 2f
Garwick Glen	13m 0f
Baldrine	13m 6f
Halfway	14m 1f
Groudle Glen	15m 0f
Derby Castle............	17m 6f

220 yards = 1 Furlong;
8 Furlongs = 1 mile

LAXEY To Douglas

⌐	=	Private Right-of-Way
┴	=	Roadside reservation with wall or hedgerow between
⊥	=	Roadside reservation
⊢	=	'Request Stop' Board
o	=	No lineside indication
F	=	Fare Stage
▲	=	Substation
✦	=	Colourlight signals

Scale in Miles
0   ¼   ½   1   1½

Manx Electric Railway

Left: Car No. 7 on layover at Laxey Goods Shed siding in 1977, resplendent in its last traditional MER repaint. *Mike Goodwyn*

Below: Car No. 6 and Trailer 41 running past Laxey Car Depot in 1981 with "Isle of Man Railways" lettering. *W P Cubbon*

Douglas cable tramway in 1895. 1895 was occupied almost entirely by the building of this cable line, made no easier by the endless squabbling and dissention that surrounded its construction, as well as the creation of the Snaefell Mountain Tramway, which is dealt with in detail in chapter eight.

THE EXTENSION TO RAMSEY

Notwithstanding the application to Tynwald for the independent Laxey and Ramsey Railway Co. scheme, the Isle of Man Tramways & Electric Power Co. Ltd., petitioned on 25th March 1897 for their own extension along the same route, and this was duly embodied in the Douglas & Laxey Tramway (Extension to Ramsey) Act passed on 13th May 1897. The official date of the commencement of construction work on this section is often given as 1st November of that year, but it is quite clear that considerable work had been in hand ever since August. Through the ensuing year, over 1,000 men were at work on the new extension, with three steam locomotives engaged on hauling material and spoil trains. One of the locos was an Andrew Barclay 0–4–0T engine, owned by the IoMT&EP and later sold to Douglas Corporation for use on their Injebreck Reservoir scheme; the other two consisted of Isle of Man Railway locomotive No. 2, DERBY, and Manx Northern Railway No. 1, RAMSEY.

The work involved in driving the new line to Ramsey was on a large and expensive scale, and despite the clouds of financial anxiety that began to gather, was well carried out. A series of three viaducts was built, at Laxey, Ballaglass and Ballure, just outside Ramsey, to which point the tramway was essentially complete by July 1898. Various changes of plan had affected the actual route across Maughold and the approach to Ramsey town. The original scheme involved the line running down to the shore at Port-e-Vullen and some of the civil engineering earthworks were partially completed and may still be seen; this projected route was then to have run along a new promenade and enter Ramsey along the seafront to terminate close to the Queen's Pier. The Ramsey Commissioners, having rejected an exploratory proposal for the line to terminate at Walpole Drive, then agreed to the shore line and proposed an extension between the Queen's Pier and the Harbour. In the event the present route into Ramsey, crossing Ballure Glen by means of a twin-span viaduct built some distance inland from the shore was adopted, and cut through to Walpole Avenue before making its final approach to the terminus behind the Palace (later Plaza) building, along the backs of the houses in Waterloo Road. The presence of unstable geological conditions along the shoreline immediately south of the Ballure stream may well have played a far more significant part in the decision to site the present route than has hitherto been appreciated.

The electric tramway to Ramsey, which was still single track through

Left: IMR Loco No. 2 'DERBY', built by Beyer Peacock in 1873, was hired in 1897 for the building of the Laxey-Ramsey line. It is shown here just south of the Little Egypt curve, alongside Ramsey Road, Laxey.
Manx Museum Archives

Right Car No. 5 and wagon V3 at Derby Castle on 2nd September 1954.
Mike Goodwyn

Left: One of the two 19'' gauge steam locos ('BEE') of the Great Laxey Mining Co, whose main line tunnelled underneath the MER at Laxey. The mouth of the tunnel from the upper Washing Floors may still be seen. *A D Lamberton*

Below: MANX ELECTRIC STEAM: The IoMT&EP's own 0–4–0ST built by Andrew Barclay in 1892 was used in construction work, but later sold to Douglas Corporation Waterworks who named it 'INJEBRECK' for building the new West Baldwin Reservoir in 1900–5.

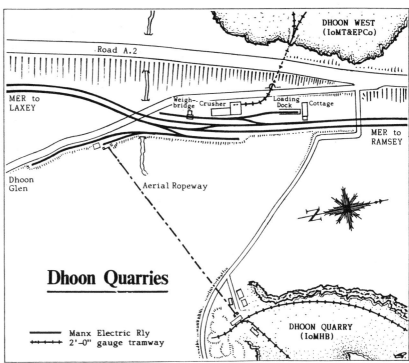

Dhoon Quarries

———— Manx Electric Rly
+++++ 2'–0" gauge tramway

Ballagorry cutting, was completed as far as a temporary terminus on the south side of Ballure Glen and passenger services commenced to this point on 2nd August 1898. A shed for six cars was erected in the field by the side of the line; although the building was later dismantled and re-erected as the present Ramsey Car Depot at Parsonage Road, the pits are still discernible in the public garden at the original site today.

The line finally reached its present extent in the summer of 1899, when the terminus at Parsonage Road, Ramsey, was suitably inaugurated (in pouring rain) on 24th July 1899. This brought the coastal line's length to 17¾ miles all of which was by now double track throughout. A section in Walpole Avenue in Ramsey was constructed in grooved Belgian tram rail and equipped with bracket arm side poles because the Ramsey Commissioners insisted on planning to surface the entire width of the road; nine decades later the work still remains to be carried out. The final section from Queen's Pier Road to Parsonage Road in Ramsey was roughly graded and temporary track laid in to enable the service to be introduced for the 1899 season. It was evidently the intention to ease the grades and curves on this section as part of the forthcoming winter's programme of work, but this, like several other intentions, was overtaken by the course of events.

COMMERCIAL ACTIVITIES & FREIGHT TRAFFIC

The Isle of Man Tramways & Electric Power Co. Ltd. had a number of intentions – not all of them related to utilities, that pointed the way to a very sizable conglomerate. In addition to their transport and electricity supply businesses, the company also set out to develop the Dhoon granite quarry and an additional quarry at Ballajora; licensed hotels and refreshment rooms were built at Laxey, Douglas, the Bungalow, Snaefell Summit and Dhoon Glen, and plans were evidently afoot to supply the liquid requirements of these and other hostelries from a new brewery, perhaps part of a much wider involvement that was destined to get no further.

The Tramway's goods and stone traffic was energetically developed into an important segment of the business as a whole. The output from Dhoon Quarry was originally handled by two-wheeled horse carts with a capacity of 1,700 lbs. and these carried the stone to the railway wagons, and again from the rail wagons to the quays in Ramsey for loading aboard ship. In an endeavour to avoid this intermediate handling as well as for reasons of political expediency (after the Ramsey Commission demanded 5% of the gross earnings of the tramway's half-mile length within their boundary and disputed terminal arrangements in the town) the IoMT&EP Co. then placed an order for four patent road-rail wagons with the Bonner Rail Wagon Co. of Toledo, Ohio, USA, in May 1899. It seems that only three such wagons arrived from across the Atlantic, and these entered service on 1st September 1899. The Bonner wagon itself consisted of a four-wheeled horse cart 13' 0" long, 6' 0" wide and with drop sides and ends 30" deep. Each wagon was equipped with a separate four-wheeled railway underframe, onto which the road carts were loaded by means of inclined ramps. Some ramps were portable but it would appear that semi-permanent sets of ramps were provided at Douglas and Ramsey. Once in position on its

underframe, the road wagon was locked into position by means of latches. One account states that the hand-operated latch gear had to be closed after loading, but other sources indicate that the latch gear was kept in the closed position by gravity and had to be operated by hand only in order to release the carts for unloading. At the time of the Bonner wagons' introduction to the Island, it was stated that similar vehicles were in fairly widespread use in Toledo, Detroit and elsewhere in the United States; an illustrated article on the Manx use of Bonner wagons appeared in STREET RAILWAY REVIEW for 15th February 1900. Shortly before this date, Bruce had placed a further order for an additional six Bonner wagons, but the order was repudiated at the Company meeting of 24th May 1900, in the light of the financial chaos that had by then arisen.

Of the three Bonner wagons delivered, all existing photographs show only any two being hauled on the railway, usually by one of the 19–22 or 24–27 class cars, and it seems more than likely that three fully laden Bonner wagons would have been beyond the tractive (or braking) capacity of any passenger car. The Bonner wagons were not numbered or listed in the official freight rolling stock lists. Although documentation is scanty, the wagons appear to have been well used until an accident on 24th January 1914, at the curve above Minorca, Laxey, everafterward known as "Bonner Corner" which apparently eliminated not only two of the Bonner wagons, but also the MER's electric locomotive (from which only the centre cab apparently survived) as well. The fate of the third Bonner wagon is unknown. Horse carts were eventually eliminated at the Dhoon quarries when a 2' 0" gauge tramway was built from the Dhoon West quarry through a narrow tunnel to the MER sidings, and an aerial ropeway was erected to similarly carry the output from Dhoon Quarry.

A former Blackpool & Fleetwood Tramroad car photographed in the early 1920s, showing an obvious similarity to the MER's Winter Saloons.

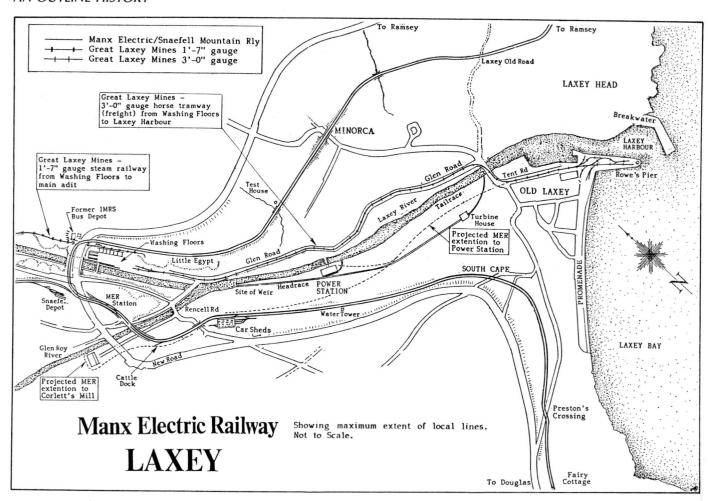

Great Laxey Mines –
3'-0" gauge horse tramway
(freight) from Washing Floors
to Laxey Harbour

Great Laxey Mines –
1'-7" gauge steam railway
from Washing Floors to
main adit

Projected MER
extention to
Power Station

Projected MER
extention to
Corlett's Mill

Manx Electric Railway
Showing maximum extent of local lines.
Not to Scale.
LAXEY

Two views of the MER's Bonner patent Road-Rail wagons of 1899 in use. The upper view shows two of the wagons being towed by a car of the 14–18 class whilst the lower picture shows the road wagons being unloaded from their four-wheeled underframes. *Manx Museum Library & Archives collection*

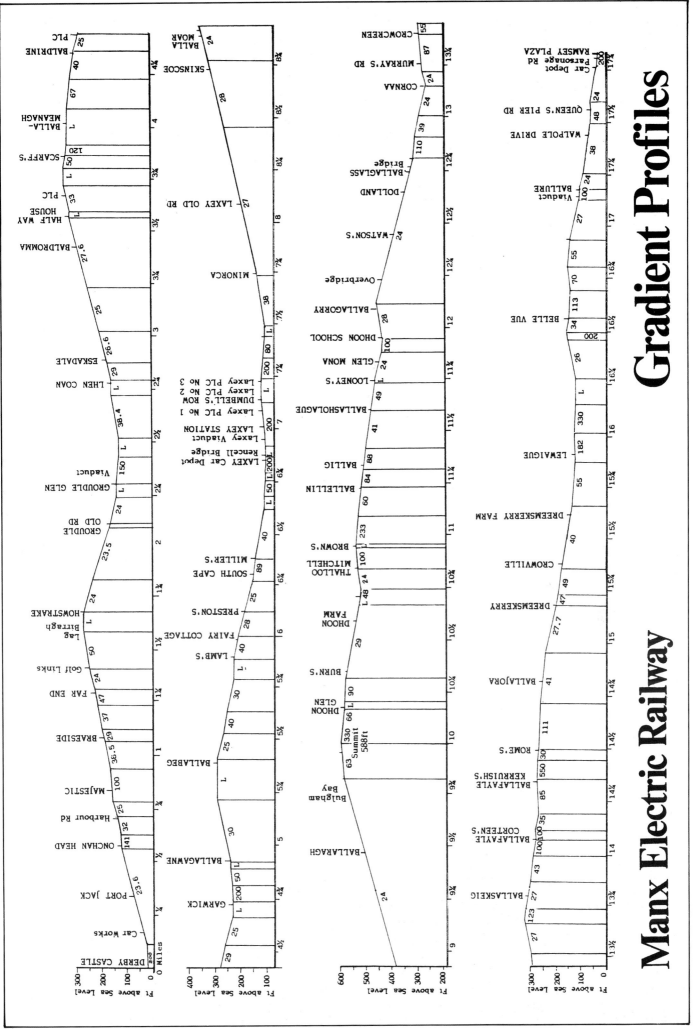

Gradient Profiles

Manx Electric Railway

Left One of the MER's three Ford Model 'T' char-a-bancs. Registered No. MN 4418 of 1926, unloading passengers from the Bungalow at the Alt entrance to Tholt-y-Will, Sulby Glen in the late 1920s.
Manx Electric Railway

Below: Seventy-four years after the photograph on page 5 was taken, Car No.2, in use as a winter works car with a snow gang, waits for the first northbound car of the day to pass at Dhoon Quarry in January, 1967. *Mike Goodwyn*

Quite outside these insular financial and other problems, some of those involved in the IoMT&EP Co. had considerable interests elsewhere. A syndicate formed in 1895 to build an eight-mile electric tramway north from Blackpool along the Fylde coast issued a prospectus as the Blackpool & Fleetwood Tramroad Co. Ltd., in June 1897, listing Alexander Bruce (by this time chairman of the IoMT&EP) as a director, whilst Mather & Platt were to supply the electrical equipments under the personal supervision of Dr. Edward Hopkinson, whilst Dick, Kerr were to be contractors for the permanent way and buildings. This line was duly authorised under the Blackpool and Fleetwood Tramroad Act, 1896, and construction started at the Fleetwood end on 19th July 1897. In March 1898 the company appointed Mr. John Cameron from the Isle of Man as its Secretary and Manager. Mr Cameron had started his professional life as a ganger on the Midland Railway's Settle and Carlisle line, then under construction, but since 1878 had been resident in the Island, firstly as a sub-contractor for the construction of the Manx Northern Railway, and from 1879 (the year this line opened) as Secretary and Manager. Under his control, the MNR became the cheapest-worked railway undertaking anywhere in the British Isles. In 1886 he was responsible for the new St John's and Foxdale line (under a nominally separate concern, and opened the same year). He was later employed as a consultant during the building of the Douglas and Laxey electric tramway, and in the construction of the Snaefell Mountain Railway in 1895.

Mr. Cameron was held in very high esteem in the Island and his departure for the Fylde was marked by many recognitions of respect and public regret. There was an enormous parting banquet at the Mitre Hotel, Ramsey, followed by a presentation by the entire MNR staff at the Masonic Hall, Ramsey, on the following day. A group of 43 Manxmen and their families followed Mr. Cameron to the Fylde, where they were employed on the Blackpool and Fleetwood line which opened for traffic on 30th July 1898. To work this hugely successful undertaking, the B&FT bought thirteen open crossbench cars, later joined by five "Winter Saloons" and all of which possessed a remarkable similarity to the curious rolling stock of the MER, albeit for the wider 4' 8½" gauge. The Blackpool and Fleetwood line passed into municipal ownership in 1919 and remains in operation today. It is an odd coincidence of traction history that both the Blackpool & Fleetwood and the Manx Electric, which had a good deal in common, should both have survived to the present day, outliving the rise and eclipse of traditional electric tramways in the British Isles.

LIQUIDATION

By the time the Bonner wagons had been put into service, and the route to Ramsey fully open, the enormous capital investment involved in the whole of the IoMT&EP Company's business meant that time would be needed for trade to build up and provide a healthy return, but time was not on the side of the undertaking. The costs of funding this enormous enterprise had far exceeded estimates and, as was later to be proved in Court, some dividends had been paid out of capital and not earnings. The first signs of really serious trouble occurred in January 1899, when the Company Secretary, Mr W.E. Young, resigned after making his objections known to the Auditors in respect of what would nowadays be referred to as "creative accounting" or worse. On 1st February 1900, Parr's Bank withdrew its underwriting of Dumbell's Bank, and two days later this Douglas bank, being unable to meet its obligations, closed its doors and sparked off the bankruptcy and liquidation not only of the IoMT&EP Co., but a significant number of other Manx businesses as well.

As a result of the financial disaster that closed upon the IoM Tramways & Electric Power Company's empire, both the horse and cable tramways in Douglas passed to Corporation ownership, whilst the rest was acquired from the Liquidator by the newly formed Manx Electric Railway Co. Ltd., which took over the Douglas–Ramsey and the Snaefell Mountain lines and their associated hotels and glens from 18th August 1902.

THE MANX ELECTRIC RAILWAY Co. Ltd.

The new company soon found itself faced with considerable problems: Because this electric tramway had, in all respects, been an electric traction pioneer, much if not most of its original equipment was obsolete, outdated and outmoded by the technical advances and developments that had taken place in the preceding decade. To bring the line's technology up to date, the MER Co. brought in leading consultants Kincaid, Waller, Manville and Dawson to advise. The consultants' subsequent recommendations were extensive. Much of the rolling stock was re-equipped with new equal wheel bogie trucks, Belgian traction motors, American General Electric control gear and American air brakes. Major changes in power generation and distribution saw an end to direct current dynamos, with high tension a.c. generation instead, working through four lineside sub-stations equipped with rotary converters. The original Power House at Douglas was superseded altogether and the generating stations at Laxey (partly hydro-electric) and Ballaglass thenceforth became the main sources of supply; the seasonal Snaefell power station was retained. By the end of 1906, the Manx Electric was as technically up-to-date as any of its contemporaries and despite being grossly overcapitalised, produced a reasonable return on investment.

Over the years that followed, the Manx Electric system became a most valued Island institution, serving both resident and visitor alike. With its operating methods, its exquisite environment and its unusual and increasingly antique rolling stock, the MER had no parallel in the British Isles. Economically it managed to worry its way through the late twenties and the troubled thirties, although the 1928–32 period proved to be exacting for a number of reasons, with the onset of bus and coach competition, one serious accident and three major setbacks.

MISHAPS

Despite an accident on 17th September 1908, which resulted in some injuries, and the death of a conductor who fell between a car and trailer near the Douglas Bay Hotel on 3rd August of the following year, the Manx Electric had been remarkably free of serious mishaps.

Accident at Ballabeg 1928.

On 8th August 1928, Car No. 1 and Trailer 39 were running heavily laden down from Ballabeg, and had reached a point some distance south of Fairy Cottage when they were hailed by two members of the "Poles and Wires" gang, who wanted a lift down to Laxey. The carset came to a dead stand and was held whilst the workmen tied their ladder onto the footboard of the trailer. Just as the carset was ready to move, Car 16 and Trailer 56, also heavily laden, came round the curve running at its normal speed. Car 16's motorman could only have sighted the standing cars as he rounded the bend, a matter of only 90 ft ahead. He applied the brakes (and bailed out) before a severe rear-end collision took place. The rear part of Trailer 39 was "reduced to matchwood" whilst the Douglas end platform of Car 16 was severely crushed by its trailer, in addition to the direct impact damage between the front of Car 16 and Trailer 39. A total of 32 people were injured in the accident, four seriously, and a combination of a Douglas-bound MER car and a passing Manxland motor bus took the injured to hospital in Douglas. The most seriously hurt was 22-year-old Lillian Edith Stillard of Alum Park, Birmingham, who suffered severe leg injuries. Others had compound fractures or impact injuries, some caused through jumping off car 16 onto the lineside just before the collision.

With one Manx exception, all of the injured were holidaymakers equally divided between Manchester and Birmingham. The accident provoked an official inquiry under the Regulation of Railways Act, 1896, and this opened in Douglas on 13th September 1928, under the chairmanship of Mr. W.H. Blaker, AMICE. The Inquiry heard from the MER Manager, Mr. Frank Edmondson, that over 60 million passengers had been carried on the line without incident, and that steps had been taken to ensure that nothing like this would ever happen again. Amongst these measures was the erection of red and white "Curve Boards" at the entry and exit to each blind curve, between which cars are not permitted to come to a stand, or, if forced to do so, the conductor must at once be sent back to the entry board, ready to stop any following car. The only other noteworthy accident occurred on 3rd August 1955, when Cars Nos. 14 and 22 contested the right-of-way near Lewaigue, whilst single-line working was in force owing to track repairs. Both cars were damaged and four people were hurt, fortunately none seriously.

Fire at Laxey Car Depot 1930.

The first of the three major setbacks of the 1930–2 period occurred on the night of Saturday 5th April 1930, when losses estimated to exceed £10,000 were incurred by a disastrous fire at Laxey Car Depot. The depot was normally unstaffed after 12.30 p.m. on Saturdays, but about 11.00 p.m. the alarm was raised when the building was found

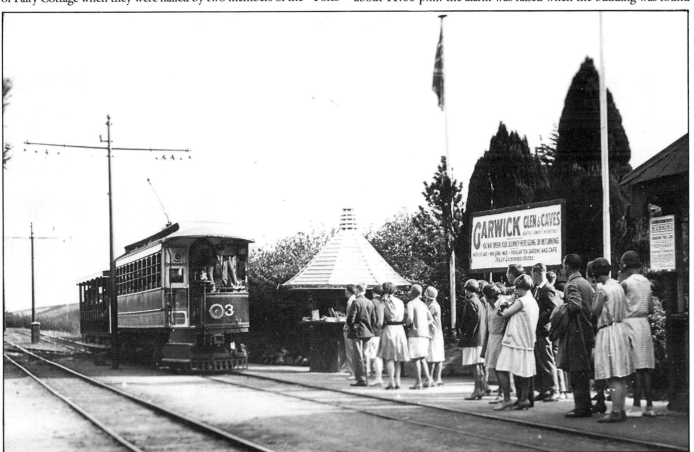

Car No. 3 and a lightweight trailer coming to a stand at Garwick Glen station in the 1920s. This car was a victim of the Laxey Depot fire of 1930.
Manx Electric Railway

Left: The 70-hp. Victor Water Turbine installed at Laxey in 1899. The casing housed two independent 12″ diam. horizontal turbines with direct-coupled shafts. The plant was remotely controlled from the main Power Station by two ¼ hp. Lundell valve motors (one of which can be seen on the plating at the centre of the picture). The 720 rpm. turbine drove the 520-volt bipolar dynamo and booster (on the extreme right) producing 160 Amps.

Manx Electric Railway

Left: The twin 400 hp. Bellis & Morcom triple expansion compound steam engines installed at Laxey Power Station in 1903–4, were coupled to 7,000-volt 300 kW revolving field alternators designed by Societé l'Electricité et l'Hydraulique, Charleroi, Belgium.

Manx Electric Railway

Below left: The Ballaglass rotary converters, showing part of the switchgear supplied by Witting Eborall in the background. To the right of the switch panels in the far background can be seen the tops of the pair of 75 kW Kolben transformers, fed from the high-tension supply from Laxey, and used to supply the transformers.

Manx Electric Railway

Below: The Traction Battery House at Laxey, with 250 Chloride cells and a capacity of 560 Amp-hours at 500 Volts. Similar batteries were also maintained at Groudle and Ballaglass at the time.

Manx Electric Railway

Left: The morning after the Great Laxey Flood of 1930, with (above) the scene near St George's Woollen Mill, where the River had left its bed and taken to the Glen Road.
Manx Electric Railway

Left: Winter Saloon in winter: Car No.20 in a blizzard in January 1964, having arrived from Ramsey seven minutes late whilst all other out-of-town transport was at a standstill owing to icy roads.

Below: The northern limit of the line at Ballaragh South during repairs after the collapse of part of the retaining wall at Bulgham Bay. The 18-month-long civil engineering repair work at the site, which was sufficiently complete for tramcars to run through again from 10th July 1968.
Mike Goodwyn

to be well alight. A maroon was fired to summon the Laxey Fire Brigade whilst Mr J.P. Grime, a member of the Laxey Commissioners, sought to locate the nearby fire hydrant cover. This proved to have been covered over with a layer of tarmacadam by the incompetent Highways Board; whilst the Laxey Fire Brigade stood by impotently, frantic efforts were made for half-an-hour with picks before the hydrant was uncovered. By this time the building and its contents were engulfed in flames and the one hose that the Laxey Fire Brigade brought into play was ineffective. The doors of the Depot were opened in an effort to rescue some of the cars and two trailers, one already alight, were manhandled out of the building, but the opening of the doors had swept the blaze to the other end of the building, where it "devoured everything in its course." The height of the flames which burst through the roof were estimated at 55 ft. and glass windows in nearby properties were shattered by the heat. The Douglas Fire Brigade had by now arrived and got three hoses into play, fed by damming and pumping from the Glen Roy River. The fire was finally brought under control, but the depot and its contents were effectively destroyed. Four motor cars, Nos. 3, 4, 8 and 24, together with Trailers Nos. 34, 35, 38, 39, 40, 41 and 44, all three tower wagons, a mail van and tools and equipment had been consumed by the flames. Of the two trailers pushed out of the burning building, one, thought to be No. 50, was only scorched, but the other, No. 60, was substantially damaged, but later repaired. The cause of the fire was thought to have been a burning cigarette end or something inside one of the cars that had been put away on the Saturday lunchtime. As it was, the insurance cover was sufficient only to rebuild the depot and to purchase three new trailer car bodies from English Electric. The attendance of the Douglas Fire Brigade was charged at £20.1s.0d.

The Great Laxey Flood 1930.

The next disaster of the period was the Great Laxey Flood. At about 8.00 p.m. on the night of 17th September 1930, a major rainstorm began, and lashed the Island until 4.00 a.m., causing widespread and extensive damage to an extent unknown in living memory. Rainwater draining off the Island in torrents caused a swath of destruction with Castletown Harbour damaged and a bridge destroyed; Rushen Abbey and Ballasalla lay under four feet of floodwater; the centre section of Pulrose Bridge, near Douglas, was swept away and the nearby Power Station lay lifeless as the fires had had to be drawn as water reached the furnaces. The Ramsey rain-gauge had recorded 4.35" during the storm, and there was fearsome destruction at Glen Auldyn, Tromode and elsewhere. Countless cows, pigs, sheep and poultry had been washed away to be found drowned many miles away or out at sea, where bloated carcasses were to be seen from passing ships for many weeks thereafter.

The greatest concentration of damage had occurred in lower Laxey, where the devastation had resulted in the wholesale destruction of property and most of the district was by now devoid of electricity, water or sewerage. The course of the floodwater pouring down from the hills above Laxey had followed the rivers, but a weir, built by the IoM Tramways & Electric Power Co. Ltd. in 1899 to serve the then-new hydro-electric plant, had at some stage become so silted up by debris that as a result, the river had simply taken to the Glen Road instead, destroying hundreds of yards of the river bank, damaging premises and leaving behind over 4,000 tons of rubble. The river bridge at the MER's Power Station in Laxey had been swept away, the Power Station itself was useless, and a large portion of Rowe's Pier down at Laxey Harbour had also been damaged.

Since the commencement of the Laxey miners' strike in 1919 (which lasted for over three years until the Great Laxey Mining Company declared bankruptcy), the valley area had not been prosperous and many people were in no position to afford substantial property repairs and several had lost all of their household effects as well. Relief funds for the victims were set up and a series of law suits were entered against the Manx Electric Railway Co. blaming their weir as the direct cause of the swollen river leaving its normal course.

The case against the MER Co. was first set down in the Chancery Court in Douglas on 3rd November 1930, and commenced in earnest on 7th January 1931, before Deemster La Mothe, KC. The weir in question had actually been erected by the Assistant Engineer of the time, Mr. R.B. Newall, who had left the MER in 1916 to become the Engineer of the Londonderry & Lough Swilly and Letterkenny Railways in Ireland, and who appeared as a defence witness in Douglas to testify that the weir had been built by him under the direction of Josua Shaw, with a Mr. F. Nell as consultant. Some difficulty had evidently been experienced in getting a 40 ft. head of water to drive the hydro-electric turbine plant, and it became clear that modifications to the weir had been effected in 1899–1900, and again in 1910 for

reasons unknown. The MER's Advocate, Mr W P Cowley (later His Honour Deemster Sir Percy Cowley, a major figure in the campaign to save the MER in the 1950s) introduced several expert witnesses to testify that the damage done in Laxey was simply an Act of God. One of the experts, Mr. A.C. Dean, a Manchester consulting engineer, quoted the flow of floodwater at its peak as being 3,200 cubic feet (or 90 tons) per second. By the first week in February, the case had become the longest-running hearing in Manx legal history, and after the close of presentation, Deemster La Mothe said that he would deliver a written judgement, but granted an immediate and mandatory injunction against the MER Co. to remove at once the 4–5,000 tons of rubble and debris still blocking the river bed, and which was "level with the roadway." The judgement, handed down on 11th February 1931, held the Manx Electric wholly to blame for failing to keep the river bed clear after it became silted up through the action of their weir, which slowed down the natural flow of water, encouraging it to drop whatever sediment it was carrying. The Court ruled that the MER Co. must pay the considerable legal costs of the case.

Fire at Dhoon Glen 1932.

It is often said that misfortune is never a solitary traveller and often comes in threes, and the third disaster of the period involved the destruction by fire of the extensive Hotel and refreshment rooms at Dhoon Glen. The entire building was found to be on fire early on 3rd April 1932, and despite attempts to fight the blaze, the building was completely gutted. Since it was far beyond economic repair, and the insurance cover insubstantial, its remains were demolished, without replacement.

THE SECOND WORLD WAR

The Second World War brought a measure of unexpected prosperity as the Island was intensively used by the Royal Air Force, the Royal Navy and the Army for training and other purposes, and the movement of materials, personnel and their supplies provided a welcome source of revenue. In addition the Isle of Man fulfilled a major role as a vast internment camp, and was later used for large numbers of prisoners-of-war.

POST-WAR DECLINE

In 1945 the Manx Electric Railway featured in a motion picture produced by Independent Films Ltd. starring Deborah Kerr and Trevor Howard, and directed by Frank Lauder, called "I See a Dark Stranger." Placed on general release in 1946 the film was notable for innumerable Manx sequences, including one at Laxey station, where Deborah Kerr boarded an MER car.

The immediate postwar period saw the MER (and Island tourism) enjoying an Indian summer, but the Island's visiting industry began to decline markedly in the early 1950s. At first this was ascribed to the counter-attraction of the Festival of Britain in London, and the dismal failure of a local "Festival of Mann" but in fact was the start of the secular decline of the ensuing thirty years. Reduced visitor arrivals affected the MER with diminished revenue, and on the other side of the Railway's balance sheet was the rise in operating and other costs which precluded anything in the way of major renewals. An attempt to remove the statutory obligation of 1893 to operate winter services was made in 1954 but rejected in Tynwald. By the following year, 1955, the overall financial condition of the MER was giving rise to considerable concern, with overwhelming arrears of debenture stock payments, and precious little help could be expected from the Island's legislature which for years had regarded the MER Company (but not the local personnel) as a hated outsider in the Manx corridors of financial power, partly because of the ethnic origin of Mr. Schenk, (later Remnant) and others with the 1902 company, almost all of whom were now dead anyway. Unable to carry on indefinitely, the Company told Tynwald in December 1955 that in view of their deteriorating position, they would be quite unable to continue trading after 30th September 1955, but were willing to offer the entire property for sale at £70,000.

NATIONALISATION

Rightly perturbed by the threat to what had by now become one of the Island's major internal lifelines as well as a growing tourist facility of considerable merit, Tynwald then commissioned an "expert" report on the line and its future from British Railways. This report materialised as not so much an opinion on the cost of keeping the MER, but more an estimate for the construction of a new railway on the same site, built broadly to Southern Region standards. This inept and inappropriate report was widely savaged and quickly consigned to the wastebasket, and a new report commissioned, this time from people who

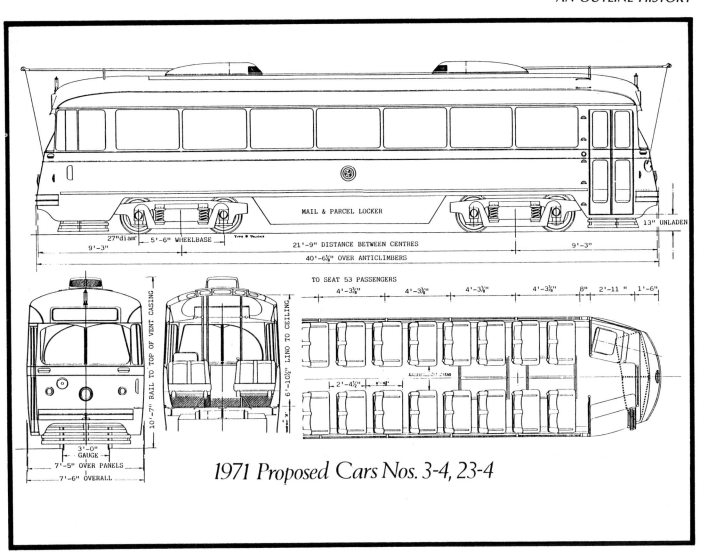

1971 Proposed Cars Nos. 3-4, 23-4

actually knew something of the operation and maintenance of electric tramways. After many vicissitudes the later report led to the nationalisation of the MER by Tynwald in its session of 6th November 1956. Authorisation, in the form of the Manx Electric Railway Act was signed on 17th April 1957, and which created a new Manx Electric Railway Board of Tynwald.

The first twenty years of government ownership and control of the MER saw a decade of relative plenty, where considerable sums of money were forthcoming and spent, although little seemed to be allocated to means of reducing the ever-increasing annual deficits. Examples of undesirable and unnecessary expenditure during this period would include the ill-advised painting of part of the rolling stock fleet in a lurid shade of green, and the restoration of the poorly-patronised motor bus service between the Bungalow and Tholt-y-Will with two elderly ex-Douglas Corporation Leyland Cubs. This period was followed by a lean decade, where only the most essential expenditure was permitted, and little investment or development of any sort was possible. On 20th January 1967, a suspect length of the retaining wall at Bulgham Bay (just north of Ballaragh, where the line is climbing to its summit of 588ft, higher than Blackpool Tower) finally collapsed, followed by an even more serious fall on 28th January. This effectively severed the Railway, but services were promptly rearranged so that cars from Ramsey and Douglas met simultaneously at "the Gap" and passengers transferred from one tramcar to another by walking along the adjacent roadway, which was also closed to all traffic. Two crossovers were installed on the Laxey side of the Gap to enable cars to reverse at the end-on terminii, and to shunt their trailers. This arrangement continued until 10th July 1967, when the enormous task of repairing and stabilising the cliff face along the formation level of the Railway had been sufficiently completed. The first car to reinstate the service was the 7.10 a.m. from Douglas to Ramsey consisting of car 21 and trailer 43.

In the face of increasingly likely outright closure on economic grounds, the MER was the subject of an unsuccessful privatisation bid by Rapid Transit Technical Services Ltd in 1971, which proposed a wholesale revision of the undertaking in an attempt to return it to viability, in conjunction with the manufacture of specialised electrical switchgear. The RTTS proposals were very detailed and involved the replacement of Derby Castle Carworks (not the running sheds) by a new, compact, works at Laxey where it could serve both the 3' 0" and 3' 6" gauge rolling stock; a rationalisation of rolling stock and the building of some new cars; the conversion to right-hand running to enable the (suitably equipped and modified) existing saloons to become front-entrance one man-operated cars; the single line and (lengthy) loop conversion and operation of the Laxey–Ramsey section and centralised traffic control by means of radio telephones. It also intended to vacate the then head offices and to re-equip the Snaefell cars to operate without the need for the Fell rail; other detail improvements related to marketing, ticketing, stations, power supply and distribution, permanent way and overhead equipment and much else.

THE TRANSMARK REPORT – CLOSURE & REOPENING

Despite the evident approval of the government, the last option dates demanded by the company expired without appropriate government action, and on 10th November 1972. Tynwald appointed "Transmark" to advise on the feasibility of the MER and the RTTS propositions, presumably with a view to implementing some of the ideas themselves. Transmark was a wholly-owned subsidiary of British Railways, a body scarcely noted for its acumen or successful innovation. It was as if the lessons of the 1955 reports had never been learned (by either side) for, once again, the British Railways and London Transport personnel responsible for the preparation of the new report proved to have a scant and deficient grasp of either the technology or the insular commerce involved, and broadly concluded that the MER would cease to be a problem as soon as it was closed. Despite very widespread protests, Tynwald decided to partly implement Transmark's illogical recommendations, and the Laxey–Ramsey section was closed on 30th September 1975. The Isle of Man Railway's remaining route between Port Erin and Douglas (which had also been "Transmarked") was also closed down except for a futile shuttle between Castletown and Port Erin. As the Manx Electric Society stated at the time: "Both operations were busily proving that half a railway could produce twice the losses."

The fate of the Island's railways became a major issue in the Tynwald general election of 1976 as a result of intense activity on the part

Summer smiles at Ramsey on 25th June 1977, when the Laxey – Ramsey section of the MER was re-opened after a two-year campaign for its restoration.
Mike Goodwyn

of the local railway lobby and a substantial number of former Members of the House of Keys were not re-elected. Thereafter, no-one was in any doubt as the wishes of the electorate and rapid moves were made by the new House to re-open both lines throughout their lengths. A ceremony on 25th June 1977, marked the re-opening of the Laxey–Ramsey services and indeed 1977 proved to be a most satisfactory year with both the MER and the IMR flourishing under experienced professional management. At the close of 1977 however, the MER Board lost the services of Mr. Harold Gilmore, Secretary and Manager since 1967, and were equally unable to procure the gifted services of Mr. A.H. Stewart, the IMR General Manager, when the newly nationalised steam railway was absorbed and administered by the MER Board in January 1978. Mr. William Jackson, formerly of consultants Sloan & Lloyd Barnes of Liverpool (and one of whose partners was the government's "Inspector of Railways" – but the reports to government on the technical condition of the Laxey–Ramsey line varied according to the political temperature, not the hardware) was appointed as "chief executive" in December 1977. He left in July 1987.

Most surprisingly, the MER Board took over the nationalised bus undertaking in April 1980, and adopted the title of "IoM Passenger Transport" in 1982. The MER Board of Tynwald was reformed as the IoM Passenger Transport Board in 1983. With the onset of "ministerial government" the Board found itself as part of Isle of Man Government Department of Tourism and Transport in 1986. On 1st December 1987, Mr. Robert H. Smith took charge as Transport Executive to the Department; MANX TRANSPORT REVIEW noted that "it was the first time in ten years that the Board's management team had been headed by someone with professional knowledge and experience of transport and management."

CENTENARY YEAR

Somehow, however, the Manx Electric Railway has managed to survive it all For the centenary of the Manx Electric, a large and imposing programme of special events was initiated, with Mr. Alan Corlett in charge of planning as Co-ordinator. During 1992, as preparations were put in hand, a specially-adapted Leyland National exhibition bus toured the British Isles visiting many transport venues and creating a good deal of interest in the island's railways and in what by this stage had been elevated to the "Year of Railways".

The celebrations and events commenced with a special Travelling Post Office run between Ramsey and Douglas (and then on by other means to Port Erin) to mark the introduction of a set of new postage stamps featuring the MER, issued by the Isle of Man Post Office Authority on 3rd February 1993. The programme really got underway at Easter, with the Lieutanant Governor and an official party travelling out from Douglas on Car No. 1 of 1893, the commissioning of car No. 9 as an illuminated tramcar – the first in MER history and the operation of IMR loco. No. 4 LOCH to provide a service unique in the annals of electric tramways, when it operated steam-hauled excursions from Laxey to Dhoon Quarry. In addition there were many other attractions, including depot and workshop open days for visitors and even motorman training lessons.

The preparations for the Island's "Year of Railways" involved very extensive work, with the entire line substantially improved, and stations and facilities rebuilt. The Groudle station in particular has benefitted from a major facelift, being restored to its original 1893 colours and illuminated by night. Even the illuminated sign on the hillside above Derby Castle carworks was rebuilt and restored.

The efforts and expense involved has been more than justified, for the celebrations mark the 100th anniversary of the opening of a pioneer electric tramway that really has no equal. It is a unique and remarkable institution to be cherished and cared for, enjoyed and revered with great and lasting affection.

COMPOSITION OF THE MANX ELECTRIC RAILWAY BOARDS OF TYNWALD

Under the statutory provisions of the Manx Electric Railway Act, 1957, the MER Board was, under the terms of Section 1, to consist of the following:

(a) A chairman (being a Member of Tynwald) appointed by Tynwald;
(b) two persons to be elected by Tynwald; and
(c) two persons to be nominated by the Governor and approved by Tynwald.

By definition, those in sub-sections (a) and (b) were elected Members of Tynwald, but the persons in sub-section (c) were not, and were intended to consist of those who had some specialised knowledge appropriate to the MER. In later years, it was customary to appoint the Governor's nominees of sub-section (c) from either local commissioners or the ranks of past or future politicians. At least one nominee was a case of mistaken identity. It will be noted that numerous later boards did not appear to fulfil the Section 1 requirements, but under the first schedule to the Act (Section 7), the same legislation provided (under sub-section F) that "the proceedings of the Board shall not be invalidated by reason of any vacancy or vacancies amongst their members, or by any defect in the mode of appointment of the Board or any means thereof."

The same Act provided (under Section 5) for the removal of Board members that were absent without leave for over three months, became bankrupt or incapacitated by physical or mental illness, or otherwise unable or unfit to discharge their duties, etc. A Petition to the Governor asking for the invocation of this Section was made in 1981.

Under the Isle of Man Passenger Transport Act, 1983, the Board is to comprise of three Members of Tynwald only.

Appointed from May 1957 until 30th November (later extended to 30th December) 1961.
All members, except Mr Kneale, resigned *en bloc* on 18th June 1958.
    Sir Ralph Stevenson, GCMG., MLC., chairman
    R.C. Stephen, MHK.
    A.H. Simcocks, MHK.
    T.W. Kneale, M.Eng., Governor's Nominee
    T.W. Billington, FCA., Governor's Nominee

Appointed 8th July 1958, to 1962:
    Hugh H Radcliffe, MHK., JP., chairman
    W.E. Quayle, MHK.
    Lt Cdr J.L. Quine, MHK.
    R.Dean, JP., Governor's Nominee
    T.W. Kneale, M.Eng., Governor's Nominee

Appointed 8th March 1962 to 1966:
    T.H. Colebourn, MHK., chairman
    Maj-Gen Sir Henry H C Sugden, KBE., CB., DSO., MHK.
    E.R. Moore, MHK.
    R. Dean, JP., Governor's Nominee
    T.W. Kneale, M.Eng., Governor's Nominee (Died 12.1.66)

Appointed November 1966 to 1971:
    Maj-Gen Sir Henry Hesketh Clapham Sugden, MHK, chairman
    Miss J.C. Thornton-Duesbury, JP., MHK.
    J.R. Gelling, Governor's Nominee
    E.R. Moore, Governor's Nominee
    M.F. Strickett, Governor's Nominee
Note: The composition of this Board was irregular and unconstitutional in having three Governor's Nominees, who could theoretically have outvoted the two elected Tynwald members.

Appointed November 1971 to 1976:
    Hugh H. Radcliffe, MLC., chairman
    Miss J.C. Thornton-Duesbury, JP., MHK.
    J.R. Creer, MHK.
    E. Ranson, MHK.
    J. Lancelot Kneale, Governor's Nominee
Note: The composition of this Board was irregular and unconstitutional in having three elected Tynwald Members against the two laid down by Section 1 (b) of the Act. Mr Radcliffe died in 1974 and was succeeded by Mr John C Clucas, MHK. Mr M. Ward, MHK., succeeded Bert Creer in 1975.

Appointed November 1976 to 1981:
    John J. Christian, MHK., chairman
    P.A. Craine, MHK.
    J.J. Radcliffe, MHK.
    M. Ward, MHK.
    R.L. Watterson, MHK.
Note: The composition of this Board was irregular and unconstitutional in having five elected Tynwald Members, ignoring the provisions of Section 1 (c) of the Act.

Appointed November 1981:
    D.F.K. Delaney, MHK., chairman
    J.A.C.K. Nivison, MLC.
    M. Ward, MHK.
    R. Payne, MHK.
    G.C. Swales, MHK.
    J.D.Q. Cannan, MHK.

Note: The MER Board was officially dissolved on 30th March 1983; until then the constitution of this Board was irregular and unconstitutional in having elected Tynwald Members only, ignoring the provisions of Section 1 (c) of the 1957 Act.

The provisions of the Isle of Man Passenger Transport Act, 1983, were implemented on 1st April 1983, and three members of the former MER Board became Members of the IoMPT Board until 1986:
    D.F.K. Delaney, MHK., chairman
    R. Payne, MHK.
    J.D.Q. Cannan, MHK.

Appointed November 1986:
    Alan Bell, MHK., chairman
    Dr John Orme, MHK.
    Bernard May, MHK. (Succeeded by Mr D Cretney, MHK. from 1988)

Appointed November 1991:
    The Rt. Hon Alan Bell MHK, Minister
    Alex Downie MHK.

Note: MHK = Member of the House of keys (the Manx Parliament).

MANX ELECTRIC RAILWAY MANAGEMENT OFFICERS

1894: Manager: J. Aldworth
       Secretary: W.E. Young
       Engineer: Josua Shaw
       Traffic Supt: Mr. Ching
1895: Snaefell Engineer: Mr. Cartner
1899: Manager & Engineer: Josua Shaw
1902: Manager: Harold Brown
       Resident Engineer: Frank Edmondson
1908: Engineer & Manager: Frank Edmondson (died January 1936)
       Chief Assistant Engineer: Bertram Kelly (to Douglas Corp. Electricity Dept 1922)
1922: Chief Assistant Engineer: E. Barnes
1936: Engineer & Manager: E. Barnes (died 2.11.52)
       Secretary: S.A. Young (River Plate House, London)
       Chief Assistant Engineer: John F. Watson
1949: Secretary (Douglas): J. Rowe
1953: Engineer & Joint Manager: J.F. Watson
       Secretary & Joint Manager: J. Rowe
       Chief Assistant Engineer: Harold Gilmore
       Traffic Superintendent: Walter Corran
       Rolling Stock Supt: Alfred Callister
       Assistant Engineer (from 1957): A.R. Cannell
1961: Rolling Stock Supt: Lewis E. Gale
       Chief Asst Engineer & Traffic Supt: Harold Gilmore
       Asst Traffic Supt: George Pressley
1964: General Manager, Engineer & Secretary: J.F. Watson
       Chief Asst Engineer & Traffic Supt: Harold Gilmore
       Asst. Traffic Supt: John R Gordon (from 1962)
       Asst Engineer: A.R. Cannell
       Accountant: E. Halsall
1967: General Manager, Engineer & Secretary: Harold Gilmore (from 31/12/67)
       Traffic Supt: John R. Gordon
       Chief Asst Engineer: A.R. Cannell
       Accountant: Vincent Cove
1970: Rolling Stock Supt: Alan McMullen
1975: Rolling Stock Supt: Darryl Gribbin
1977: General Manager & Engineer: (W. Jackson, "chief executive")
       Engineering Supt: A.R. Cannell (retired 1983)
       Operations Supt: John R. Gordon
1987: Transport Executive: Robert H. Smith
       General Manager: J.R. Oates
       Operations Supt: John R. Gordon
       Asst Operations Supt: M. Graham Warhurst
       Engineering Supt: J. Maurice Faragher
       Asst Engineering Supt: George Lawson
       Rolling Stock Supt: Darryl Gribbin
1990: Operations Supt: M. Graham Warhurst
       Asst Operations Supt: M.P. Ogden

The Manx Electric Railway Co., Ltd.

WINTER SERVICE
Between Douglas, Laxey, and Ramsey.

On the Advertised Winter Service, the **Cars are due to pass** the intermediate points as shown below. The Times given are for the general guidance of the Public, and are based upon **Greenwich Time** as exhibited at Ramsey, Laxey, and Douglas Stations.

SPECIAL NOTE—While the Cars will not pass **previous** to the indicated time, the company will not accept any responsibility for unavoidable delays en route.

Cars marked thus ※ will be liable to Delay at Douglas awaiting Arrival of Steamer.

At the intermediate points (with the exception of Laxey), the Cars Stop on request only.

UP CARS.

Week Days.

	a.m.	a.m.	a.m.	noon	p.m.	p.m.	p.m.	p.m.	p.m.	Saturdays only
Dep. DERBY CASTLE	7 0	8 15	10 0	12 0	2 30	4 15	5 15	6 0	8 0	8 30
Pass Groudle	7 9	8 24	10 9	12 9	2 39	4 24	5 24	6 9	8 9	8 39
" Half-Way House	7 14	8 29	10 14	12 14	2 44	4 29	5 29	6 14	8 14	8 44
" Garwick	7 18	8 33	10 18	12 18	2 48	4 33	5 33	6 18	8 18	8 48
" Ballabeg	7 23	8 36	10 23	12 21	2 51	4 36	5 36	6 21	8 21	8 48
" South Cape	7 30	8 40	10 25	12 25	2 55	4 40	5 40	6 25	8 25	8 51
Dep. Laxey	7 33	8 45	10 30	12 30	3 0	4 45	5 45	6 30	8 30	8 55
Pass Minorca	7 45	8 48	10 33	12 33	3 3	4 48	5 48	6 33	8 33	
" Dhoon	7 50	9 5	10 45	12 45	3 15	5 0	6 0	6 45	8 45	9 0
" Glen Mona	7 50	9 5	10 50	12 50	3 20	5 0	6 0	6 50	8 50	9 20
" Ballaglass	7 54	9 9	10 54	12 54	3 24	5 4	6 4	6 54	8 54	9 24
" Ballajora	8 1	9 16	11 1	1 1	3 31	5 16	6 16	7 1	9 1	9 31
" Belle Vue	8 7	9 22	11 7	1 7	3 37	5 22	6 22	7 7	9 7	9 37
Arr. Ramsey	8 15	9 30	11 15	1 15	3 45	5 30	6 30	7 15	9 15	9 45

Sunday.

	a.m.	p.m.	p.m.	p.m.	p.m.
Dep. DERBY CASTLE	9 45	2 30	4 0	6 0	8 0
Pass Groudle	9 54	2 39	4 9	6 9	8 9
" Half-Way House	9 59	2 44	4 14	6 14	8 14
" Garwick	10 3	2 48	4 18	6 18	8 18
" Ballabeg	10 6	2 51	4 21	6 21	8 21
" South Cape	10 10	2 55	4 25	6 25	8 25
Dep. Laxey	10 15	3 0	4 30	6 30	8 30
Pass Minorca	10 18	3 3	4 33	6 33	8 33
" Dhoon	10 18	3 15	4 45	6 45	8 45
" Glen Mona	10 35	3 20	4 50	6 50	8 50
" Ballaglass	10 39	3 24	4 54	6 54	8 54
" Ballajora	10 46	3 31	5 1	7 1	9 1
" Belle Vue	10 52	3 37	5 7	7 7	9 7
Arr. Ramsey	11 0	3 45	5 15	7 15	9 15

DOWN CARS.

Week Days.

	a.m.	a.m.	a.m.	a.m.	p.m.	p.m.	p.m.	p.m.	p.m.	Saturdays only
Dep. RAMSEY	6 45	7 15	8 30	10 30	12 30	2 30	4 30	6 0	8 0	8 30
Pass Belle Vue	6 51	7 21	8 36	10 36	12 36	2 36	4 36	6 6	8 6	8 36
" Ballajora	6 57	7 27	8 42	10 42	12 42	2 42	4 42	6 12	8 12	8 42
" Ballaglass	7 4	7 34	8 49	10 49	12 49	2 49	4 49	6 19	8 19	8 49
" Glen Mona	7 8	7 38	8 53	10 53	12 53	2 53	4 53	6 23	8 23	8 53
" Dhoon	7 13	7 43	9 0	11 0	1 0	3 0	5 0	6 30	8 30	9 0
" Minorca	7 22	7 52	9 8	11 8	1 8	3 8	5 8	6 38	8 38	9 8
Dep. Laxey	7 25	7 55	9 15	11 15	1 15	3 15	5 15	6 45	8 45	9 15
Pass South Cape	7 28	7 58	9 18	11 18	1 18	3 18	5 18	6 48	8 48	9 18
" Ballabeg	7 32	8 6	9 22	11 22	1 22	3 22	5 22	6 52	8 52	9 22
" Garwick	7 36	8 12	9 25	11 25	1 25	3 25	5 25	6 55	8 55	9 25
" Half-Way House	7 42	8 17	9 31	11 31	1 31	3 31	5 31	7 1	9 1	9 31
" Groudle	7 47	8 21	9 35	11 35	1 35	3 35	5 35	7 5	9 5	9 35
Arr. Derby Castle	8 0	8 30	9 45	11 45	1 45	3 45	5 45	7 15	9 15	9 45

Sunday.

	a.m.	p.m.	p.m.	p.m.	p.m.
Dep. RAMSEY	9 30	2 30	4 30	6 0	8 0
Pass Belle Vue	9 36	2 36	4 36	6 6	8 6
" Ballajora	9 42	2 42	4 42	6 12	8 12
" Ballaglass	9 49	2 49	4 49	6 19	8 19
" Glen Mona	9 53	2 53	4 53	6 23	8 23
" Dhoon	10 0	3 0	5 0	6 30	8 30
" Minorca	10 8	3 8	5 8	6 38	8 38
Dep. Laxey	10 15	3 15	5 15	6 45	8 45
Pass South Cape	10 18	3 18	5 18	6 48	8 48
" Ballabeg	10 22	3 22	5 22	6 52	8 52
" Garwick	10 25	3 25	5 25	6 55	8 55
" Half-Way House	10 31	3 31	5 31	7 1	9 1
" Groudle	10 35	3 35	5 35	7 5	9 5
Arr. Derby Castle	10 45	3 45	5 45	7 15	9 15

F. EDMONDSON, General Manager.

Winter Service, 1908

Isle of Man Tramways & Electric Power Co.
LIMITED (In Liquidation).

TIME TABLES,
COMMENCING JULY 13th, 1901, AND UNTIL FURTHER NOTICE.

Douglas & Laxey.

A Service of ELECTRIC CARS will leave DERBY CASTLE for LAXEY at 8-15 a.m., 9 a.m., and every half hour until 9 p.m., with a LATE CAR on Wednesdays & Saturdays only at 11 p.m. Leaving LAXEY for DERBY CASTLE at 7-35 a.m. (Royal Mail Car) 9-15 a.m., 10-15 a.m., and every half hour until 9-45 p.m.

On SUNDAYS Cars will leave DERBY CASTLE for LAXEY at 10 a.m., and afterwards the same as on Week-days, with a late Car at 10 p.m. (in connection with the Sacred) From LAXEY for DOUGLAS at 10-15 a.m., 11-15 a.m., and afterwards the same as on Week-days.

Additional Cars will run at intervals between the above stated times to meet the traffic requirements.

Douglas & Ramsey.

A Service of THROUGH CARS will leave DERBY CASTLE STATION for LAXEY & RAMSEY at

8-15 a.m., 9 a.m., 10 a.m., 10-30 a.m., 11-30 a.m., 12 noon, 12-30, 1 p.m., 1-30 p.m., 2 p.m., 2-30 p.m., 3 p.m., 3-30 p.m., 4-30 p.m., 5 p.m., 5-30 p.m., 6 p.m., 6-30 p.m., 7 p.m., 8 p.m., with a LATE CAR on Wednesdays and Saturdays only at 11 p.m.

THROUGH CARS will leave RAMSEY for LAXEY and DOUGLAS at

6-50 a.m. (in connection with the Sacred), 8-30 a.m., 9-30 a.m., 10-30 a.m., 11 a.m., 11-30 a.m., 12 noon, 12-30 p.m., 1 p.m., 1-30 p.m., 2 p.m. (in connection with the Sacred), 2-30 p.m., 3 p.m., 3-30 p.m., 4 p.m., 4-30 p.m., 5 p.m., 5-30 p.m., 6 p.m., 6-30 p.m., 7-30 p.m., 8-30 p.m., and on Wednesdays and Saturdays only, 9 p.m.

On SUNDAYS Cars will leave Derby Castle Station at 10 a.m., and afterwards the same as on Week-days, until 8 p.m., with a LATE CAR at 10 p.m. (in connection with the Sacred) From RAMSEY at 9-30 a.m., and afterwards the same as on Week-days until 8-30 p.m.

Additional Cars will run at intervals between the above stated times to meet the traffic requirements.

Croudle, Garwick, Laxey, Dhoon, Glen Mona, and Ballaglass.

Also SNAEFELL MOUNTAIN TRAMWAY,
On which Cars Run at frequent intervals throughout the Season.

The Electric Cars are the Cheapest, most Convenient and Pleasant means of reaching the beautiful Glens of

Douglas Bay.

A Service of Horse Cars will run every few minutes between the Electric Tramway Station and Victoria Pier, starting from the Tramway Station in the morning in time to catch the Fleetwood, Barrow, and Liverpool Steamers, the Last Car Leaving Derby Castle at 11 p.m., and Jubilee Clock at 11-20 p.m.

On SUNDAYS the First Car will leave the Tramway Station at 9-15 a.m. and Victoria Station at 10-30 p.m. and Victoria...

CHAPTER TWO

TRAFFIC

The Traffic Department of the Manx Electric is (or in a few cases-was) responsible for a very wide range of duties and activities. It is primarily concerned with collecting sufficient revenue to finance the costs and expenses of the undertaking and for the everyday superintendence of traffic working. This involves schedules, duty rosters and records, the recruitment, selection, training and supervision of platform and station staff; planning, operation and traffic control, marketing, publicity and advertising, tickets and fare collection, maintenance of statistics and internal revenue control, uniforms, time sheets and wage bills, superannuation, liaison with trades unions, local authorities, pressure groups and others, and in earlier days also included the responsibility for goods and parcels too. It is virtually responsible for everything and everybody that moves on the Line, outside of the Engineer's Department.

What ultimately became the Manx Electric Railway was evidently conceived primarily as a passenger-carrying operation, and indeed it was only at the behest of Tynwald that a statutory obligation to convey freight was incorporated into the 1893 Act, which authorised the building of the extension to Laxey. The Act also stipulated maximum rates for goods as well as passengers and all subsequent legislation for the final extension to Ramsey included these provisions.

TRAFFIC DEPARTMENT ORGANISATION

For the greater part of its existence to date, the traffic organisation of the Manx Electric consisted of the Traffic Superintendent and an assistant, together with a chief inspector and one or more travelling inspectors. These inspectors, in conjunction with the Station Masters at Douglas, Laxey, and Ramsey (and at the Bungalow and Summit on the Snaefell section) are responsible for everyday working arrangements, and for the general supervision of traffic. Each departure from any main station is then advised by telephone to the next control point. In earlier times there were also Station Masters at Groudle Glen, Garwick Glen and (for some time) at Dhoon Glen. A series of three "traction telephone circuits" was also provided from about 1912 or possibly earlier, covering the Douglas–Laxey, Laxey–Snaefell, and Laxey–Ramsey sections using apparatus supplied by Western Electric (USA). Each section had its own system of bell codes and for example the Douglas–Laxey circuit code was as follows:

Station

Douglas General Office	Two rings
Douglas Booking Office	One short, one long
Douglas Yard Office	Three
Car Works	Three short
Groudle	Four
Garwick	Six
Laxey Station	One long
Laxey Sub Station	Five

Lineside telephone boxes were also provided at every crossover to enable inspectors or platform staff to make contact with the respective stations in case of necessity. Since 1982 these arrangements have been superceded by the use of radio telephones; all main stations and the head office have transceiver sets, and all of the Winter Saloons together with Cars Nos. 5, 6 and 9 are equipped with mounting brackets and aerials for mobile sets.

PASSENGER TRAFFIC

The total number of passengers aboard each car is counted at Douglas, Laxey and Ramsey, and the figure entered on a daily traffic summary; short stage passengers travelling between intermediate points only can be determined from the conductors' waybills.

The pattern of high-season traffic on the Manx Electric has altered little over the years, despite the decline in overall numbers and the need for extreme resilience in catering for wide variations in demand according to the weather. Each normal summer morning sees an exodus from Douglas to Laxey and Ramsey; the early afternoon sees a similar demand, but with heavier bookings to Laxey rather than Ramsey. Beginning at about 3.00 p.m. there is invariably very heavy traffic southbound until about 5.45 p.m., as tourists return to Douglas. The intervention of poor weather can make substantial differences, all of which have to be coped with. The normal "tidal flow" is catered for by a combination of "service" cars, which appear in the published timetables, and "special" cars which do not, but which operate from point to point according to demand. Many of the specials are loaded and despatched from Douglas to Laxey, where they may be sent on up the Northern line to Ramsey if demand requires, or returned to Douglas for yet another load of passengers, or kept at Laxey until they are needed to cope with the lunchtime or afternoon build-up of crowds returning to Douglas. Carsets awaiting further instructions at Laxey are first shunted into the siding by the side of the old goods shed at the east end of the station, where they can be quickly called down into the station as needed; later arrivals are required to shunt back along the main line outside Laxey Car Depot, again to be called down as required. In the case of specials stacked at the Depot, there is a strict "first in, first out" rule to ensure a fair and equitable distribution of duties. All of these local movements come under the control of the Laxey Station Master. Similarly, a special carset that gets to Ramsey may be kept there at the discretion of the Station Master until needed for a southbound journey.

Whilst the overall traffic pattern along the line has remained stable, the very intensive short-stage workings of earlier years has now largely vanished. Up until the outbreak of World War II it was quite normal to maintain a five-minute service in both directions as far as Groudle, in order to cope with the demands of passengers to and from Derby Castle and Onchan Head (White City) and Howstrake Holiday Camp, as well as Groudle Glen itself. These shuttle services were normally operated primarily by the "ratchet" or "scratcher" cars (hand-braked crossbench type) hauling a lightweight trailer, and local traffic in this district came under the control of the Groudle Station Master. With the disappearance of this short-stage traffic, the need for close-headway working waned, but it is still possible to maintain a minimum headway between cars of five minutes between Douglas and Laxey, and ten minutes between Laxey and Ramsey.

PROVISION OF TRAIN SETS AND CREW

Cars for traffic are officially delivered by the Engineering Department from Derby Castle depot each morning; those cars required by the schedules to be based at Laxey or Ramsey Car Depots are only (usually) away for a single night, and the platform crews will change over from one car to another en route, so that the personnel and cars find themselves at the right places at the end of the day. Platform crews are rostered according to demand, availability and circumstances, and are divided into those allocated to "service" cars and those to crew the "special" cars. In earlier times both of these groups were divided into "early" and "late" shift men, but today's reduced timetables mean that in general the line can be operated on a single shift basis. There is a further difference between the "service" and "special" car crews in that those rostered to work the "service" cars sign on fifteen minutes before they are booked to take over their cars even if starting out cold from the depot, this will have been prepared and oiled up ready for use. On the other hand, the "special" crews are required to book on at 8.00 a.m. in order to prepare their own cars prior to going out in traffic. This involves oiling up the axlebox and motor bearings, check-

Manx Electric Railway

TIME TABLE

DOUGLAS, LAXEY & RAMSEY

Commencing Tuesday, 18th September, 1934, and until further notice.

FROM DOUGLAS — WEEK DAYS / SUNDAYS

		a.m.	a.m.	a.m.	noon	p.m.	p.m.	p.m.	p.m.	p.m.	p.m.	p.m.	p.m.	p.m.	SUN p.m.	SUN p.m.
DOUGLAS (DERBY CASTLE)	dep.	9 0	10 0	12 0		2 30	4 30 A	5 30	6 30	9 0 To Laxey B	9 15 D	9 30 B	11 0 C		2 45	8 30
GROUDLE GLEN	,,		Mail Car													
BALDRINE	,,															
GARWICK GLEN	,,															
LAXEY	,,	7 45	9 25	10 30	12 30	3 0	5 0	6 0	7 0	9 30 STOP	9 45	10 0 From Dhoon	11 30		3 15	9 0
DHOON	,,											9 15 B				
GLEN MONA, BALLAGLASS	,,															
RAMSEY (PALACE)	arr	8 30	10 5	11 10	1 15	3 45	5 45	6 40	7 40		10 25	9 45	10 40	12 10	3 55	9 40

FROM RAMSEY — WEEK DAYS / SUNDAYS

		a.m.		a.m.	a.m.	a.m.	p.m.	p.m.	p.m.	p.m.	p.m.	p.m.	p.m.	SUN p.m.	SUN p.m.
RAMSEY (PALACE)	dep	7 0		8 30	10 30	12 15	2 15 Mail Car	4 30	6 45	8 45 To Dhoon 9 15	9 45 C	10 30 To Laxey D	10 30 B	2 30	8 30
GLEN MONA, BALLAGLASS	,,	Mail Car													
DHOON	,,		From Laxey												
LAXEY	,,	7 40 For Liverpool Boat	8 30	9 10	11 10	1 0	2 55	5 10	7 30	B	10 25	11 10 STOP	11 10	3 15	9 10
GARWICK GLEN	,,														
BALDRINE	,,														
GROUDLE GLEN	,,														
DOUGLAS (DERBY CASTLE)	arr.	8 10	9 0	9 40	11 40	1 30	3 20	5 40	8 0		10 55		11 40	3 40	9 40

Reduced Winter Fares: Douglas & Laxey, or Laxey & Ramsey, 1/- Return; Douglas & Ramsey, 2/- Return

(Return Journey for Single Fare Thursday all Day)

A—Liable to delay awaiting arrival of Boat Passengers.   B—Saturdays only.   C—Thursdays and Saturdays only.   D—Saturdays excepted.

Goods Merchandise and Parcels conveyed between all Stations. Goods and Parcels collected and delivered every hour within Douglas Town Boundaries. Advance Luggage, Goods, Merchandise, and Parcels conveyed by Road Motor Service to and from Douglas, Onchan, Garwick, Laxey and intermediate points.

Parcels may be left at Mr. E. Hudson's Shop, King Street, and at Mr. Newby's Shop, 58 Buck's Road, Douglas—Collections at 10 a.m. and 3 p.m.

Rates and all other information from Goods Department General Office and Station-Masters.

General Offices: 1 Strathallan Crescent, Douglas.   Telephones: Douglas 61, Laxey 26, Ramsey 49.   F. EDMONDSON, General Manager.

Norris Modern Press Ltd., 6 Victoria Street, Douglas.

ing brakes, lights, control gear, trolley and trolleywheel, filling the sand hoppers and generally ensuring that the car is in good working order. Platform crews are no longer usually responsible for the cleaning of their cars, which are swept out by the night watchman/cleaner at Derby Castle; cars are washed down theoretically on a rota basis by "special" motormen on any weekday morning except mondays, when they are fully occupied in oiling up and checking the trailer cars. Although the evening cars are usually swept out prior to taking the service, it is no longer usual for each of the saloon cars to carry its own brush; similarly the snow shovels that used to be kept behind the plat-form doors of the winter saloons and certain other cars, are no longer mandatory. Platform crews do not carry out any adjustments, and any defects are noted in a register as the cars return to the depot. In earlier times, a night fitter was responsible for carrying out brake adjustment and clearing minor defects before morning.

The actual order in which power cars are coupled to trailers depends on circumstances, and although theoretically any car could couple any trailer or freight vehicle, there is in fact a fairly strict pecking order for the mating of cars and trailers, owing to differences in the heights of couplers and step-boards. Oddly, even cars and trailers delivered at the same time from the same builders, such as Cars 32–33 and trailers 61–62, feature slight differences in heights. As not all of the air-braked power cars are equipped with trailer coupling air hoses and cocks, the heavy saloon trailers Nos. 57 and 58 are usually only hauled by the 19–22 class; they cannot be coupled to Cars Nos. 1, 2 or 9 or 32–3. Trailer No.59, when in regular use, was frequently tied to Car No. 5; trailers Nos. 61–62 do not appear with Nos. 1, 2 or 9 either. The lightweight 1893 trailers of the 49–54 series were in use primarily with the ratchet crossbench cars of the 14–18 and 28–31 series. The lightweight trailers were also notable in being the only passenger trailers that were hauled (unladen) in twos behind a winter saloon to and from winter storage at Ramsey Depot. Trailer Cars Nos. 40–48 are invariably allocated to any of the Winter Saloons or the "Tunnel" cars. Nos. 6, 7 or 9, or Nos. 1 and 2. Since the restoration of trailer No. 51 to its c.1895 condition (as Trailer No 13) this has usually been matched with either Car No.1 or No.2. Trailer Cars Nos. 55–56 seem to always be matched to any of the three "paddlebox" crossbench cars, Nos. 25–27.

Trailer cars are shunted around their motor cars at turnaround points by hand and invariably aided by a favouring gradient. The three trailers supplied by English Electric in 1930 to replace some of those lost in the Laxey Depot fire of that year are perceived as (and are!) particularly heavy when compared with similar cars from other carbuilders.

MANX ELECTRIC RAILWAY - DOUGLAS, LAXEY AND RAMSEY

COMMENCING SATURDAY, 15th SEPTEMBER, 1962, and until further notice

WEEKDAYS — SUNDAY SERVICE SUSPENDED

Connecting Bus from Central Bus Station, Lord Street	8.15	9.35	11.35	1.	5.	2.35	4.	5.35	7.	8.35
DOUGLAS (Derby Castle) dep.	7. 0 a.m.	8.45	9.45	11.45	1.15 p.m.	2.45	4.15	5.45	7.15	8.45
Majestic Hotel										
Groudle Glen										
Baldrine										
Garwick Glen										
LAXEY	7.25	9.10	10.10	12.10	1.40 p.m.	3.10	4.40	6.10	7.40	9.10
Dhoon										
Glen Mona, B'glass										
RAMSEY (Plaza) arr.	8.10	9.55	10.55	12.55	2.25	3.55	5.25	6.55	8.25	9.55

RAMSEY (Plaza) dep.	6.55	8.25	10.25	11.55	1.25	2.55	4.25	5.55	7.25	8.25
LAXEY	7.35	9.	11.	12.35	2.	3.35	5.	6.35	8.	9.
DOUGLAS (Derby Castle) arr.	8.15	9.35	11.35	1.	5.	2.35	4.	5.35	7.	8.35
Connecting Bus to Victoria Pier and Cent'l Bus Station Lord Street		8. 9	9.39	11.39	1. 9	2.39	4. 9	5.39	7. 9	8.39	9.39

Return Fares — RAMSEY to: Groudle 7d.; Ballajora 1/-; Garwick 1/6; LAXEY 1/6; Dhoon 1/3; Glen Mona 1/5; Ballaglass 2/-; DOUGLAS 3/6.

DOUGLAS to: Groudle 10d.; Garwick 1/6; LAXEY 2/-; Dhoon 2/1; Glen Mona 2/6; Ballaglass 3/-; Fairy Cottage 2/6; Halfway House 2/6; Ballajora 3/-; RAMSEY 3/6.

WEEKLY TICKETS and CONTRACT TICKETS available at Reduced Rates

Goods, Merchandise and Parcels conveyed between all Stations. Goods and Parcels collected and delivered everywhere within Douglas Town Boundaries. Goods and Merchandise and Parcels conveyed by Road Motor Services to and from Douglas, Onchan, Garwick, Laxey and Ramsey and intermediate points.

Parcels may be left at Mr. E. Hudson's Shop, King Street, and Lowey's, Newsagents, Rosemount, Douglas—Collections Daily. Rates and information from Goods Department General Office and Station Masters.

General Offices: 1 Strathallan Crescent, Douglas.   J. ROWE / J. F. WATSON, Joint Managers
Tels. Douglas 61; Laxey 226; Ramsey 2249

This timetable also applied upto and including 1970–1.

The order in which cars are committed to traffic from Derby Castle has also remained largely unchanged since the early years of the present century. The 48-seat Winter Saloons (Nos. 19–22) maintain the service schedule, augmented as necessary by Saloon Cars Nos. 5, 9, 7 and 6 in that order. Of the crossbench cars, Nos. 32–33 were normally always despatched first, in the hands of a known expert motorman, on the eminently sensible basis that since these were and are the fastest cars in the fleet and they can be there and back before anything else. The two UEC-built cars are then followed by Cars Nos. 16, 25, 26 and 27, after which, if traffic demand requires, one or more of the non-air-braked "ratchet" cars would be called out. In fact these cars are nowadays seldom used in normal traffic, and then only by arrangement.

STAFF

For very many years the MER has depended upon a hard-core nucleus of permanent staff, supplemented as necessary by seasonal personnel. In earlier times it was also perfectly normal for engineering staff to be loaned or even transferred to traffic duties as required in the season, and this process could at times result in the workshops being almost totally devoid of any staff, on a particularly busy summer's day, when everything that would run was out in traffic. Nor was this process restricted to what might be termed "wage staff", for, in extremes, it was not unusual up to 1977 to find senior members of the management acting as platform crew (usually Motormen) at times of acute traffic pressure.

The serious imbalance between winter and summer traffic, and its direct effect on permanent staff duties meant that it was entirely normal to find Station Masters and other senior traffic personnel acting as motormen and conductors during the winters, and summertime platform crews out on winter track gangs.

The recruitment, selection, training and supervision of platform crews and station staff was and remains the responsibility of the Traffic Department. Most training involves several weeks of tutorial guidance under senior personnel, and in the case of Motormen was formerly a prolonged and extremely thorough process, taking many weeks and extended as necessary until an acceptable level of proficiency was reached and proved. The aim was to ensure that any motorman was not only entirely competent to meet any normal demand, but was also totally proficient in dealing with almost any conceivable difficulty ever likely to arise somewhere in the wilds of Maughold on a dark and stormy winter's night, many miles from any source of assistance. For a time after 1977 training was abbreviated but an adequate training and competency assessment programme for all recruits is now in place, and the training of Motormen is dealt with in greater detail elsewhere in this volume. Conductors have to satisfy the Traffic Department as to their competence before being allowed out in sole charge of a car.

UNIFORMS

From the beginning the Line's outdoor staff and platform crews were provided with a uniform tunic, more or less in keeping with contemporary tramway practice, and consisting of a uniform jacket, trousers and a cap. However, by the late 1940s, those in receipt of full tunics had diminished to Station Masters, some other station staff, travelling inspectors and perhaps a few of the most senior platform crews. The remainder of the car crews were issued with full-length khaki dust coats, black uniform trousers and caps. This arrangement survived for many years, indeed until after the nationalisation of 1957, when the new government Board introduced a curious dark green uniform for supervisory staff. The style featured wildly exaggerated lapels and other accoutrements and was erroneously rumoured to have been acquired from the closing-down sale of an unsuccessful firm of theatrical costumiers. Thereafter a reversion to the original style took place, and lasted until 1978 when proper uniforms were dispensed with altogether in favour of a short blue nylon jacket and a shapeless cap, and which prompted unkind enquiries about convict garb and penal battalions. In 1987 platform crews were equipped with new standard lightweight overalls of what was termed "the zoo-keeper" variety, in camouflage green, and the complete issue consisted of two pairs of trousers, two jackets, two cream shirts, one brown tie and a pair of black, steel-capped shoes. A green anorak with hood and waterproof protective clothing was also available to motormen, as were some long blue dust coats. By this time, Station Masters had a semi-uniform suit made from a peculiar blue cloth, which had also been issued to bus personnel. In 1989, dark blue anoraks, jackets, trousers, shirts and clip-on Isle of Man Government ties; became standard issue for platform crews. Jackets featured a curious "Isle of Man Railways" device.

With a return to professional management and traditional values,

a welcome reversion to a proper uniform tunic for MER staff, fully in keeping with the line's rolling stock and historic infrastructure, has subsequently been made.

TIMETABLES AND SCHEDULES

Because of the imbalance between summer and winter traffic, the MER has always had two or more separate timetables for the year. usually for summer and winter (and with reduced rates and fares during the off-season) and sometimes also for the "shoulder" periods at one or both ends of the main season,

No timetables of the services provided between Douglas and Groudle in September 1893 appear to have survived and only sketchy details exist of the 1894–5 services to Laxey. By 1899, with the completion of the line to Ramsey (Plaza), the IoM Tramways & Electric Power Co. Ltd. were advertising a half-hourly headway in each direction between Douglas and Ramsey, from 7.00 a.m. to 9.00 p.m. on weekdays, and from 9.30 a.m. to 8.00 p.m. on Sundays. The adult return fare between Douglas and Ramsey was 3s. 6d. (17½p), a not inconsiderable sum in those days. In order to encourage off-peak travel, this fare was reduced to 2s. 6d. (12½p) a not inconsiderable sum in those days.

From the opening of the Ramsey line, the journey times were scheduled at 40 to 45 minutes between Douglas and Laxey, and 50–55 minutes between Laxey and Ramsey. The bankruptcy of the IoMT&EP Co. early in 1900 did not affect the standard of services, save only that the timetable for 13th July 1901, onwards showed departures for Ramsey at 8.15 a.m., 9.00 a.m. and then every half-hour up to 7.00 p.m., then 8.00 p.m., with an additional departure at 7.35 p.m. for Laxey, this being billed as a "Royal Mail Car." On Sundays the service was maintained at half-hourly intervals between 10.00 a.m. and 8.00 p.m., with a "Late Car" at 10.00 p.m. "in connection with the Sacred Concert at the Palace" in Douglas.

The technical re-equipment programme of the 1902–4 period resulted in a considerable acceleration of services, and brought the Douglas–Ramsey journey time down to 75 minutes, or 70 minutes for Boat Cars, and 65 minutes for Mail Cars. Whilst the opening of the electric line had had some effect on the amount of traffic carried by the IMR-Manx Northern Railway steam train services, the fast new timings of the MER produced a reaction, whereby the IMR and MNR

MANX ELECTRIC RAILWAY

DAILY REGISTER OF CARS

STATION *Derby Castle*. DAY *Tuesday*. DATE *16th August 1988*

Motor No.	Trailer No.	Time of Departure	Destination	Number of Passengers	Remarks	Vans
9	44	9.43	Laxey	71		
7	47	9.55	✓	57		
22	42	10.03	Ramsey	46		
33	61	10-15	Laxey	74		
21	.48	10.26	Ramsey	92		
26	62	10.35	Laxey	56		
6	41	10.50	✓	75		
20	45	11.01	Ramsey	87		
9	44	11.11	Laxey	90		
7	47	11.26	✓	57		
33	61	11.45	✓	74		
19	46	12.03	Ramsey	811 92		
26	62	12.34	Laxey	46		
22	42	1.01	Ramsey	68		
9	44	1.16	Laxey	26		
7	47	1.33	✓	33	Ramsey Spec.	
6	41	1.46	✓	47		
21	48	2.02	Ramsey	28		
33	61	2.18	Laxey	27		
20	45	2.31	Ramsey	33		
16	40	2.41	Laxey	14		
26	62	2.50		6		
9	44	3.02	✓	1235 36		
19	46	3.15	Ramsey	15		
6	41	3.49	Laxey	25		
22	42	4.03	Ramsey	16		
33	61	4.11	Laxey	–		
21	48	5.03	Ramsey	33		
20	–	5.45	✓	11		
19	–	7.00	Laxey	20		

-1355-

MANX ELECTRIC RAILWAY
DERBY CASTLE STATION (Terminus of Horse Tramway)
TIME TABLE
DOUGLAS, LAXEY and RAMSEY
SATURDAY, 24th MAY and until 14th SEPTEMBER, 1969

THE SNAEFELL MOUNTAIN RAILWAY OPEN from 19th May until 19th Sept., 1969 — Cars as Required by Traffic

Passengers Change at Laxey for the Glorious Trip to the Summit of SNAEFELL Mountain (2,034 feet above sea level)
A Welcome awaits you at the SUMMIT HOTEL — Fully Licensed — Teas and Refreshments

From DOUGLAS
Time from Derby Castle :— Groudle 12 minutes ; Garwick 20 minutes ; Dhoon 45 minutes ; Ballaglass 55 minutes

DOUGLAS (DERBY CASTLE)	Sundays....dep.	7 0			10 0		11 0			1 0	2 0	2 30	3 15	4 0			5 30	6 30	7 30	9 0		10 30
White City, Majestic Hotel, Howstrake Camp ,,	Weekdays dep.	7 0	8 50	10 0	10 30	11 0	12 0		1 0	2 0	2 30	3 15	4 0	5 0	5 30	6 30	8 0	9 0	10 30		
GROUDLE GLEN ,,		a.m. BOAT CAR					noon	p.m.									BOAT CAR	A				
BALDRINE ,,																						
GARWICK GLEN ,,																						
LAXEY (Change for Snaefell Mountain Summit)	Sundays....dep.	7 30			10 30		11 30			1 30	2 30	3 0	3 45	4 30		6 0	7 0	8 0	9 30		11 0
DHOON GLEN ,,	Weekdays dep.	7 30	9 15	10 30	11 0	11 30	12 30		1 30	2 30	3 0	3 45	4 30	5 0	6 0	7 0	8 30	9 30	11 0	STOP	
GLEN MONA ,,		B																				
BALLAGLASS GLEN ,,																						
BALLAJORA, LEWAIGUE ,,																						
RAMSEY (PLAZA)	Sundays....arr.	8 15			11 15		12 15			2 15	3 15	3 45	4 30	5 15		6 45	7 45	8 45	10 15		
	Weekdays arr.	8 15	10 0	11 15	11 45	12 15	1 15		2 15	3 15	3 45	4 30	5 15	6 15	6 45	7 45	9 15	10 15	11 45		

From RAMSEY
ALL THE CHARMING GLENS EN ROUTE ARE IN MAGNIFICENT FOLIAGE

RAMSEY (PLAZA)	Sundays....dep.		8 20			11 30		12 30	1 45	2 30	3 30	4 0	4 30	5 30		7 15	8 30	9 30		
LEWAIGUE, BALLAJORA ,,	Weekdays dep.	7 15	8 20		10 30	11 30	12 0	12 30	1 45	2 30	3 30	4 0	4 30	5 30	6 30	7 15	8 30	9 30	10 30	
BALLAGLASS GLEN ,,		a.m.	B				noon	p.m. BOAT CAR											B	
GLEN MONA ,,																				
DHOON GLEN ,,																				
LAXEY (Change for Snaefell Mountain Summit)	Sundays....dep.		9 0	10 15		12 15		1 15	2 30	3 15	4 15	4 45	5 15	6 15		8 0	9 15	10 15		
GARWICK GLEN ,,	Weekdays dep.	8 0	9 0	10 15	11 15	12 15	12 45	1 15	2 30	3 15	4 15	4 45	5 15	6 15	7 15	8 0	9 15	10 15	11 15	
BALDRINE ,,																			STOP	
GROUDLE GLEN ,,																				
Howstrake Camp, Majestic Hotel, White City ,,	Sundays....arr.		9.30	10 45		12 45		1 45	3 0	3 45	4 45	5 15	5 45	6 45		8 30	9 45	10 45		
DOUGLAS (DERBY CASTLE)	Weekdays arr.	8 30	9 30	10 45	11 45	12 45	1 15	1 45	3 0	3 45	4 45	5 15	5 45	6 45	7 45	8 30	9 45	10 45		

Sunday Service Shown in Red
A—Terminates Laxey 24th May to 28th June and after the 23rd August
B—Operates from 29th June to 24th August

RETURN TICKETS are available for Break of Journey at all the Charming Glens en route, both going and returning
For Particulars of the ROVER TICKET TWO DAYS' UNLIMITED TRAVEL INCLUDING ONE RETURN Journey to SNAEFELL MOUNTAIN SUMMIT **see Handbills**
EXTRA CARS WILL ALSO RUN BETWEEN THE ADVERTISED TIMES AS REQUIRED BY THE TRAFFIC

Strathallan Crescent, Douglas. Phone Nos. Douglas 4549 ; Laxey 226 ; Ramsey 2249. Telegrams : Electric Douglas.

H. GILMORE, General Manager

managed to reduce their journey time to 68 minutes and the endless nonsense at St. John's Junction (which for years maintained a frontier checkpoint aura, which also included a train for Ramsey having to make two stops at the individual companies' stations there) ceased, but the bulk of the traffic from Douglas to Ramsey all too clearly preferred the fast, direct, electric line. This competition, added to the deepening economic problems of the MNR and its Foxdale line, and ultimately led to the IMR–MNR amalgamation of 1905. Quite what intentions the MER's proprietors had in respect of the Manx Northern have never become clear, although on two occasions (once in 1898 and again in April 1904) the IoMT&EP Co. and the MER Co. respectively had tried to acquire the undertaking; the first attempt even prompted a clear undertaking to electrify the MNR and to build a separate electric line from St John's to Douglas.

The Manx Electric's public timetables from about 1910 set the standard for traffic operation throughout the ensuing half-century, save only for the period of the two World Wars.

From 1906 it had become necessary to operate no less than three Boat Cars from Ramsey each summertime weekday. The first, leaving Ramsey at 6.45 a.m. served the Isle of Man Steam Packet's sailings for Dublin and Fleetwood, and also the Barrow Steam Navigation's departure for Barrow-in-Furness. The second car, at 7.15 a.m. connected with the Steam Packet's Liverpool steamer, whilst the third, leaving Ramsey at 7.45 a.m. was specifically to connect with the Midland Railway's Douglas–Heysham route, introduced in 1905. As it happened, the Midland's own publicity heavily featured the MER and its services and through ticketing was available from all Midland stations to Laxey and Ramsey. About 1906 too, the MER timetables referred to "Up" cars to Ramsey and "Down" cars to Douglas, a reversal of the convention whereby "Up" usually referred to the direction of the capital, or at least (as in the Midland Railway's case) to the administrative centre of the railway.

Year-round passenger traffic on the Manx Electric remained relatively stable until well after the Second World War. The onset of massive bus competition after the mid-1920s was countered most successfully by the advent of new facilities such as the "Rover Tickets" which were introduced in 1928, improved advertising and the introduction of improved services, such as the "Royal Mail Express" referred to later in connection with the postal contract. These and other measures ensured a high penetration of the tourist market of the period. In the aftermath of World War II, the Manx Electric profited from the ongoing petrol rationing and the restrictions on motor coaches, but after 1950 tourist traffic declined, and the residential traffic also began to diminish. The increasingly poorly-patronised winter Sunday services were abandoned completely after the spring of 1951 and late evening services were steadily withdrawn. The nationalisation of the Line in

MANX ELECTRIC RAILWAY — DOUGLAS AND LAXEY
Timetable commencing Monday, 2nd May 1977 and until 4th June, 1977. Also 17th September until 30th September, 1977

WEEKDAYS												
Douglas Dep. D/castle	10.00 a.m.	10.30	11.15	12.00 Noon	1.00 p.m.	2.00	2.30	3.15	4.05	4.45	5.30	
Laxey Arr.	10.30	11.00	11.45	12.30	1.30	2.30	3.00	3.45	4.35	5.15	6.00	

WEEKDAYS												
Laxey Dep.	9.15 a.m.	10.35	11.15	12.15 p.m.	1.00	1.45	2.35	3.30	4.00	4.45	5.30	
Douglas Arr. D/castle	9.45	11.05	11.45	12.45	1.30	2.15	3.05	4.00	4.30	5.15	6.00	

NO SUNDAY SERVICE. EXTRA CARS WILL ALSO RUN AS REQUIRED BY TRAFFIC.
DATES FOR 1977 SEASON
30 MINUTE SERVICE TO LAXEY COMMENCES SUNDAY, 5th JUNE AND UNTIL FRIDAY, 16th SEPTEMBER.
EVENING CARS COMMENCE MONDAY, 11th JULY AND UNTIL FRIDAY, 19th AUGUST.
SNAEFELL MOUNTAIN RAILWAY OPEN MONDAY, 16th MAY & UNTIL 30th SEPTEMBER, 1977.

Tel: Douglas 4549
Laxey 86226

H. GILMORE, General Manager.

MANX ELECTRIC RAILWAY — TIME TABLE — Douglas, Laxey, Ramsey & Snaefell

SATURDAY, 12th MAY, and until further notice — 1934

The Snaefell Mountain Railway and Motor Coach Service between Snaefell Bungalow Station and the Manx Switzerland, Tholt-e-Will, Sulby Glen, now open. Cars as required by Traffic

Change at Laxey for the Glorious Trip to the Summit of Snaefell Mountain (2,034 feet above sea level). The run on the Open Cars by the Royal Mail and Direct Coast Route to Ramsey through magnificent Woodland and Marine Scenery is of unrivalled popularity.

(Timetable grids for 1934 — From Douglas and From Ramsey, Weekdays and Sundays.)

RETURN TICKETS ARE AVAILABLE FOR BREAK OF JOURNEY AT ALL THE CHARMING GLENS EN ROUTE BOTH GOING AND RETURNING

1 Strathallan Crescent, Douglas. Phone Nos.: Douglas 61; Laxey 226; Ramsey 2240. Telegrams: Electric, Douglas. E. BARNES, General Manager and Engineer.

MANX ELECTRIC RAILWAY — Douglas, Laxey, Ramsey & Snaefell

TIME TABLE—Saturday, 26th May, 1973 until 15th September, 1973

Time from Derby Castle:— THE SNAEFELL MOUNTAIN RAILWAY OPEN from 14th May until 21st September, 1973. CARS AS REQUIRED BY TRAFFIC. Groudle 12 mins.; Garwick 20 mins.; Dhoon 45 mins.; Ballaglass 55 mins.; Change at Laxey for the Glorious Trip to the Summit of Snaefell Mountain (2,034 feet above sea level).

(Timetable grids for 1973 — From Douglas and From Ramsey, Weekdays and Sundays.) A—Operates from 2nd July to 31st August. B—Boat Car.

RETURN TICKETS ARE AVAILABLE FOR BREAK OF JOURNEY AT ALL THE CHARMING GLENS EN ROUTE BOTH GOING AND RETURNING

1 Strathallan Crescent, Douglas. Phone Nos.: Douglas 4549: Laxey 226: Ramsey 2249. Telegrams: Electric Douglas. H. GILMORE, General Manager

1957 inevitably led to political interference: In April and May 1958, the MER Board was savaged in Tynwald for its increasing deficits and the Railway survived an outright closure bid by only one vote; the permanent closure of the Laxey–Ramsey section was advocated during this dismal debate, as was permanent winter closure of the rest. It was finally resolved to run the line purely as a "scenic railway" for tourists, and with no early or late cars. A month later this Board introduced an eleven-journey timetable, operating only between 10.00 a.m. and 6.00 p.m. and scheduling complete winter closure from 19th September. Not unnaturally the reaction of the Island in general and the now-abandoned residential passengers of the period reacted bitterly and in the uproar that ensued, four of the five members of the Board resigned. A new Board was appointed on 10th July, and the full twenty-journey timetable was restored two days later on 12th July. Plans for winter closure were also abandoned, but just as the strikes and troubles of the 1956–7 period inflicted irremedial damage to Britain's motor bus industry, this Island episode severely shook the confidence of the residential traffic, and inflicted injury from which it never recovered.

Although the winter timetable remained relatively stable for many years, the evening services were pared down and latterly suffered from the lack of any connecting buses to or from the centre of Douglas; neither the 8.30 p.m. or the 9.35 p.m. arrivals at Derby Castle had connecting buses, and at one stage it became the practice for the MER Board's own black Ford Prefect (XMN 666) to collect any stranded passengers and take them on down the Promenades. In this respect, the line was paying the penalty imposed by the failure to complete the route through to Victoria Pier.

The Winter schedule introduced on 13th September 1971, eliminated the last two journeys between Douglas and Ramsey each weekday evening, and for the first time in nearly eighty years, the MER did not provide the time-honoured "Boat Car" from Ramsey to Douglas each morning. This timetable reduced the number of journeys per day from 20 to 14 and whilst some reduction in direct costs resulted,

it also discouraged many regular travellers who sought other means of transport. With declining patronage, the winter services were still further eroded with the timetable commencing on 29th September 1973, and still further a year later, when only six through journeys a day were scheduled, and two of these operated only on Tuesdays and Fridays. As detailed elsewhere, the entire line closed to all traffic on 30th September 1975. Although the Ramsey line was intended to be closed permanently, a single car continued to operate along it mornings and evenings, for MER staff, until a local newspaper correspondent enquired if this car could be permitted to carry fare-paying passengers as well. The MER Board of the time reacted swiftly, by eliminating the car and forcing even its own staff to use road transport.

TIMETABLE: SEPTEMBER 13 1971 until further notice WEEKDAYS ONLY - SUNDAY SERVICE SUSPENDED							
Douglas	7.15	10.00	11.45	1.15	2.45	4.15	5.45
LAXEY	7.45	10.25	12.10	1.40	3.10	4.40	6.10
Ramsey	8.30	11.10	12.55	2.25	3.55	5.25	6.55
Ramsey	8.35	10.25	11.50	1.25	2.50	4.25	5.45
LAXEY	9.15	11.05	12.35	2.05	3.30	5.05	6.30
Douglas	9.45	11.35	1.05	2.35	4.00	5.35	7.00

(Also applied during winter of 1972-3)

TIMETABLE: SEPTEMBER 29 1973 until further notice WEEKDAYS ONLY - SUNDAY SERVICE SUSPENDED							
Douglas	–	8.45	10.00	11.45	1.15	3.00	4.15
LAXEY	7.45	9.10	10.25	12.10	1.40	3.25	4.40
Ramsey	8.30	9.55	11.10	12.55	2.25	4.10	–
Ramsey	8.35	10.25	11.50	1.25	2.50	4.25	
LAXEY	9.15	11.05	12.35	2.05	3.30	5.05	
Douglas	9.45	11.35	1.05	2.35	4.00	5.35	

Although the MER's winter services did incur a considerable direct loss, there were and are cogent and compelling engineering and other reasons why it is highly desirable that even a regular skeleton service be maintained throughout the length of the Line. These are in no way connected with any assertions relating to the avoidance of statutory inspections.

The truncated seasonal service between Douglas and Laxey in 1976 commenced on 2nd May, with 22 scheduled journeys between 9.15 a.m. and 6.00 p.m. and continued until 30th September. Between 5th June and 16th September the service was augmented to provide a half-hour headway. No service operated during the winter of 1976–1977 and a timetable similar to that of the preceding year was operated during the early season of 1977. On 25th June, however, the Northern Line to Ramsey was once again reopened, and from 26th June a 24-journey schedule was introduced, and operated up to the end of September, when once again services were suspended altogether until the following spring. At the end of the 1980 season, however, a skeletal winter service was reintroduced from 6th October, and has continued ever since, subject to minor alterations.

FREIGHT & GOODS

The Traffic Department was also responsible for the handling of freight, goods and parcels, which for many years contributed substantial profits to the general undertaking. Whilst traffic of this nature might not have been part of the original 1893 concept, the IoMT&EP Co. espoused any means of revenue, and rapidly built up a significant business in freight tonnage. Much of this related to the output from the associated quarries at Dhoon and Ballajora, from which a vast tonnage of stone setts was exported. Business developed to the extent where by 1900 it had become necessary to produce Locomotive No. 23 and at least two other passenger cars were also used throughout the off-season solely to haul freight. At a slightly later stage some rolling stock (viz the 10–13 class cars) were converted for freight purposes, and large goods sheds were provided at Laxey, Ramsey (1903) and Douglas (1908). Much of the freight traffic consisted of livestock, milk, bagged corn, wheat, flour, fertilizer, coal, stone and other materials in addition to wet and dry goods of all descriptions.

Although the carriage of milk, livestock and heavy freight diminished after the First World War, the MER retained and indeed developed an enormous parcels and "smalls" collection and delivery service throughout the north of the Island, with other major segments being dealt with on a station-to-station basis, or to and from a series of MER Parcels Agents in Ramsey, Laxey and Douglas. The vast bulk of the goods and parcels traffic to or from the Island was handled by the Isle of Man Steam Packet Co., who maintained a limited distribution system of its own in Douglas and as far as the Manx Arms in Onchan, only. Items for the west or south of the Island were handled by Peel Carriers Ltd, and Southern Carriers Ltd respectively, for many years, but the entire east coast and the north of the Island was MER Co. territory. Off-line collection and delivery was originally carried out by horse carts, and later by road motor lorries and vans based at Douglas and Ramsey, where loads were transhipped into or out of rail vans as required. During the post First World War period until the early 1960s, freight mileage on the MER accounted for over 10% of all mileage operated and represented a significant proportion of the business as a whole.

The last major heavy freight contracts concerned the haulage of vast quantities of rubble spoil or "deads" from the Laxey Mines, either south to Douglas for their promenade widening schemes, or northward to Ramsey for transhipment into lorries for the construction of the wartime RAF airfields at Jurby and Andreas. By 1956 much of the freight rolling stock was derelict, with the exception of the vans and a few open wagons. The comprehensive parcels services were abandoned on and after 1st April 1966, officially because the road motor vehicles needed replacement; perhaps more important would have been a major revision of the supervisory arrangements of those directly dealing with the parcels business. The MER's statutory obligations as a common carrier were maintained even in the 1983 Act, and parcels and goods are still conveyed on a station-to-station basis, and the vans are available for use if the quantity so warrants.

MAIL TRAFFIC

The Manx Electric was also almost unique in its provisions for the carriage and even the collection of the Royal Mail. Shortly after the inauguration of services to Laxey in 1894, the IoMT&EP Co, secured a contract for the carriage of mails between Douglas and Onchan, Lonan and Laxey. Postmen and telegraph boys were also to be carried between Douglas and Baldrine. The mail, carried in locked bags, was transhipped at Derby Castle between the horse trams and carts, and speedy

and convenient handling might have benefited still further by the proposed electrification of the promenade horse tramway, which would have given virtually direct access to the main Post Office in Regent Street.

Once the IoMT&EP Company's northern extension to Ramsey had been completed in 1899, it was clear that a substantial saving in journey time over the Manx Northern Railway's circuitous line could be made by switching the Douglas–Ramsey mails to the new electric line. The MNR had been awarded a Mail contract when it opened in 1879, but by this time it had become involved in serious financial difficulties, brought about by the failure of the lead and silver mines at Foxdale, as a result of its own involvement with the Foxdale Railway. These troubles were eventually to lead to the MNR's amalgamation with the Isle of Man Railway Company in 1905.

In the wake of the IoMT&EP Company's own bankruptcy in 1900 and the formation of the Manx Electric Railway Co. Ltd. in 1902, a major effort was made to maximise the line's revenue, and on 30th July 1903, an Agreement between the MER Company and H.M. Postmaster General, the Rt. Hon. J.A. Chamberlain (father of Neville "Peace in our time" Chamberlain) which appears to have formalised some provisions already extant, but which was possibly unique in British postal history in that MER Conductors became auxiliary postmen. Under this arrangement Conductors were duly sworn in and signed a statutory declaration not to open, delay, impede, mutilate or endanger the post, and to expedite His Majesty's Royal Mail with all despatch. They were also reminded of the quite terrifying consequences of any transgression. No additional payment to the conductors was involved, and the GPO issued none of the badges usually associated with Postmen and nor was any additional time allowed on MER journeys which were now to make the actual collections from a total of eight lineside GPO letterboxes. In addition, the MER was given a monopoly for the carriage of bagged mail between the Douglas and Ramsey sorting offices.

These new arrangements apparently worked to everyone's satisfaction, and in the ensuing years some of the wayside letterboxes were relocated to positions closer to the lineside stops, in some cases onto land belonging to the MER Co.

In 1904 the MER Co. applied to the GPO to formalise mail arrangements for items posted at the Snaefell Summit Hotel. Ever since these premises had been opened in 1895 it had been the practice to sell endless souvenir postcards and lettercards which bore a special "Snaefell Summit" cachet or (rubber) impress stamp. A private letterbox was provided inside the Hotel and the box was cleared daily by MER staff at 4.00 p.m., and the contents sent down to Laxey for onward transmission via the official GPO arrangements. Under the 1904 Agreement the GPO paid the MER to convey one locked bag of Snaefell mail which was put on the old 4.45 p.m. departure from Laxey for Douglas, along with the mails from the north.

As the collection and carriage of the mail by the MER provided the GPO with a very good service in return for what the company described as "a very moderate payment', the contract rates were revised as and from 10th May 1908, and this was worth £225 per annum; it was terminable by six months notice on either side. Additional provisions included in this Agreement involved the conveyance of a Postman (or Postlady) from Laxey to Baldrine each weekday. This duty, for many years carried out by Mrs. Janie Cannell, actually involved meeting the northbound car at Baldrine to take off the bag containing the mail for delivery in that district.

Whilst the MER's Royal Mail contract was subject to minor revisions over the years, and the sum received by the company gradually increased, the basic arrangements changed little. Vans for parcels and bagged mail were provided on the 10.00 a.m., 5.15 p.m. and 8.00 p.m. journeys from Douglas to Ramsey, whilst the 6.45 a.m. and 2.30 p.m. cars from Ramsey not only involved a mail van, but also carried out the lineside collections. For these purposes the Conductors were provided with a red mail bag into which the contents of the letterboxes were to be put, along with a smaller cloth bag containing the batch of letterbox keys and collection time tablets, to be changed as collection took place at each box. The GPO regulations required that the mail bag had to be taken to each box and that otherwise it had to be kept chained and padlocked to the handbrake stanchion or such other immovable structural component as was found expedient. When the last letterbox had been cleared, the little cloth bag with the keys and time tablets had to be secured inside the neck of the red mail bag, ready for handing over to the Postman who would be waiting at Derby Castle for the car to arrive.

The First World War had little effect on the MER's postal contract, save only that the Snaefell section remained closed until the end of hostilities. From 1919 onwards some through mail runs were introduc-

The Manx Electric Railway

(Derby Castle Station---Terminus of Horse Tramway)

WHERE TO GO
this Afternoon !

THE MOST ENJOYABLE TRIP
ON THE ISLAND IS TO . .

LAXEY

by the popular

OPEN ELECTRIC CARS
from
DERBY CASTLE STATION

RETURN **3/-** RETURN

Travelling Time - 30 minutes each way

*Exhilarating Air - - Sylvan Glens
Magnificent Mountain and Marine Scenery
all the way*

YOU MAY BREAK THE JOURNEY AT *GROUDLE GLEN*
AND *GARWICK GLEN.* CARS EVERY FEW MINUTES

DON'T MISS THIS *Ideal Afternoon's Excursion !*

1 Strathallan Crescent,
Douglas.

J. ROWE,
J. F. WATSON,
(Joint Managers)

"Courier" Works, Ramsey

MANX ELECTRIC RAILWAY

Where to go To-day !

TRAVEL ELECTRIC . . . . . .
on the Popular Open Cars of MANXLAND'S
Famous Scenic Railway
from
DERBY CASTLE STATION
DOUGLAS (Terminus of Horse Tramway)
to

RAMSEY

Book
Return Fare **4/6** Book
Return Fare

The Ticket entitles the holder to break the journey
both going and returning at all the Charming Glens
en route : GROUDLE, GARWICK, LAXEY, DHOON,
GLEN MONA and BALLAGLASS. Ballajora for
Port Moar and Maughold Lighthouse

*Gorgeous Inland and Marine Scenery throughout :: Bracing
Sea and Mountain Air ! :: Frequent Service of Electric Cars !
Refreshments obtainable at all points !*

For all in search of Health and Pleasure
Do not miss this Delightful . . . .

Whole Day's Outing !

1 Strathallan Crescent,
Douglas.

J. ROWE,
J. F. WATSON,
(Joint Managers)

"Courier" Works, Ramsey

The Manx Electric Railway

(Derby Castle Station---Terminus of Horse Tramway)

Why not a Whole Day on the Island's Scenic Railway ?

NO. 1 TOUR
A WHOLE DAY'S GLORIOUS OUTING

DOUGLAS TO LAXEY

change for the SUMMIT of

SNAEFELL MOUNTAIN

return to LAXEY ; on to

RAMSEY

and back to DOUGLAS

You have the option of BREAKING YOUR JOURNEY
at all or any of the Numerous and Beautiful GLENS
WONDERFUL SEACOAST AND MOUNTAIN SCENERY

FARE **8/-** RETURN

*Children under 5 years, not occupying a seat—Free ;
over 5 years and under 15 years—Half Fare*

High Class Refreshments at All Principal Stopping Places
Licensed Hotels en route

1 Strathallan Crescent,
Douglas.

J. ROWE,
J. F. WATSON, } Joint Managers.

"Courier" Works, Ramsey.

IMPORTANT TO VISITORS

MANX ELECTRIC RAILWAY

The Direct Coast Route to LAXEY AND RAMSEY

A Continuous Panorama of Mountain, Glen and Marine
Scenery

2 Day Excursion
'ROVER' TICKET

ANYWHERE . . . ANYTIME
(Within Seven Days of Date of Issue)

Including ONE RETURN JOURNEY to

SUMMIT OF SNAEFELL
MOUNTAIN

Don't miss this golden
opportunity to see
MANXLAND'S FINEST SCENERY

TICKETS obtainable at the SEFTON BOOKING OFFICE
DERBY CASTLE STATION, LAXEY and RAMSEY

ASK FOR AN M.E.R. 'ROVER' TICKET

1 Strathallan Crescent
Douglas

H. GILMORE, General Manager

The Norris Modern Press Ltd., Douglas, Isle of Man

```
            TIMETABLE: SEPTEMBER 30 1974 until further notice
            MONDAY-FRIDAY ONLY - SATURDAY & SUNDAY SERVICE SUSPENDED
            SDO           TFO
Douglas     –     10.00   12.15   –      3.00
LAXEY       7.45  10.25   12.40   12.40  3.25
Ramsey      8.30  11.10   1.20    1.20   4.10

Ramsey      8.35  11.50   11.50   1.25   4.25
LAXEY       9.15  12.35   12.35   2.05   5.05
Douglas     9.45    –     1.05    2.35    –
            SDO           TFO

            SDO = School Days Only
            TFO = Tuesdays & Fridays Only
```

ISLE OF MAN TRANSPORT

MANX ELECTRIC RAILWAY

**During the Winter period the following timetable will operate
Monday – Friday**

Dep Douglas		A		11.20	1.30 pm	4.40
Dep Laxey	8.45 am	A	10.35	11.50 STOP	2.00	5.10 STOP
Arr Ramsey	9.30		11.20		2.45	

A — Tuesday only depart Derby Castle 10.00 a.m., arriving Laxey 10.35
to connect with 10.35 for Ramsey.

Dep Ramsey	9.45 am			12 noon	3.15	
Dep Laxey	10.30 STOP	B	12 noon	12.40 pm	4.00	
Arr Douglas		B	12.30 pm	1.10	4.30	

B — Tuesday only depart Laxey 10.35 a.m., arriving Derby Castle 11.05 a.m.

Motorists are reminded that in addition to the timetable, extra cars on maintenance and other duties are likely to run at any time, including Saturdays and Sundays. Also that parking on the railway track is strictly forbidden.

W. JACKSON, C.Eng.F.I.Mech.E.,
Chief Executive.

ISLE OF MAN TRANSPORT

MANX ELECTRIC RAILWAY

COMMENCING Monday, 8th December, the MER winter timetable will be amended to read as follows :—

CONNECTING Bus Dep Lord St.				1.05 p.m.	4.25 p.m.
Dep Derby Castle				1.30 p.m.	4.40 p.m.
Dep Laxey	8.45 a.m.	10.45 a.m.		2.00 p.m.	5.10 STOP
Arr Ramsey	9.30 a.m.	11.30 a.m.		2.45 p.m.	
Dep Ramsey	9.45 a.m.		12.10 p.m.	3.00 p.m.	
Dep Laxey	10.30 STOP		12.55 p.m.	3.45 p.m.	
Arr Derby Castle			1.25 p.m.	4.15 p.m.	
CONNECTING Bus Dep Derby Castle				1.42 p.m.	4.22 p.m.

ed on Sundays, and from some point in the later 1920s (almost certainly May 1928), an MER version of the "Postal Limited" was introduced. This departure was advertised (particularly on the IoMSPC steamers) as "The Mail Express" and was scheduled to stop only at Baldrine, Laxey and Ramsey, doing the complete journey in just under one hour. This service left Douglas at 3.30 p.m., or as soon thereafter as passengers and luggage from the steamer had boarded, and the train invariably consisted of a Winter Saloon and a van. The departure was demoted about 1937 and thereafter was indicated in the official timetables (along with certain other departures) simply as a "Boat Car" but with a 70-minute journey time.

By the 1930s the GPO Mail contract was worth £525 per annum and mail was conveyed by trains leaving Douglas at 7.00 a.m., 3.00 p.m. and 8.00 p.m., (9.00 a.m. and 3.30 p.m. in the winter) and leaving Ramsey by the 7.00 a.m., 1.30 p.m. and 4.30 p.m. cars in summer and the 7.00 a.m. and 2.15 p.m. in winter. On Sundays, vans were attached to the 8.00 p.m. Boat Car for Ramsey, and the 7.50 p.m. car to Douglas, for the conveyance of bagged mail.

The postal contract brought benefits not only to the GPO and the MER but also helped to provide an economic rural postal service of considerable merit. The contract was renegotiated with the GPO in 1958–9, following the nationalisation of the MER, and increased the payment to £657 10s. 0d. per annum. During the time that the Douglas–Ramsey line was severed by the cliff fall near Ballaragh, all of the through mail was temporarily diverted to road vehicles, although the MER cars still continued to make their normal lineside collections. In the autumn of 1972, the MER Board of the period substantially

reduced the winter timetable to an extent where it was no longer possible to meet the GPO requirements, and the 4.25 p.m. car from Ramsey on 9th September 1972, cleared the lineside letterboxes at Laxey, Baldrine, Halfway House, Groudle and Onchan Harbour (Majestic) for the last time.

This left the MER with a residual contract to clear the remaining letterboxes at Belle Vue, Ballajora and Glen Mona; this was done by the 11.50 a.m. car from Ramsey each weekday, and a GPO motor van met the car at Laxey to receive the single mailbag. This arrangement continued up to the outright closure of the Laxey–Ramsey line on 30th September 1975, when for the last time, the Royal Mail was collected and carried by the MER and seventy years of a unique contractual agreement came to a close. As and from the same date, the letterboxes at Belle Vue and Glen Mona were closed altogether. It is a matter of considerable surprise that the MER postal facilities were not recorded by the GPO (later Crown) Film Unit. At one stage in the 1960s a budding scriptwriter came up with the scenario for a full-length motion picture based on the "Great Mail Tram Robbery" and to feature the MER, but in the wake of the real "Great Train Robbery" of the time the idea was severely frowned upon by the GPO and got no further.

MARKETING & PUBLICITY

The Line's advertising and publicity is deserving of a special study in its own right, for an enormous effort was made not only to attract and procure custom and increase revenue, but also to provide and market what might be termed "terminal purposes" for excursionists, and ranging from the organisation or sponsoring of events, exhibitions and displays, to the development of the lineside glens. Whilst Groudle and Garwick Glens were owned and operated by nominally independent proprietors, the extensive Laxey Glen Gardens complex was acquired by the MER sometime later; Dhoon and Ballaglass Glens were developed by the MER from the beginning and attracted vast patronage until the Second World War, and all of these attractions were featured in the Railway's advertising.

For the greater part of eighty years the MER primarily relied upon handbills and posters; during the period when the same concern owned the horse and cable cars in Douglas, these inevitably carried advertisements for the electric line, and indeed, the MER continued to advertise on the horse trams until relatively recently. The winter and summer timetables were printed and distributed in very large numbers; indeed, the order for the pocket-size summer timetable of 1959 ran to 150,000 copies. In addition there were display timetables (approximately 12" by 16" and 12" by 10" in size) which were distributed to shops, hotels and so on, as well as being posted in the cars and at each wayside shelter.

In addition to the traditional handbills and posters, the MER at one time also decorated the front of their general offices at Nos. 1 and 2, Strathallan Crescent, Douglas, with a canvas advert for the Snaefell line. The Company was quick to try new advertising media and distributed lantern slides to the cinemas in Douglas and Ramsey for many years. They also produced attractive folders extolling the beauties of the Line and its wayside attractions, and at one stage also sold a guide book which described the route in some detail. A great deal of excursion business was procured by the MER booking office at the Sefton Hotel on Harris Promenade in Douglas. With an overhaul of publicity arrangements in the post-nationalisation period, the Board produced in 1959 a 20-minute 16 mm promotional colour film, which showed the MER's most spectacular views and settings. For some years the film was exhibited on a suitable screen in the Sefton booking office, until it was superceded by a series of colour slides. Other MER advertising ranged from the erection of the giant illuminated sign on the hillside above Derby Castle Carworks, to the use of Manx Radio. The illuminated sign originally showed 'M.E.R FOR SCENERY' but after a gorse fire damaged some of the letters, it was rearranged to show 'ELECTRIC RAILWAY.' The sign itself was dismantled having been out of use for some time, but an entirely new one was commissioned in 1993.

Competition from local motor coach operators reached very serious proportions in the 1950s, but the MER successfully retaliated and maintained its share of the market. One promotional idea, tried out about this time, was the use of "soap coupons" which were distributed in very large numbers to hotels and boarding houses, and which entitled the bearer to a 25% discount on normal fares on any Thursday, Friday or Saturday. The Island's Road Traffic Act of 1966 substantially curtailed some of the wild excesses of local motor coach operations.

In addition to the advertising of their normal services, the MER has always tried hard to participate and promote joint ventures of one sort and another. Before the Second World War there was a provision whereby passengers could go one way or the other between Douglas

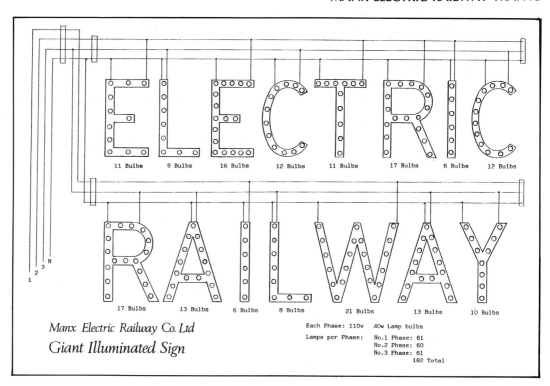

11 Bulbs 9 Bulbs 16 Bulbs 12 Bulbs 11 Bulbs 17 Bulbs 6 Bulbs 12 Bulbs

17 Bulbs 13 Bulbs 6 Bulbs 8 Bulbs 21 Bulbs 13 Bulbs 10 Bulbs

Manx Electric Railway Co. Ltd
Giant Illuminated Sign

Each Phase: 110v   40w Lamp bulbs
Lamps per Phase: No.1 Phase: 61
                   No.2 Phase: 60
                   No.3 Phase: 61
                        182 Total

Below: The "Grand Tour" operated for the last time in 1958, run in conjunction with the Isle of Man Railway Co.

MANX ELECTRIC RAILWAY

THE most popular day's outing in the Island is the Personally Conducted Tour through the MANX SWITZERLAND and Peak District by SPECIAL ELECTRIC CAR, MOTOR COACH and Narrow Gauge STEAM TRAIN

(Particulars on the other side)

FIVE SEPARATE KINGDOMS can be viewed FROM THE TOP OF SNAEFELL MOUNTAIN

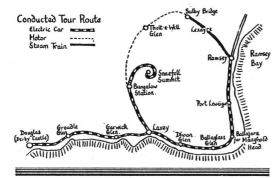

Conducted Tour Route
Electric Car
Motor
Steam Train

TO SPEND A PLEASANT HALF-DAY BOOK TO

GARWICK
GLEN AND CAVES

THE ISLAND CAN BOAST NO MORE BEAUTIFUL SPOT

ON THE MANX ELECTRIC RAILWAY

Full of Interest and Charm from its own Station to the Sea

BREAK YOUR JOURNEY if holding THROUGH or "ROVER" Tickets

RETURN FARE from DERBY CASTLE 2/6 ONLY

(See over)

NMP 114.

Finest for Scenery . . .
Manx Electric Railway

Personally
CONDUCTED TOUR

(DISTINCTIVE FROM ALL OTHER TOURS IN THE ISLAND)

OF ALMOST 50 MILES THROUGH

The Manx Switzerland
INCLUDING HOTEL LUNCHEON

The Most Popular Whole Day's Outing in the Island!

EVERY WEEKDAY

(WEATHER AND OTHER CIRCUMSTANCES PERMITTING)

A RESERVED ELECTRIC CAR leaves Derby Castle Station at 10 a.m. accompanied by a Guide to explain the interesting points en route. Seats are limited to 50 Daily

ITINERARY—Leave Derby Castle by Special Electric Car at 10 a.m. for Laxey Glen Gardens and the thrilling climb to the Summit of Snaefell Mountain (2,034 feet) where a first class five course Luncheon will be served in the famous Summit Hotel, thence to Snaefell Bungalow Station, where Saloon Motor Coaches will take the party to the renowned Tholt-e-Will Glen. The party will be conveyed from the Glen by Saloon Motor Coaches through the charming Vale of Sulby to Sulby Glen Station, thence by narrow gauge Steam Train to Ramsey where, after a full opportunity of exploring this ancient Northern Town, a special Electric Car will be waiting for the return journey to Douglas by the Coast Route, through magnificent marine and mountain scenery, arriving back in Douglas at 5.30 p.m.

As the number of the Party is limited to 50, to avoid disappointment Tickets should be booked in advance at the Derby Castle Terminus or the Branch Office at Sefton Hotel, Harris Promenade, Douglas. (Money willingly refunded in full if weather unfavourable and Tour postponed).

INCLUSIVE FARE **14/-** NO EXTRA CHARGE

A Most Charming and Romantic Spot is **GARWICK**

A BEAUTIFUL GLEN running down to the Sea, with wonderful Caves, Romantic Shore and Headlands, Wish-Stone, Maze, Water Lily Ponds, famous Tea Gardens, Boating and Fishing. On the Manx Electric Railway. Devote another day to it. Book direct, or break your journey, if holding the "Rover" Tickets.

1 Strathallan Crescent,
Douglas.

J. ROWE, Secretary.
J. F. WATSON, Chief Engineer.

---

and Ramsey by MER, and return via any IoMSPC ship calling at Ramsey's Queen's Pier. This provision was suspended with the outbreak of war in 1939, but was restored in 1966. However by then the number of steamers calling at Ramsey had dwindled, and very few took advantage of this unusual facility. Other examples from the 1960s would include special tickets which included not only a Douglas–Ramsey return but also admission to the Ramsey Town Commission's Mooragh Park bowls and putting, golf and motor boats. Similarly, special events such as the Royal Manx Agricultural Show in Ramsey was heavily adver-

tised and joint rail and admission tickets sold in quantity.

Quite apart from the endless souvenirs sold by the MER at the Snaefell Summit Hotel, one of the most enduring aspects of publicity material consisted of the very wide range of official commercial postcards. These were sold in colossal quantities and all bore the crest or title of the Manx Electric. With at least three major series, the MER's official postcards have proved to be exceedingly difficult to record, but those that are known are listed in Appendix 3.

BYE-LAWS

The Manx Electric Railway Co. Limited.

MADE WITH REFERENCE TO

The Douglas, Laxey, and Ramsey Electric Tramway

UNDER ACTS OF TYNWALD

By the I.O.M. Tramways & Electric Power Co., Ltd., whose powers and undertakings are now vested in THE MANX ELECTRIC RAILWAY CO., LTD.

WHEREAS the DOUGLAS & LAXEY COAST ELECTRIC TRAMWAY, LIMITED, were empowered by, inter alia, the 133, 134 and 135 sections of the Isle of Man Railway Act, 1872, incorporated with the Douglas and Laxey Electric Tramway Act, 1893, from time to time, and subject to the provisions, restrictions, modifications, variations, and qualifications in such Acts contained to make such Bye-laws as they should think fit for the purposes by the said Acts authorised.

And whereas, the name of the said Company was subsequently changed to "The Isle of Man Tramways and Electric Power Company, Limited" (hereinafter called "The Company.")

Now, the Company do hereby ordain and declare that the following Bye-laws shall be the Bye-laws made under and by virtue of the said Acts:—

1.—The Bye-laws hereinafter set forth shall extend and apply to all places and carriages with respect to which the Company have power to make such Bye-laws.

2.—Every passenger shall enter or depart from a closed carriage by the hindermost and from an open carriage by the footboard of such carriage, and not otherwise.

3.—No passenger shall smoke tobacco inside any closed carriage or waiting-room of the Company not set apart for that purpose by the Company, and every person persisting in smoking in any such closed carriage or waiting-room, after being warned by any servant of the Company to desist, may, in addition to incurring the penalty hereinafter provided, be immediately removed from the Company's closed carriage or premises, and forfeit any fare he may have paid.

4.—No passenger or other person shall, while travelling in or upon any carriage, play or perform upon any musical instrument.

5.—Any person in a state of intoxication shall not be allowed to enter or mount upon any carriage, and if found in or upon any carriage, station, or elsewhere upon the Company's premises, may be immediately removed from such carriage or premises, by or under the direction of the conductor, or other duly authorised servant of the Company, and, if a passenger, forfeit any fare which he may have paid.

6.—No passenger shall swear or use obscene or offensive language whilst in or upon any carriage, or commit any nuisance, in or upon or against any carriage, or wilfully interfere with the comfort of any passenger.

7.—No person shall wilfully cut, soil, damage, remove, or deface any cushion, number plate, printed or other notice, or break or scratch any window of, or otherwise wilfully damage any carriage. Any penalty to which any person may be subject under this Bye-law shall be in addition to the amount of any damage for which he may be liable.

8.—Any person whose condition or clothing is such as to soil or injure the carriage or the clothing of any passenger, or any person who is for any other reason offensive to passengers, shall not be entitled to mount, enter, or remain upon, and may be prevented from mounting upon or entering any carriage, and if found in or upon any carriage, shall, on the request of the conductor, leave the carriage, upon the fare, if previously paid, being returned.

9.—Each passenger shall, upon demand, pay to the conductor, or other duly authorised officer of the Company, the fare legally demandable for the journey.

10.—Each passenger shall show his ticket, when requested so to do, to the conductor, or any duly authorised servant of the Company, and shall also, when required so to do, either deliver up his ticket or pay the fare legally demandable for the distance travelled over by such passenger.

11.—Personal or other luggage (including the tools of artisans, mechanics, and daily labourers) shall, unless otherwise permitted by the conductor, be placed in a compartment specially set apart for the conveyance of parcels, and not in the interior of any carriage.

12.—No passenger or other person not being a servant of the Company shall be permitted to travel on the steps or platforms of any carriage, or stand in the interior, or sit on any rail or any other part of a carriage not intended for passengers, and shall cease to do so immediately on request by the conductor.

13.—No person shall sell or offer for sale any goods or merchandise of any sort in or upon any carriage or premises of the Company.

14.—When any carriage contains the prescribed number of passengers, no additional persons shall enter, mount, or remain in, upon any such carriage when warned by the conductor not to do so.

15.—No person shall enter, mount, hang on, or leave any carriage whilst in motion.

16.—No dog or other animal shall be allowed in or upon any carriage in any case in which the conveyance of such dog or other animal is offensive or an annoyance to passengers. No person shall take a dog, or other animal into or upon any carriage after having been requested not to do so by the conductor. . . Any dog or other animal taken into or upon any carriage, in breach of this Bye-law, shall be removed by the person in charge of such dog or other animal from the carriage immediately upon request by the conductor, and, in default of compliance with such request, may be removed by or under the direction of the conductor.

17.—No person shall travel in or upon any carriage of the Company with loaded firearms.

18.—No person shall wilfully obstruct or impede any officer or servant of the Company in the execution of his duty upon the Tramway, or upon or in any of the stations or other works or premises connected therewith; and no person shall wilfully obstruct or interfere with the traffic upon the Tramway or endanger the safety of any person travelling by any carriage upon the Tramway.

19.—The expression "conductor" shall include any officer or servant in the employment of the Company having charge of a carriage.

20.—A single journey ticket shall be available only in respect of the journey in which the car for which such ticket is issued, and not by any other car.

21.—Any passenger travelling by a car which is making a journey other than that for which his ticket has been issued, shall be liable to pay another fare, calculable from the point at which the journey on which he is so travelling commenced.

22.—Any person offending against, or committing a breach of, any of these Bye-laws, shall be liable to a penalty not exceeding five pounds.

"Examiner" Printing Works, Hill Street, Douglas.

CHAPTER THREE

TICKETS

The Manx Electric's ticketing system is as unique as the Railway itself, combining aspects of pure railway, tramway and omnibus theory with a curious blend of ancient and modern practice. It has often been said that from a very early stage the MER's ticketing system provided the missing link between the original Edmondson railway-type card tickets and the geographical or numerical stage-type Bell Punch tickets that were once so familiar on every tram or bus. For sheer complexity and the provision of little-known facilities, the entire Manx Electric ticketing system probably has no equal.

The purpose of any ticket and fare collection system is to provide the operator with a fraudproof means of recording the receipt of cash, and to provide the passenger with a receipt for the fare paid, usually denoting the stage or station boarded, and indicating the point to which that fare entitles the passenger to travel; it may also carry other details, including the date, to guard against improper or fraudulent use. The serially-numbered tickets may be cancelled by punching (either by machine or hand-nippers) either on issue or on presentation; they may also be taken off the passenger at the end of his ride. With printed stock tickets of this nature, the conductor or booking clerk must finish his day with his remaining stock and cash equal to the value of stock sold, an utterly convincing set of reasons, or the sack.

TICKET SYSTEMS

For those unfamiliar with the various species of ticket, it is perhaps worth outlining the various systems in roughly chronological order. In railway practice, with its complex classes, types and routings, printed stock tickets made their appearance as the familiar pasteboard oblong, approximately 1 3/16" wide and 2¼" long, and known as the "Edmondson card" after its inventor, Thomas Edmondson, born in Lancaster in June 1792. This system became almost universal throughout the railways of the world, and was in use by BR until fairly recent times. In the early days of the horse tram or bus in public transport, fares were collected in a box into which coins were deposited, with no ticket or receipt in exchange. Such a system had obvious and elementary flaws, and printed receipts or tickets in roll or pad form made their appearance in order to prove that each passenger had paid his fare. With human nature the way it is, it quickly became necessary to introduce some form of cancelling device to prevent the re-issue of used tickets (or "Joeys" as they seem to be known). Initially tickets were cancelled with a hand punch or nippers, but these measures were insufficient to counter fraud by employees, and a mechanical punch, which would ring a bell only when it actually punched a hole, as well as counting the number of punches made, was introduced. One of the earliest bell punches in use in the Island was the BARKER, of circa 1895 and closely followed by the more common BELL PUNCH and WILLIAMSON punch. It is important to appreciate that all of these punches had a device that detected the type of paper between the jaws, and would not work at all if the wrong type of paper was offered. In addition, the same sensing device ensured that the punch would not ring if an already punched ticket was offered to the machine. These and other safeguards largely eliminated fraudulent re-issue.

Tickets for punch systems were printed on relatively thick paper of different colours, according to value, and the tiny particles punched from each ticket were kept in a chamber inside the machine so that in the event of a discrepancy they could be taken out and stuck on sheets of gummed paper in colour (and therefore value) order to prove the exact total of the tickets punched, and thus the total sum owing. Bell punch type tickets were printed to show stages either by number or by geographical designation according to the operator's practice. The old geographical stages tended to disappear many years ago, although Douglas Corporation retained them long after almost everyone else.

Later ticket printing machines such as the GIBSON (used by London Transport and Douglas Corporation), T.I.M. (Ticket Issuing Machines Ltd) and the SETRIGHT SPEED print the value, type, class and validity of the ticket onto a roll of paper at the time of issue. All of these expensive machines also calculate the total value of tickets issued, and this and other information is displayed in a series of windows; in this way, and unlike the earlier (and perhaps better) systems, the conductor knew precisely how much cash was owing. Of these types, only the Setright Speed machine has been used on the Manx Electric.

ROLL tickets consist of printed stock, originally torn off by hand, but later mechanised, usually by the AUTOMATICKET machine (more familiarly used by cinemas) or by the ULTIMATE machine, where a bank of appropriate values was issued from a machine carried by the conductor. The Manx Electric used an AUTOMATICKET machine in the period prior to and after the Second World War at Onchan Head Station to cope with the intensive local traffic from this point. Persistent rumours that this or a similar machine was also installed at Groudle have not been confirmed. The Automaticket stock used by the MER were standard stock rolls, showing only the value and serial number, with no title.

MANX ELECTRIC RAILWAY PRACTICE

The ticket arrangements during the early years of the Line have not been well documented and it appears that the IoMT&EP Co. used a combination of Bell Punch and Edmondson tickets, apparently depending on their value. From about 1902, the Edmondson type ticket, in its various forms, became almost universal.

The bulk of MER tickets (with a few exceptions to be dealt with later) still consist of Edmondson cards of traditional size and thickness, but laid out in Bell Punch style. The spaces for punching and clipping are numerous and represent intermediate points which may be used for breaks of journey, a facility for which the MER has long been famous. The points listed on the tickets do not necessarily always relate to fare stages.

The majority of MER tickets are purchased from booking offices before boarding the car. There are booking offices at the stations at Derby Castle, Laxey, Ramsey, the Bungalow, Snaefell Summit and the Sefton town office in Douglas. Those boarding a car at intermediate points along the route can buy tickets from the car conductor, as is also the case when the booking offices are closed. In the case of tickets purchased from booking offices, these are validated for travel when presented to the conductor, who cancels this validity as required by the passenger. In cases where the passenger exercises his right to unlimited stop-overs or breaks of journey, it is by no means impossible to finish up with a ticket having eight or more different clips.

The printed card ticket stocks consisted until recently of a very substantial range, covering every main stop or station; this has now been reduced to the stops at Douglas, Onchan Head, Groudle, South Cape, Laxey, Dhoon Glen, Glen Mona, Ballaglass, Ballajora and Ramsey on the coastal line, and Laxey, the Bungalow and the Summit on the Snaefell section. The stocks consist of singles and returns for adults and child half-fares. Formerly the car conductors carried the same basic range, but with the main stops preprinted, and over-printed with the cash value, until the end of October 1980 when an assortment of Setright Speed ticket machines were introduced. Some of the early paper rolls for these machines were made of poor quality yellow paper and the equally poor standard of production meant that it was not unusual to find the printed title running along the middle of the roll instead of at the head.

The MER's Edmondson card tickets have long been famous for the comprehensive range of overprints, and nearly all card stocks still have blocked overprints in different colours. In addition, overprinted route or type codes are used, formerly in contrasting hues but nowadays commonly in black. The overprint code for journeys consist of the following:

DR   Douglas and Laxey section
DRS   Douglas–Ramsey Single
DRR   Douglas–Ramsey Return
RS   Ex-Ramsey single
RR   Ex-Ramsey Return
DSS   Douglas–Snaefell Single
DSR   Douglas–Snaefell Return
LSS   Laxey–Snaefell Single
LSR   Laxey–Snaefell Return
SS   Bungalow–Snaefell Single
SR   Bungalow–Snaefell Return

TICKET NIPPER PATTERNS

Each individual ticket nipper makes a distinctive punch-mark which enables the conductor concerned to be instantly identified by head office. At least 35 patterns are known to have been used, and the above is a representative selection. The nippers themselves, which are inordinately expensive, were supplied for many years by Tools and Equipment Ltd. of Highgate, and Williamsons of Ashton, but are nowadays purchased from the old-established firm of Thos. Newey & Co. of Birmingham.

The prefix "½" before any of these overprints denotes a child or half-fare rate ticket. In earlier times, when the MER operated a char-a-banc or motor coach service between the Bungalow and Tholt-y-Will Glen, there was a further set of overprint codes, using 'TS' and 'TR' to denote Bungalow–Tholt-y-Will single or return tickets respectively.

Some of these sectional/geographical tickets were gradually superceded in part by new and more recent issues, having an overprint of the fare value, originally in shillings and pence, and then after February 1971 in the decimal equivalent. Most if not all of the early decimal overprints were actually hand-stamped with rubber stamps by the Traffic Office staff.

In addition to the standard range of tickets, the MER Co. and later the Board issued "Voucher" or "Name" tickets to regular travellers, in booklets of 20 pre-paid coupons and which were sold at discounted winter and summer rates. These coupons were torn out of the booklet by the conductor as required, and the passenger received a no cash value exchange ticket in return. "Name" tickets were obtained from the booking offices at Douglas, Laxey or Ramsey on demand, or in the case of passengers who lived in remote parts and rarely got to any of the main stations, they could be obtained via the conductor on a day's notice. "Name" tickets were officially valid only for travel by the person(s) named inside the front cover of the booklet, and only between the points written on the cover. In an era where the Manx Electric was fighting to retain every passenger, chapter and verse were not always rigidly adhered to, and it was not unknown for a conductor to settle for say two Douglas–Laxey coupons for a journey from Douglas to Ramsey. Quite apart from these tickets, the MER also offered long-term Contracts at extremely attractive rates. In 1966 for example, the "Any Station to Any Station" three-month Contract rate was £5. and it was calculated that a really dedicated passenger, travelling all day and every day could, if he survived, clock up almost 16,000 miles in the period of validity, a remarkable transport bargain by any standard.

Staff and Privilege MER tickets were and remain standard Edmondson cards, normally on yellow board with a bar overprint in green; some were overstamped with 'REPTA' indicating the MER's participation in the organisation that used to be responsible for negotiating railway employees' privilege travel facilities.

Until well into the 1960s, it was the practice for Inspectors to board cars travelling towards Douglas at Groudle, Howstrake or Onchan Head (or for the car to be stopped at Onchan Head) for the express purpose of collecting all tickets from passengers. This procedure tends to explain why some types of ticket very rarely found their way into private collections, although any interested parties enquiring about used tickets at the old Head Office were usually rewarded by having a number of cardboard boxes, filled with tickets, thrust into their arms.

All of the MER tickets issued from booking offices were invariably arranged to provide a space for dating across the head, by means of a ticket date press or date stamp. Dating was largely unnecessary, except for the Rover and similar tickets, and ceased many years ago.

TOURS, ROVERS AND SPECIAL FACILITIES

From a date well before the First World War the MER offered two inclusive tour tickets: No. 1 Tour covered a journey from Douglas to Laxey, up to the Summit of Snaefell and back to Laxey, then on to Ramsey, and return from Ramsey to Douglas. The No. 2 Tour consisted of Douglas to Laxey, Laxey to the Bungalow and to Tholt-y-Will, back to the Bungalow and then to the Summit, and down to Laxey and home to Douglas. The tickets for these popular trips were white with a red circle overprint for the No. 1 Tour. and an overprinted outline figure '2' for the No. 2 Tour. Whilst the No. 2 Tour is no longer possible, the No. 1 Tour ticket was still available in 1988 at a price of £5 and is popular amongst enthusiasts who are aware of this otherwise little-known facility. The third variety, of "Personally Conducted All-Day Tour" tickets, issued up to 1939, were substantially larger than normal and made up into a small book of coupons, torn out for collection as required, and including meal tickets. MER Tour passengers visiting Tholt-y-Will Glen were given small brass tokens at the Bungalow, which entitled the bearer to gain free admission to the Glen. Otherwise the admission price was 4d.

The MER also successfully promoted a "Rover" ticket giving two (not necessarily consecutive) days' unlimited travel on the line, including one return trip to the Summit of Snaefell. Although there was some form of similar ticket in existence in earlier times, the "Rover" as it now exists was first introduced on May 26, 1928 (at a price of 5s. 0d.) with the intention of countering the growing menace of motor buses; at this date the "Personally Conducted Tour" ticket (which also included luncheon) was being sold at 8s. 6d.

For many years the MER was also prepared to deliver individual newspapers which, in the case of people dwelling by the lineside, could be thrown off as the car passed; others were left in private nooks and crannies or dropped off at wayside shelters for collection. Car conductors necessarily acquired considerable skill in flinging the rolled newspapers towards their intended destinations, and the force and aim had to be adjusted according to the wind and other circumstances. Quite how much force was necessary could be open to some doubt, and a remarkably unpleasant recipient had her parlour window broken on more than one occasion when her newspaper arrived with all the force of a missile; malevolent intent under these circumstances was unusually difficult to prove afterwards. The fee for MER newspaper deliveries appears to have originated at 2d. per week, later rising to ½d. per day and latterly to 1d. Newsagents wishing to use this service could buy small batches of pre-paid wrappers. This individual service is not to be confused with the carriage of newspapers in bulk, which were conveyed aboard the passenger cars as express parcels.

With the vast range and multiplicity of special provisions involved in MER tickets, and the system that has naturally evolved over the past ninety years, the need for economy and reduced costs resulted in a well-known authority on ticket and fare collection systems being asked in the 1960s if he could think of a suitable replacement scheme which would also have enabled most of the tickets to be issued on the car. After many months of evaluation. it was suggested that the only foolproof system readily available at the time was an adaptation of the "Willebrew" system, using three main types of pre-printed tickets in conjunction with their machines and over-reach nippers. At that time the Willebrew machine rental was less than £1 per year, and the tickets were approximately 1.2p. per 100.

Another little-known facility was available on the MER for a number of years from about 1964 until the demise of the winter service in 1975, whereby passengers travelling to Derby Castle, and intending to continue their journey along the Promenade by Douglas Corporation bus, could purchase an "Extension" ticket from the MER conductor. Douglas Corporation Bell Punch tickets were used for the purpose, and supplied to the MER in pads of 100 from DCTD stocks. They were sold at a small discount, and if the standard bus fare was 6d, the tickets could be bought by MER passengers at 5d. The ticket was sold unpunched by the MER conductor, and cancelled by the DCTD conductor aboard the bus.

In 1977, as a result of efforts by the local railway associations, a new joint "Rail Rover" ticket was introduced, valid on both the steam and electric railways. With the nationalisation of the Isle of Man steam Railway early in 1978 and the takeover of IoM National Transport's buses in 1980, the somewhat curious direction and management of the time introduced an amazing assortment of other types of "Rover" ticket, including a 3-day Rover, valid on both railways and including a return Snaefell trip, and a 5-day rover valid on both railways and on the buses as well. Initially these specifically excluded the bus routes along Douglas Promenade (!) but this has now been corrected. The validity of these tickets commences on the day of issue and is consecutive. Yet a further series of discount tickets became available in 1979 for Manx residents who could purchase seasonal contracts on the MER and IMR. None is valid on the Snaefell section. These were sold at extremely low rates, and the cost of the most expensive IMR/MER Adult, was originally only £10 and valid for unlimited travel between 5th April and 1st October. Not surprisingly, these tickets destroyed the market for "Name" and Contract tickets, although the former are still available if required.

The MER and IMR also have provision for family travel, whereby a maximum of four children travel free after paying for the adults and a first child. The tickets are overstamped "Pass 2/3/4" as appropriate.

The printed ticket stocks for the Isle of Man Tramways & Electric Power Co. Ltd. were provided by Fosters of Nottingham, a long-defunct ticket printer, but from about the turn of the century, all ticket printing was carried out by Alfred Williamson Ltd., of Ashton-under-Lyne near Manchester. MER tickets were still being provided by this historic company when it ceased to trade in the early 1980s. Thereafter the current range of printed stocks have been supplied by a number of printers, including British Railways, but since the beginning of 1987 have been handled by Bemrose & Son of Derby. This firm, although now part of a major printing group, began life and flourished as the printers to the Midland Railway Company.

WINTER FARE TABLE 1964 – 5

Top fares are return fares.

GLEN MONA – BALLAJORA
8d RETURN

Fares shown as **return / single** (top fare in the table is the return fare).

Station abbreviations for column headings:
Dgl = Douglas; OnB = Onchan Head/Braeside; How = Howstrake Camp; Grd = Groudle; Gar = H.W.House/Garwick; Bbg = Ballabeg; SoC = Fairy Cottage/South Cape; Lax = Laxey/Minorca; Blr = Ballaragh; Dho = Dhoon; GlM = Glen Mona; BGC = B'Glass/Cornaa; BSk = B'Skeig; Bjo = B'jora; Lew = Lewaigue

To \ From	Dgl	OnB	How	Grd	Gar	Bbg	SoC	Lax	Blr	Dho	GlM	BGC	BSk	Bjo	Lew
Onchan Head/Braeside	4/3														
Howstrake Camp	7/4	4/3													
Groudle	10/6	7/4	4/3												
Halfway House/Garwick	1/-·8	10/6	7/4	4/3											
Ballabeg/Fairy Cottage	1/3·9	1/-·7	10/6	7/4	4/3										
South Cape	1/5·10	1/3·9	1/-·7	10/6	7/4	4/3									
Laxey/Minorca	1/6·11	1/5·10	1/3·9	1/-·7	10/6	7/4	4/3								
Ballaragh	1/9·1/1	1/7·11	1/5·10	1/3·9	1/-·7	10/6	7/4	4/3							
Dhoon	2/1·1/2	2/-·1/1	1/7·11	1/5·10	1/3·9	1/-·7	10/6	7/4	4/3						
Glen Mona	2/3·1/3	2/1·1/2	2/-·1/1	1/7·11	1/5·10	1/3·9	1/-·7	10/6	7/4	4/3					
Ballaglass/Cornaa	2/6·1/4	2/3·1/3	2/1·1/2	2/-·1/1	1/7·11	1/5·10	1/3·9	1/-·7	10/6	7/4	4/3				
Ballaskeig	2/9·1/6	2/6·1/4	2/3·1/3	2/1·1/2	2/-·1/1	1/7·11	1/5·10	1/3·9	1/-·7	10/6	7/4	4/3			
Ballajora	3/-·1/9	2/9·1/6	2/6·1/4	2/3·1/3	2/1·1/2	2/-·1/1	1/7·11	1/5·10	1/3·9	1/-·7	10/6	7/4	4/3		
Lewaigue	3/3·1/9	3/-·1/9	2/9·1/6	2/6·1/4	2/3·1/3	2/1·1/2	2/-·1/1	1/7·11	1/5·10	1/3·9	1/-·7	10/6	7/4	4/3	
Ramsey	3/6·2/-	3/3·1/9	3/-·1/9	2/9·1/6	2/6·1/4	2/3·1/3	2/1·1/2	2/-·1/1	1/7·11	1/5·10	1/3·9	1/-·7	10/6	7/4	4/3

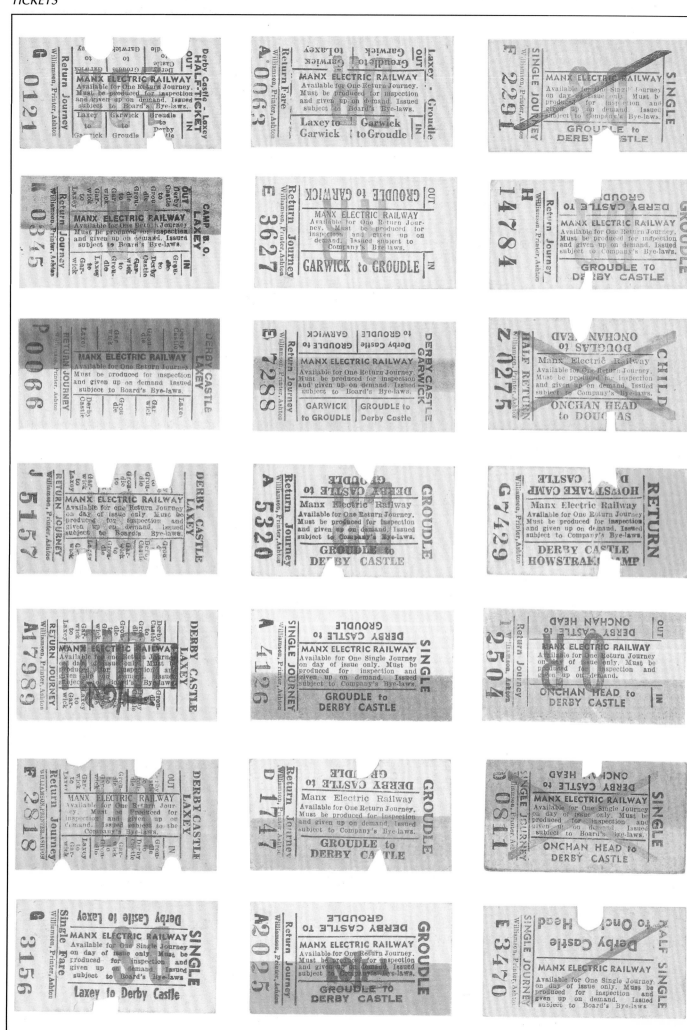

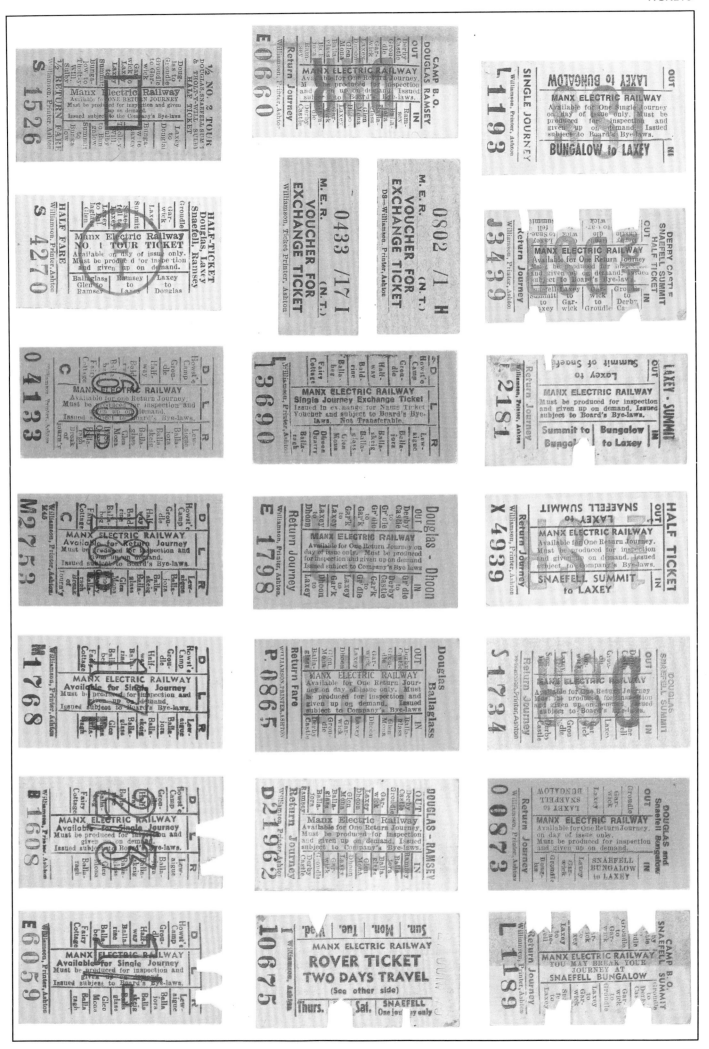

CHAPTER FOUR

ROLLING STOCK

Like so much else on the Manx Electric Railway, the line's rolling stock fleet is extremely distinctive and very unusual. With the exception of one group of four cars, and those lost in the Laxey Car Depot fire of 1930, every tramcar used on the line since its inception in 1893 still exists. Since the fleet essentially dates from the first delivery in 1893 to the last in 1906 (if the replica trailer carbodies of 1930 are discounted), the youngest car is now nearly ninety years old, a longevity that would have been impractical had it not been for high quality maintenance and the peculiar operating circumstances, in which limited seasonal use is made of a majority of the fleet. In mechanical terms, the Island winters are very long; in economic terms the summers are short and getting shorter.

1–3. UNVESTIBULED SALOONS

For the opening of the line from Douglas to Groudle in 1893, three 38-seat open-platformed saloon cars were supplied by G.F. Milnes & Co. Ltd., of Birkenhead. The cars were mounted on Milnes equal-wheel plate frame bogie trucks fitted with Mather & Platt traction motor equipment. The two surviving cars (Nos. 1 and 2) of the original three are worthy of special study not only because they are the oldest electric cars still at work on their original lines anywhere in the world, but also because of the particular era in the development of electric traction technology that they represent. The carbodies are outstanding examples of the art of contemporary vehicular coachbuilding, with a remarkably high weight/strength ratio, which was as vital to the era of horse-drawn vehicles as it was later to become in aviation. The trucks are classic examples of a design adapted from earlier steam tram trailer or cable tramcar practice, modified as necessary to incorporate traction motor gear.

These cars, numbered 1–3 on delivery, were accompanied by six open toastrack trailer cars, seating 44. It was clearly anticipated (or earnestly hoped) that each power car would be able to haul two trailers. This was not realised. A whole series of changes and modifications have taken place since these power cars made their debut: They were originally fitted with an early and experimental form of Mather & Platt control gear for some time, and received GE K.11 controllers in 1902. At the same time their original Milnes trucks were replaced by the present equal wheel Brush type D units, equipped with SEHC traction motors. Car No. 3 was destroyed in the Laxey Depot fire of 1930.

4–9. VESTIBULED SALOONS

For the extension of the line to Laxey, together with the advent of a year-round service in 1894, six more saloon cars, Nos. 4–9, were built by G.F. Milnes and featuring platform vestibules and a more fully developed design. The cars were again equipped with Milnes plate frame trucks and Mather & Platt electrical equipment. All had longitudinal seats for 36 passengers. With these cars came six additional trailers, eventually numbered 36–41; these featured crossbench seats for 56, but had bulkheads and fixed roofs. Of the 1894 delivery. Car No. 4 exchanged trucks and equipment with Car 16 in 1899. whilst Cars Nos. 5–9 received new Brush Type D trucks in 1903. together with SEHC traction motors, GE controllers and Christensen air wheel brake equipment. Cars Nos. 4 and 8 were lost in the Laxey fire in 1930 and Car No. 5 had its longitudinal seating removed and replaced by new transverse and upholstered 2+1 seating for 32 in 1932. This car was also given a saloon partition to divide it into nominally smoking and non-smoking compartments. Car No. 6 also acquired a central partition at a later date. and Car No. 9 was similarly equipped in 1982. Car No. 9 was normally relegated to works duties during the winters and was also used as a snowplough when the need arose. For this purpose a sheet iron snowplough, usually kept at Laxey Depot, was fitted to the underframe headstock (after removing the steps) at the Ramsey end. Car No. 9 is the only one of the batch which is not fitted

with compressed air cocks for trailer car air brake operation. In 1992–3 car No. 9 was fitted with over 1600 bulbs for use as an illuminated tramcar – the first illuminated car in the 100 year history of the MER. This work was carried out by Bolton Trams Ltd. The batch as a whole (less No. 5) has always been referred to as the "tunnel cars" from their interior appearance and saloon layout. However car No. 5 is often referred to as "The Shrine" or "Cathedral" on account of its interior woodwork and fittings. The cars were given Dunlopillo seat cushions in 1967–9 which markedly improved passenger comfort. The external appearance of these cars was considerably altered in 1966–8 when the original centre pillars of the twin front platform windows was sawn through, the two sash-type windows and frames discarded and replaced by a one-piece windscreen (of plain glass) instead, for the purpose of improving the forward visibility, although car No. 6 reverted to original type twin windows in 1992–3. As delivered all of the platform windows were designed to open, but with the exception of the window next to the bulkhead by the side of the motorman, all are now fixed in position and will not open. Similarly the saloon windows were arranged to drop almost fully, and to prevent damage to heads the windows were covered by twin bars. These windows too have been arranged so that they will only open partially, and the bars have been removed. As delivered and for many years these cars featured an iron gate across the top of the platform steps. These were progressively replaced over a lengthy period by half-glazed platform doors. Car No. 5 was the first to be so dealt with in the 1930s and No. 9 was the last to be equipped in 1979.

In 1969 Car No. 5 became the first in the fleet to be equipped (at the Ramsey end only) with an air-operated windscreen wiper; the Trico Mk.III unit and its associated reducing valve was provided on loan by the North Western Road Car Co. Ltd., of Stockport. Car No. 6 was involved in a collision with the Railway's hedge-cutting tractor near South Cape on 9th July 1991 and extensive damage was done to the Ramsey-end saloon and platform areas. As a result the car was withdrawn but during the autumn and winter of 1992–3 it was rebuilt.

10–13. VESTIBULED SALOONS

In 1895 four more power cars were delivered from G.F. Milnes, and numbered 10–13. These were vestibuled saloons fitted with transverse seats for 48 passengers, and built to an economy specification, costing only £260 per body. The six saloon windows were left unglazed, like the contemporary delivery of cars for the Snaefell section, with which they also shared the omission of clerestories. The 10–13 class cars were fitted with glazed vestibules, but had a wrought iron gate across the top of the step pans, rather than the usual glazed and panelled door. These cars were fitted with Mather & Platt electrical gear (the last, as it happened), and Milnes plate frame trucks. They lasted in passenger service for only a relatively short time, and photographs of them in service during this period are rare. Two of the batch were taken out of service in 1902 and stored; the others were converted into freight cars to cope with the MER's growing business. Car No. 12 emerged from Derby Castle Carworks in March 1903 as a powered cattle car, and the other re-entered service as a "Goods Motor" in 1904. The stored pair remained in Laxey Depot until 1918 when they were modified and rehabilitated as air-braked freight trailers. In this form one of them survived, disused, until 1978 when it was painted up and moved to the museum at Ramsey. The MER Society had formally proposed a scheme to restore this vehicle to full working order, but regrettably the then-Board not only ignored the proposition but ensured its demise by disposing of the car to a Midlands-based group. The other remaining specimen lay rotting for many years at the Dhoon sidings until it was broken up during one of the Line's sporadic "tidying-up" campaigns during the very late 1950s.

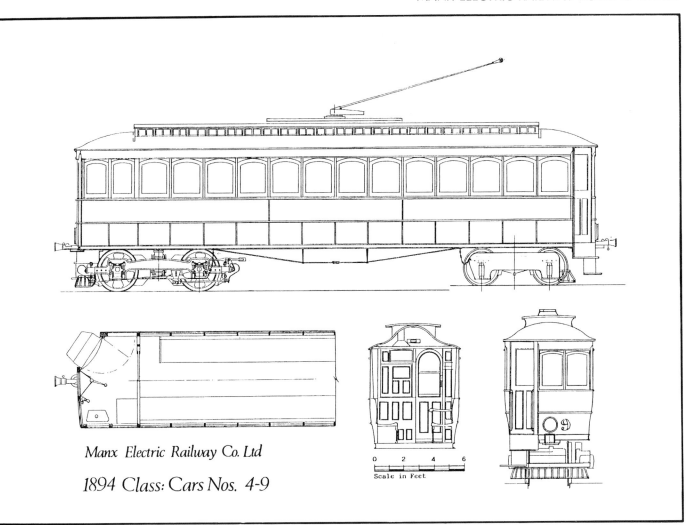

Manx Electric Railway Co. Ltd

1894 Class: Cars Nos. 4-9

0 2 4 6
Scale in Feet

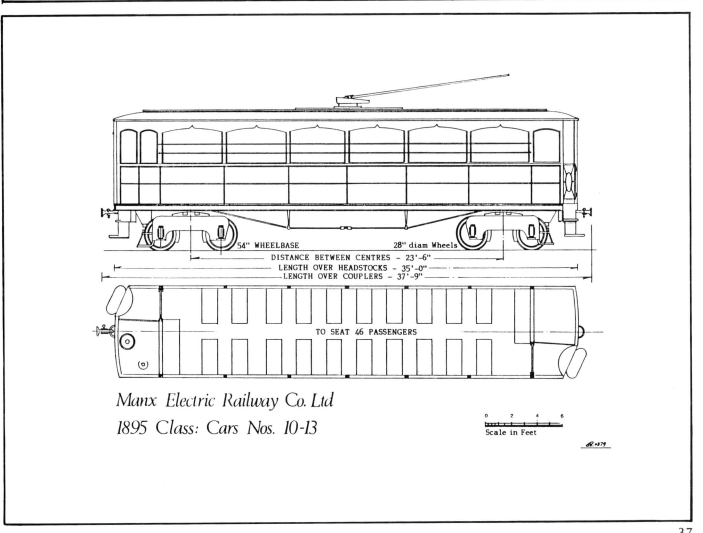

54" WHEELBASE   28" diam Wheels
DISTANCE BETWEEN CENTRES - 23'-6"
LENGTH OVER HEADSTOCKS - 35'-0"
LENGTH OVER COUPLERS - 37'-9"

TO SEAT 46 PASSENGERS

Manx Electric Railway Co. Ltd

1895 Class: Cars Nos. 10-13

0 2 4 6
Scale in Feet

Above: Unvestibuled Saloon No. 1, the oldest working electric car still at work on its original line anywhere in the world, at Derby Castle on 8th August 1990 lettered "Douglas & Laxey Coast Electric Tramway".
Bernard Mettam

Left: No. 2 in passenger service at Groudle on 29th June 1965. *Bernard Mettam*

Below Left: By 1975 No. 2 had become a service vehicle and is seen in a forlorn state at Laxey Car Shed.
Peter Fox

Below: No. 2, now restored, stands on the southbound main line at Laxey Car Sheds with trailer No. 37, prior to being reversed over the crossover and propelled into the sidings to await further traffic. *Adrian Lewis*

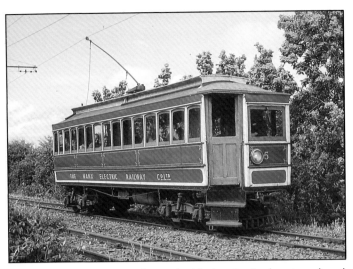

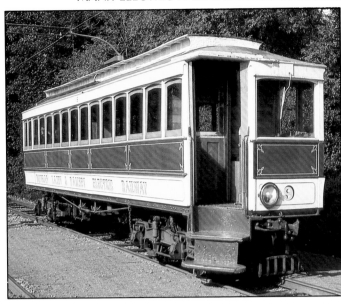

Above: Saloon car No. 5 of 1894 had its longitudinal seats replaced by 2 + 1 transverse seats in 1932, as is clearly seen in this photograph. It is regularly rostered for use on the main timetabled service, and is pictured here on the descent through north Ballaglass en route for Ramsey. *Adrian Lewis*

Above: Car No. 9 in its 'Douglas Laxey and Ramsey' livery, standing on the northbound main line just short of Minorca in 1989. *Adrian Lewis*

Above: Another photograph of No. 5 at Derby Castle on 28th May 1986. To the right can be seen the original MER booking office of 1897. Note the 'MAN' registration plate on the car on the left.
Bernard Mettam

Right: Car No. 6 at Derby Castle on 28th May 1974. Note the different headlight position as compared with No. 5. The Summerland leisure centre can be seen in the background.
Bernard Mettam

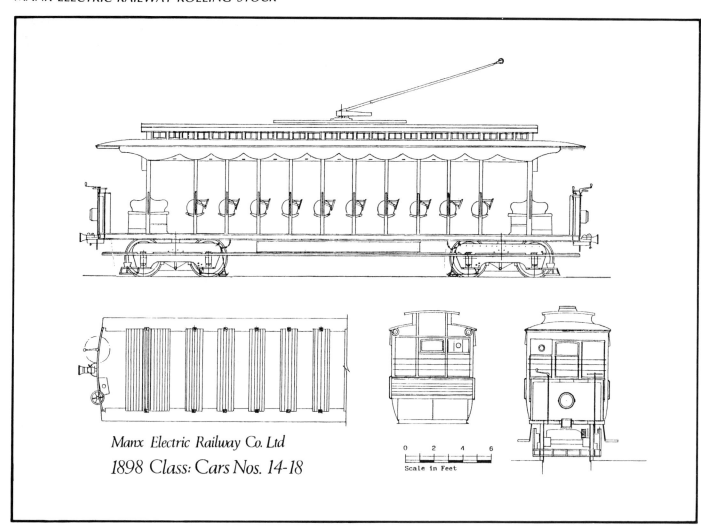

Manx Electric Railway Co. Ltd
1898 Class: Cars Nos. 14-18

0 2 4 6
Scale in Feet

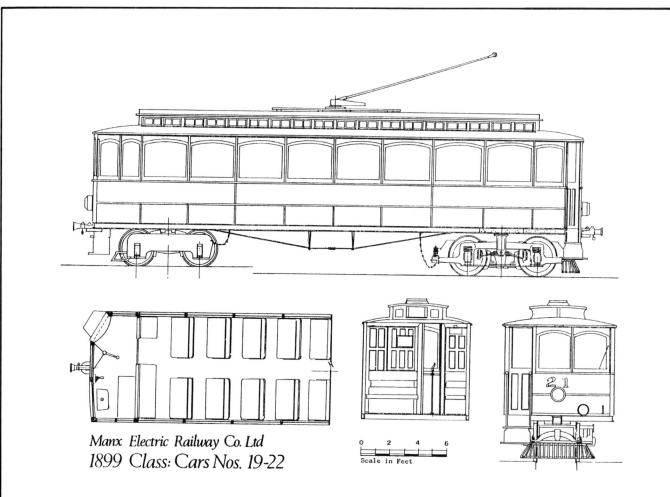

Manx Electric Railway Co. Ltd
1899 Class: Cars Nos. 19-22

0 2 4 6
Scale in Feet

14–18. UNVESTIBULED CROSSBENCH CARS

The next batch of cars to be delivered, Cars Nos. 14–18, reflected a strong Transatlantic influence in concept and materialised as unvestibuled open crossbench cars seating 56 passengers. The Milnes plate frame trucks were fitted with four 20-horsepower traction motors manufactured by the Electric Construction Company of Wolverhampton, and driving through open spur wheel and pinion gearing. These cars, delivered in 1898, were built by G.F. Milnes and were equipped from the beginning with GE K.11 controllers. As delivered these cars had an ornamental polished brass headlamp rim. They were not fitted with hand or grab rails across the platform bulkhead windows; these were fitted later at a date unknown. Car No. 16 switched its trucks and equipment with Car No. 4 in 1899. During the re-equipment programme of 1902–4, Car No. 16 was given new Brush Type D trucks, Christensen air brake equipment and SEHC traction motors, which it still retains. Car No. 16 has had platforms of unequal length ever since the Fairy Cottage accident of 1928. The whole batch was fitted with roller-blind side shutters before 1904, and which they retain. The entire class still exists: Car No. 16 is available for normal traffic; it might also be noted that this car has the remains of the 1900 Liquidator's Impress label under the Ramsey-end platform seat locker. Car No. 18 was put through the car works and restored in 1992–3 and is available for service. Cars 14, 15 and 17 are largely derelict.

19–22. WINTER SALOONS

In 1899 the line was supplied with four "Winter Saloons" numbered 19–22, and which arrived as fully glazed and vestibuled saloon cars with transverse seats for 48 passengers. Again built by G.F. Milnes & Co. Ltd. these cars were, at 37' 6'' long and 7' 4'' wide, the largest on the system and have formed the backbone of summer and winter traffic services ever since delivery. As originally supplied, they were mounted on Milnes plate frame trucks with four 20 h.p. ECC motors and GE K.11 controllers. In the autumn of 1904 the MER carried out a revision of equipment allocations and married the best trucks and equipment to the most heavily used and useful cars. In this way, Car 21 took the original Brill 27Cx trucks off Car 30 of the 28–31 class; Cars 19 and 22 received the trucks and equipments from Cars 29 and 30, whilst Car No. 20 took Car 28's original equipment. Similarly the

air wheel brake equipment was also transferred from the 28–31 class to the 19–22 cars. The saloons were also given panelled wood partitions to provide nominally smoking or non-smoking saloons. In 1932, as part of a general upgrading programme, the original wooden seats of the 19–22 class were replaced by new upholstered seat cushions; Car 20 retained its original seat frames but the remainder were given new Laycock seat frames. In 1967–8, Dunlopillo seat cushions (rescued in suitable sets from bus-breakers at Wombwell near Barnsley) were fitted. A distinctive feature of these cars was the plentiful provision of Milnes makers plates, with at least ten per car. These survived virtually intact until the 1978–87 era when they were filched and stolen, a sad commentary on contemporary values.

On 29th September 1990, car No. 22 suffered a resistance fire at Eskadale as a result of sustained wheelspin on slimy rails whilst towing winter trailer No. 57 mainly loaded with German tourists. The car was taken out of service and returned to Derby Castle Carworks where it was carefully examined. Shortly after 7.30 p.m. on the following day (when the works would have been unstaffed for the first Sunday since the beginning of the season) a nearby resident saw the carworks on fire and alerted the fire brigade. The extensive fore was extinguished and was found to have begun with the Ramsey-end of car 22, above its rheostats, and had devastated the carbody. Cars Nos. 19 and 17 were also in the building at the same time and suffered some damage. Considerable damage was also done to the roof of the building. The extent of the destruction to car No. 22 was such that only the trucks and underframe survived but these formed the basis upon which an entirely new carbody was built. The contract to supply manufactured woodwork for this was let in October 1990 to McArd Contractors Ltd. of Port Erin whilst the highly active consultant for the rebuilding project was Mr Eric Cleator, formerly a senior clerk of works to the Government Property Trustees, and a master carpenter of exceptional ability. Mr Cleator produced a comprehensive set of working drawings for the carbody construction and supervised its erection. The rebuilt car was commissioned on 22nd May 1992 and features a public address system, electric bells and a number of other improvements.

23. LOCOMOTIVE

The line's most unusual piece of rolling stock was electric locomotive No. 23, designed by the engineer, Mr Frank Edmondson and built

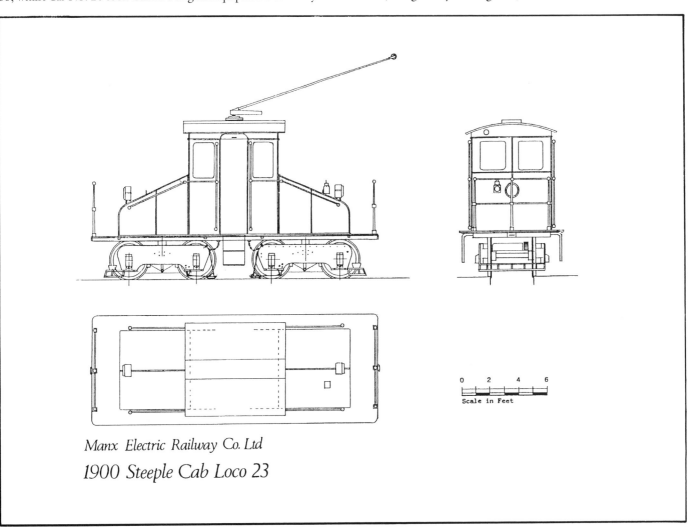

0   2   4   6
Scale in Feet

Manx Electric Railway Co. Ltd
1900 Steeple Cab Loco 23

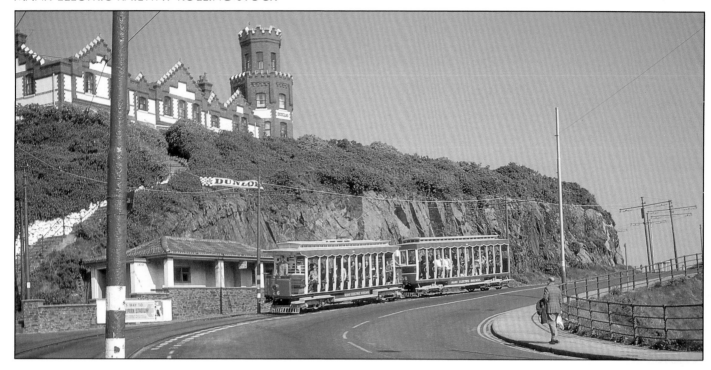

Above: Crossbench motor No. 26 with trailer at Port Jack on 31st May 1974. The Douglas Bay Hotel seen above the cliffs has since been demolished. *Bernard Mettam*

Below: In 1977, No. 25 was painted in a special livery to commemorate the Silver Jubilee of HM the Queen, as was trailer No. 55 which was temporarily renumbered '25' for the period. The two cars are seen at Derby Castle on 7th July 1977, awaiting departure at 10.11. *Peter Fox*

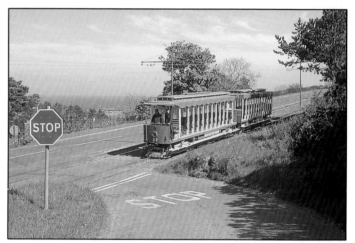

Above: From 1957–63, a green and white livery was applied to certain cars, but this was not liked by the public and they all eventually reverted to their traditional liveries. Cars 32 and 61 were repainted in this livery in 1979 for a short time. Here they are seen at Groudle on 29th May of that year. *M.R. Taplin*

Below: A view at Laxey on 29th June 1965 with 32 + 62 bound for Ramsey and 'winter saloon' 22 with crossbench trailer 42 and parcels van 4 bound for Douglas. *Bernard Mettam*

Above: On 28th June 1974, an unidentified 'winter saloon' leaves Laxey for Ramsey.   *Bernard Mettam*

Right: Rebuilt car No.22 is passed by sister No. 19 in original condition between Howstrake and Groudle.
John Symons

Below: A view of saloon trailer No. 58 as it passes the Laxey Mines Inn.
Bernard Mettam

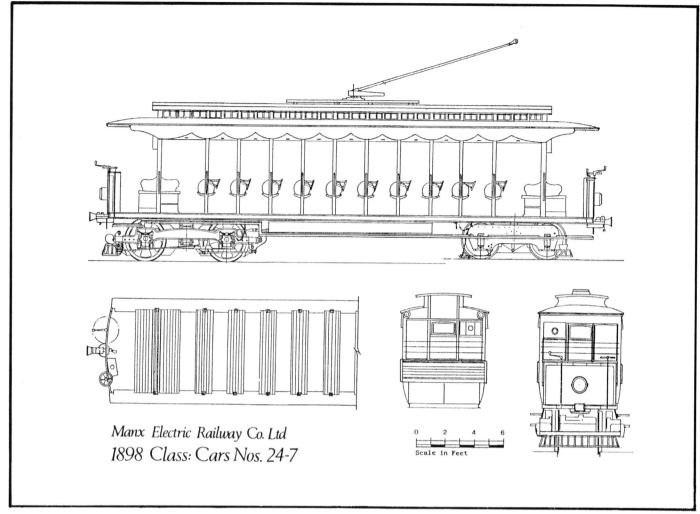

Manx Electric Railway Co. Ltd
1898 Class: Cars Nos. 24-7

Scale in Feet

at Derby Castle Carworks as a 12 ton loco to handle stone traffic and other freight. Having no trucks of its own, it borrowed those off Car 17 except during the peak summer months when it evidently sat on barrels whilst Car 17 was in revenue traffic. As built. the loco had a fine appearance, but the major collision on 24th January 1914, resulted in serious damage to it, and the remains appear to have been stored for over a decade. In 1925 a new bogie underframe was built, onto which the original loco's surviving cab was mounted, between two six ton open wagon bodies. In this guise, the loco was also fitted with an air whistle which was capable of emptying the compressed air reservoir very rapidly, leaving little to apply the air brakes. From 1928 the locomotive borrowed the Brill 27Cx trucks off Car 33 as needed, and operated until 1944 when it became disused. It spent a lengthy period of years on a siding in Derby Castle yard during the 1950s but was later stored at Laxey Depot. During the past few years it has been restored for occasional use for enthusiasts' weekends.

24–27. CONVERTED CROSSBENCH TRAILERS ("PADDLEBOXES")

The bankruptcy, receivership and liquidation of the IoM Tramways & Electric Power Co. Ltd., meant that despite the growth in traffic demand, no new rolling stock was delivered from 1899 until after the formation of the Manx Electric Railway Co. in 1902. The rehabilitation and upgrading programme launched by the new company resulted in the purchase of new trucks, traction motors and equipment for many of the existing cars, whilst four car sets of equipment were used to motorise former trailer cars, which then became the present Nos. 24–27. Of these, all save No. 24, lost in the Laxey fire, still exist in seasonal service. The fitting of the wider Brush trucks necessitated new footboards to clear the axleboxes. and the resulting configuration was responsible for the cars being referred to as "Paddleboxes" thereafter.

The depleted trailer stock was replenished by the last of G.F. Milnes orders from the Manx Electric, with Cars Nos 40–43 delivered in 1903. Growing traffic demanded additional rolling stock and in 1904 the United Electric Car Co., (Electric Railway & Tramway Carriage Works) Preston, supplied a composite order consisting of four open crossbench power cars, Nos. 28–31, two open crossbench trailers, Nos. 55–56, and two exquisite unvestibuled winter saloon trailer cars numbered 57 and 58. The entire batch was fitted with American-built Type 27Cx trucks by J.G. Brill of Philadelphia. As noted previously, the perfor-

mance of the trucks and equipment fitted to the 28–31 cars was such as to warrant their transfer to the winter saloons. Of these crossbench cars, car No. 28 has been stripped of controllers, switchgear and other items; cars 29–30 are essentially complete but stored whilst car 31 was put through the carworks in 1992–3 and is available for traffic.

32–33. UNVESTIBULED CROSSBENCH CARS

The final purchase of rolling stock was made in 1906, again from the United Electric Car Co., Preston, (a forerunner of the mighty English Electric group of companies) and comprised two further crossbench cars. Nos. 32–33, and two crossbench trailers, Nos. 61–62. All were again fitted with Brill 27Cx trucks, and the power cars were equipped with General Electric GE.60 27 b.h.p. traction motors, with four per car. As such, these were the most powerful and certainly the fastest cars in the fleet, and were able to do a return Douglas–Ramsey run in some minutes under two hours, in the days when labour was cheap and plentiful and the line's trackwork was maintained to very high standards. Both cars are heavily used each season and survive intact. As referred to later both Nos. 32–3 have their rheostats, air tanks and compressors on the opposite sides to the rest of the fleet; similarly they were for many years wired to a Ramsey-end circuit breaker. It seems most likely that the cars were placed on the rails the wrong way round on delivery.

TRAILERS

Whilst the Manx Electric's power cars are sequentially numbered roughly in the chronological order of delivery, the trailer car fleet has been renumbered (in some cases more than once) to accommodate the increasing size and composition of the power car fleet. The trailer car roster is dealt with hereunder according to their date of delivery.

Cars Nos. 49–54:

The six original 1893 trailers established the standard overall dimensions of almost all of the open crossbench trailers that followed, namely 28' 9" long by 6' 3" wide over grabrails, and 6' 9" over footboards. All seated 44 passengers on wooden seats with reversible backs according to the direction of running. The countless millions of times that the seat backs have been thrown over to reverse them has resulted in considerable wear on the stops with the result that the angle at which the backrests now lie is not what their designers intended. As original-

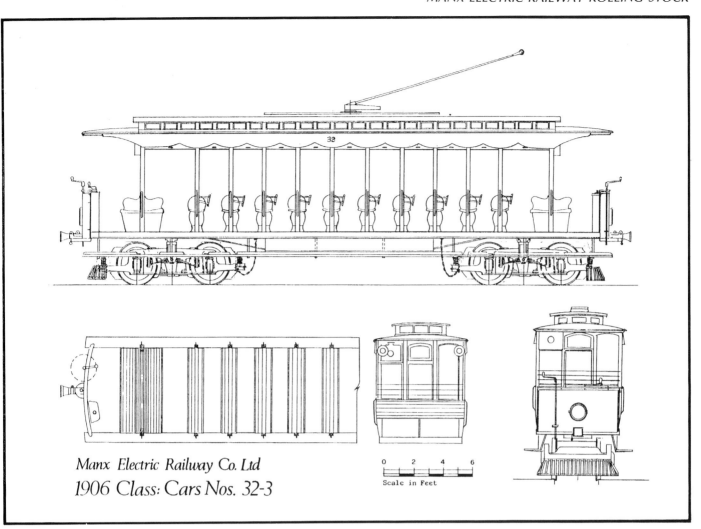

Manx Electric Railway Co. Ltd
1906 Class: Cars Nos. 32-3

0   2   4   6
Scale in Feet

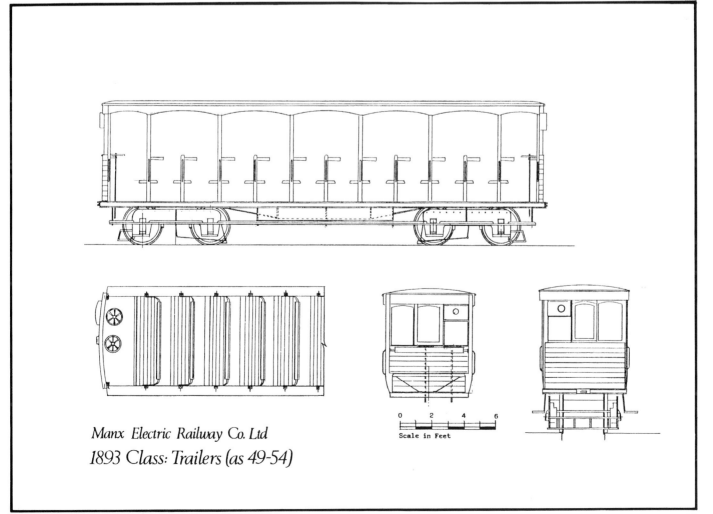

Manx Electric Railway Co. Ltd
1893 Class: Trailers (as 49-54)

0   2   4   6
Scale in Feet

Above: A view of Derby Castle terminus taken on 28th May 1974. The Douglas Corporation horse cars can be seen in the foreground with their depot on the left. In the background is the great canopy which was demolished in 1980. *Bernard Mettam*

Below: Crossbench motor No. 27 and the unnumbered tower wagon forming a 1992-version works train seen at Dhoon Quarry reconstructing the siding ready for 1993 steam working. *John Symons*

Above: Aachen car No. 1010, the only Aachen car to reach the Isle of Man, in Derby Castle Works on 7th July 1977 (see the Snaefell Mountain Railway chapter). *Peter Fox*

Below: MER No. 27 tows Snaefell Mountain Railway No. 6 (mounted on temporary bogies) towards Douglas wrong line at Onchan Head on 29th May 1986. *Bernard Mettam*

Above: A view of Derby Castle Car Works on 28th May 1986.   *Bernard Mettam*

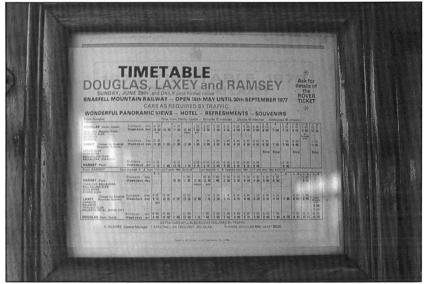

Left: Posters on the end of the booking office at Derby Castle on 7th July 1977. Note the one on the top left which proudly proclaims that the line has re-opened to Ramsey.   *Peter Fox*

Above: The timetable mounted inside a car on the same day.   *Peter Fox*

Below: The new Ramsey station built in 1964, photographed on 6th July 1977.   *Peter Fox*

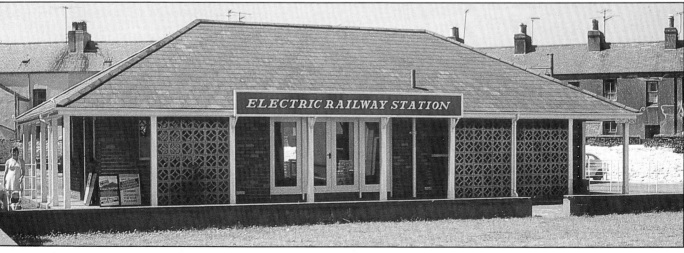

Car No.3 of 1893, destroyed in the Laxey fire of 1930, climbing the sustained 1 in 40 gradient from Laxey to South Cape, shortly after the opening of the line between Douglas and Laxey in 1894. *Mather & Platt*

ly delivered. the first trailer cars were genuine "toastracks" with no roofs and no bulkheads. By 1894 light canvas roofs on wooden frames had been added, with additional side pillars. It is assumed that these cars were delivered as Nos. 11–16, being renumbered in 1895, 1898, and again in 1904, as additional power cars were added to the fleet. About 1903 these trailers had their canvas roofs replaced by light wooden decking, and later modifications have included the provision of panelled bulkhead fittings. Car No. 52 was used minus seats for many winters as a rail carrying pw car; about 1947 or possibly earlier it ceased to be equipped with its missing parts for the summer seasons but still exists in this form, albeit with only the south end dash panel. No. 51 was restored to c.1895 condition in 1987 and has been renumbered 13; this and car No. 49 have survived to see a slowly diminishing rate of utilisation during each summer. Cars Nos. 50, 53 and 54 have been out of use, stored at Laxey for over ten years.

Left: Car No.9, seen here in May 1956, has regularly been used as a works car each winter and could be equipped with a snow plough. *Mike Goodwyn*

Cars Nos. 34–39:

In 1894 six further trailer cars arrived from G.F. Milnes, but were equipped with proper roofs and horizontal planking to their end bulkheads. As delivered they took the fleet numbers 17–22, but were renumbered as 34–39 later in 1898. Four of these cars (Nos. 34/5/8/9) were lost in the Laxey Depot fire in 1930, and only Cars Nos. 36 and 37 survive, of which the former No. 36 has not been used for at least twelve years.

Car No. 59:

Delivered by G.F. Milnes & Co. in the latter part of 1895, this unvestibuled saloon trailer is the smallest item of passenger rolling stock on the Railway, and is in many ways perhaps the most interesting. The car was originally built as a Directors' Saloon, finished to an extremely fine standard with velvet covered seats, ornamental woodwork and fittings, interior mirrors, framed photographs and carpets. It was originally mounted on four-wheel trunnion gear, which may well have provided an overall riding quality somewhat inferior to the remainder of the car's appointments. In 1900 it was remounted on spare Milnes plate frame trailer trucks, the inner frame members of which were very close together. It became known as the "Royal Saloon" after being used to convey their Majesties King Edward VII and Queen Alexandra to Walpole Drive, Ramsey. from Douglas in August 1902. Thereafter the car seems to have seen very little use until the platform entrances were transposed from side to side to coincide with those of the power cars in 1933. In this form it proved to be a somewhat uncertain runner, showing a distressing propensity for coming off the rails, particularly at Cornaa where there is a fiendish combination of acute curve and sudden change of grade. In 1945 some modifications were made to

Left: Car No.14 in immaculate condition in May 1956, outside No.1 Car Shed at Derby Castle Carworks, together with three members of MER staff in traditional uniforms. *Mike Goodwyn*

Below: The remains of one of the 10–13 class cars, derelict at Dhoon Quarry sidings in 1955, with a "Dreadnought" wagon in the foreground. They were later scrapped altogether with a number of other wagons during a tidying-up campaign shortly after nationalisation. The stone-built "Creosote Cottage" in the background was demolished in 1979–80.

increase the clearance between the tops of the wheels and the underframe cross members, and the car has been reliably used ever since, particularly for small private parties or special events. It has seating for 18 passengers, and is sometimes referred to as "The Doll's House".

Car No. 60:

At the end of 1896 a further trailer car arrived from G.F. Milnes, of the now-conventional roofed open crossbench construction with glazed bulkheads. The car was originally taken into stock as No. 27, but in the various renumberings up to 1906 it became Car 60. This trailer was severely damaged in the Laxey Depot fire but was subsequently rebuilt and repaired at Derby Castle Carworks and returned to service in 1931.

Cars Nos. 44–48:

Delivered from G.F. Milnes in 1899 for the opening of the extension from Laxey to Ramsey, these cars were purchased to make up the rather depleted trailer stock after equipping the original 19–22 crossbench cars of 1898, originally delivered as trailers, as previously noted. Trailer cars Nos. 44–48 were of substantially heavier constructional proportion, although the overall dimensions remained essentially the same. These cars were fitted with roller blind shutters in 1903. Car No. 44 was burned in the Laxey fire, but the remaining cars are in regular use.

Cars Nos. 40–43:

Manufactured by G.F. Milnes at their then-new factory at Hadley Castle, Shropshire, in 1903, these open crossbench trailer cars were mounted on the heavier "traction-type" of Milnes plate frame truck, which had been rendered surplus by the contemporary re-equipment of power cars. Of this batch, Cars Nos. 40–41 were lost at Laxey, but the other two remain in being.

Cars Nos. 55–56:

Built by the Electric Railway & Tramway Carriage Co. at Preston in 1904, in company with Cars Nos. 28–31, and designed to match, this pair of crossbench trailers arrived in Douglas mounted on Brill Type 27CxT (trailer) trucks. They are in regular use.

Cars Nos. 57–58:

By 1903 the Manx Electric Railway was being obliged to operate two of the 4–9 class power cars as winter trailers, and in order to permit these to return to their proper role, two winter saloon trailer cars were ordered from Preston. Delivered in 1904, they took the fleet numbers 57–8 and were fitted with Brill 27CxT trucks and air brake equipment. The unvestibuled saloons had cane rattan seating for 32 passengers on transverse 2+1 seats. Measuring 32' 9" in length and 6' 9" wide, they have quite exceptional interior fittings, and with their relatively low utilisation after 1936, are in outstanding structural condition. As well as air wheel brakes, the two cars also have hand wheel, scotch and emergency brake gear. One of the pair was substantially damaged many years ago, when it was accidentally towed away from the Derby Castle terminus one night, after having been incorrectly uncoupled. Unnoticed, it hung on to the power car's coupler until it reached Port Jack curve, where it broke free. The empty car then ran back down the line to the terminus, left the tracks beyond the booking office and danced across the horse tramlines and landed in the garden of one of the

houses in Strathallan Crescent, from where it was later retrieved.

Cars Nos. 61–62:

The last delivery of rolling stock from the United Electric Car Co. in 1906 consisted of power cars Nos. 32–33, together with a pair of matching trailers, which were taken into stock as Nos. 61–62. These crossbench cars are mounted on Brill Type 27CxT trucks and equipped with hand wheel and scotch brakes, although the latter have now been removed.

Cars Nos. 40/41/44 (II):

Since the Laxey Depot fire destroyed four power cars (Nos. 3/4/8 and 24) and seven trailers (Nos. 34/35/38/39/40/41/44) and since the insurance payment barely met the cost of replacing the depot building, only three car bodies were replaced. An order ("As per previous Order") was placed with the English Electric Co. Ltd., Dick, Kerr Works, Preston, in 1930 and after an English Electric draughtsman had been despatched to the Island to check details, the three new bodies were delivered later the same year and took the fleet numbers 40/41/44. They were virtually identical to the carbodies that were supplied by Preston in 1904 and were provided with Milnes plate frame trucks of the 1894 pattern.

Although it is almost impossible to determine the individual unladen car weights, it is very clear that any of the cars constructed at Preston are very much heavier than the corresponding Milnes products. Relatively few horse cars were ever produced at Preston, and the design and constructional proportion of the cars built by the Electric Railway & Tramway Carriage Co, United Electric Car Co., and finally the English Electric Co. Ltd., reflected the practice of the electric traction era.

FITMENTS

All Manx Electric power cars are fitted with platform-end sockets for trailer car lighting jumper cables, although not all trailer cars have interior lights. Trailers Nos. 49–54 have bulkhead lampbox lights only, and it is worth noting that these were originally required to show a red lamp to the front and a green tail lamp at the rear; this practice

Left: Empty carsets returning to Derby Castle Depot always propel their trailers. Here Car No. 30 pushes Trailer 53 up to the Depot in 1962. *Mike Goodwyn*

*Right:*The Hughes Patent coupler, sold by G.F. Milnes & Co., is fitted to all of the MER's power cars and was originally invented for use with steam trams and their trailer cars. These two photographs show the sequence of securing the coupler bar in the mouth of the coupler.
Alex Townsend

Left: Car No.17 and a lightweight trailer, loading at Laxey about 1968. *George Shaw, courtesy Manx Electric Railway*

Left: The interior of Winter Saloon No.19, showing the internal partition bulkhead with its Tudor-arch doorway window and ornate panelling, fitted after delivery. The reversible seat-frames were supplied by Laycock early in the 1930s.
Alex Townsend

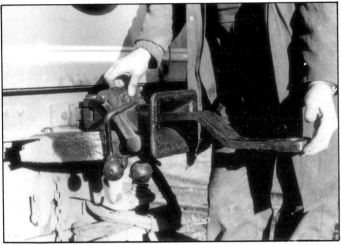

was modified during World War II to show a white light at the front and a conventional red tail-lamp. It is, however, possible to find some lamps that have not yet been modified.

Since no turning circles or reversing loops exist on the MER, it is quite impossible for a car to change ends, necessitating the orthodox 'No. 1 End' and 'No. 2 End' designations habitually found on other tramways with double-ended cars. Instead there is the "Ramsey end" and the 'Douglas end" of each car, with 'land-side' or 'sea-side' in place of the customary nearside and offside.

Power cars are equipped with a Hughes patent coupler, invented by Mr. Albert Hughes of G.F. Milnes & Co., Birkenhead. It was originally designed and used for steam tramway practice. The primitive but highly effective and reliable coupler gear features a pendulum lock which engages the coupler bar when it is pushed into the mouth of the coupler. Because coupler heights vary between the various batches of power and trailer cars (even on brand new wheels with their full diameter) it is common to marry only certain cars with certain trailers. Even then, the use of specially cranked coupler bars is needed.

As required by statute, all MER cars carried oil head and tail lamps as well as their electric lights, until 1987–8, when the then-management of the line decided that they were unnecessary.

LIVERY

The MER's rolling stock livery has traditionally been centred on red or brown and white or ivory with varnished teak mahogany and pitch pine. There remains however the possibility that these colours were not those used by the Isle of Man Tramway Co. until its demise in 1900 and it seems more than likely that cars delivered up to 1895 and possibly later were finished in Prussian blue. There are several contemporary references to "blue faced cars" which definitely related to Nos. 1 to 3 and 10 to 13. The picture is further clouded by the discovery of blue original coats on trailer car 42 a few years ago when it was being completely stripped for repainting. The paint scheme adopted by the MER has habitually featured some detail differences between the styles of individual cars even within the same batch.

With the exception of a brief recent period the MER has always used signwritten numerals and titling, employing transfers only for the MER crest itself. Over many years the style (and in some cases the sizes too) has varied slightly according to the practices of the individual foreman painter or signwriter. The onset of "historic liveries" applied

to cars nos 1, 2, 9, 21, trailer 15 etc., also reintroduced styles long surpassed.

The earliest cars nos 1–3 were lettered 'DOUGLAS & LAXEY COAST ELECTRIC TRAMWAY' which was shortly contracted to 'DOUGLAS AND LAXEY ELECTRIC TRAMWAY' when cars Nos. 4–9 arrived in 1894. The advent of the first crossbench power cars Nos. 14–18 evidently caused a problem of where to put some lettering and the cars were later equipped with a backboard fitted to the step brackets carrying the title. The arrival of cars 19–22 in 1899 brought a new 'DOUGLAS, LAXEY & RAMSEY ELECTRIC TRAMWAY' title and this also was applied to some but not all of the earlier stock. The title was further modified by changing TRAMWAY to RAILWAY about 1900. In the same year however loco No. 23 appeared painted dark blue or green and merely lettered 'IOMT&EP Co Ltd' and certain other stock also carried this title. Certain cars carried the name of the Company Secretary at one end and the General Manager at the other.

In 1902 the new company placed its title in full along the rocker panels, this time painted red with white lettering shaded black reading 'THE MANX ELECTRIC RAILWAY Co LTD' and which became the standard for many years until abbreviated to 'MANX ELECTRIC RAILWAY.' From World War II onwards the title was progressively reduced simply to 'MER' in an effort to contain costs. The MER crest which featured the three legs of Man and the national motto in an ornamental belt and buckle device was still applied to the side panels of saloon cars and to the dash panel or bulkhead of crossbench or trailer cars, sometimes above the headlamp and sometimes below it.

The nationalisation of the MER in 1957 produced the first MER Board of Tynwald which decided to replace the traditional livery with an ill-chosen green and white scheme, and the first of these repaints appeared on December 24, 1957. Disregarding the howls of protest, and the incidental danger of the cars not being as easily seen on the approach to road crossings, the Board pursued its policy until October 1958, by which time Cars Nos. 1, 20, 21, 22, 26, 27, 29, 32 and 33, together with Trailer Nos. 50, 61, 62 and Snaefell Nos. 2 and 4 had acquired the new green livery and featured white lettering and numerals shaded blue, with white and grey interiors. With the end of this Board, repaints from November 1958 reverted to the proper livery and the last green thing disappeared in September 1963. In 1977 Car 25 and Trailer 55 appeared in a red and silver livery for the Queen's Silver Jubilee; during this period the trailer was renumbered "25" as well, but the pair subsequently reverted to traditional colours. In 1979 Car No. 32 and Trailer No. 61 reappeared in green and white primarily in connection with the "Centenary of Electric traction" scheme of that year, for a short time and since 1979 various cars, such as Nos. 1, 2, 19 and 21, have appeared in "historic liveries", which were in stark contrast to another innovation of the same period whereby many motor cars and trailers were retitled 'Isle of Man Railways' using a modern faced yellow plastic stick on letter; the obscene effect was added to by the stencilled lettering, applied randomly 'OPERATED BY MER BOARD.' The use of the original crest continued until 1978 when it was superceeded by a most unfortunate creation of the then board's invention, based loosely on the former IMR crest but with a picture of car 32 added by snipping it out of a coloured postcard. These bizarre changes have now largely been expunged and the original MER crest was reintroduced in 1992.

The numerals in current use are usually 7" high characters, normally white shaded black. Cars nos 1 and 2 have more ornate numerals with gold leaf and tinted shading; for some time use was made of '3's with a flat top stroke, but these have now reverted to normal double arced figures. Each car tends to display individual characteristics and the position of the numbers vary as may also the size, spacing and style of the figures themselves.

DERBY CASTLE CARWORKS

All the line's rolling stock and other equipment is repaired and maintained at the carworks at Derby Castle. This complex which dates in part from the beginning of the line can be divided into two parts – the depot buildings used for accommodating cars from traffic or storage and the lower buildings forming the carworks. It is not possible in practical terms to divide the roles, for some work is carried out by carworks staff in the top shed and some cars for traffic are also stored in the lower shed or "hospital roads".

The carworks includes not only the three parallel hospital roads in the No. 1 Car Shed but also the Machine or "Fitting" shop based on the original engine house, which also accommodates the electrical section and a sub-station, the joiners' shop formerly No. 6 Car Shed of 1923–4, and the paint shop formerly the boiler house and converted into a goods shed in 1908.

Left: Locomotive No. 23 as rebuilt by the MER in 1925 after its accident. It spent many later years after 1944 parked on this siding at Derby Castle, where it was photographed during an LRTL visit in 1956.
Mike Goodwyn

Left: One of the three most modern cars on the MER: Trailer 44 (ii) built by English Electric in 1930 approximately to the designs of 1906, seen here at Laxey in 1979.
W.P. Cubbon

Below: Trailer No.62, built by the United Electric Car Co. Preston, in 1906, and seen here at Laxey in 1979.
W.P. Cubbon

Above: The interior of one of the Winter Trailers, Nos. 57-58, showing its original cane rattan seating and hat racks. The photo was taken by Mr Edward Hoole, a tobacconist-cum-photographer of Watery Lane, Preston, who was commissioned to record many of the products of the Preston car works. *Manx Electric Railway*

Below: Electric Locomotive No.23, as built by the Isle of Man Tramways & Electric Power Co. Ltd. at Derby Castle Carworks in 1900. This is the only known picture showing its 'IoMT&EP'' lettering. *Manx Electric Railway*

The Machine Shop measuring 60' x 37' now contains a Kendal & Gent (Manchester) wheel lathe of unknown date; it was reputed to have been bought second-hand in 1893–4 from the liquidator of an Irish narrow-gauge line; there is a hydraulic wheel press built and supplied by Miller & Co of Edinburgh, makers of chilled iron wheels, axle trees and other tramway goods: a large capacity centre lathe and a smaller more modern machine together with a planing machine, drilling machines, miller and shaping machine and a relatively recent addition, a very large vertical boring machine from London Transport. The shop is also equipped with a mechanical hacksaw which together with certain other machines is driven by the original lineshafting. A new Smithy has recently been completed on the site of the old one albeit considerably enlarged and is equipped with a hearth, anvils, foundry pit and a Berry centre lathe.

CAR TRUCKS

The most important components of any electric tramcar consist of the trucks on which it is mounted, and which reflect not only the technical development of the era of electric traction, but also contain and represent the most costly and critical part of the whole tramcar. Any electric car truck is required to provide four fundamental functions: First it must guide and carry the vehicle safely along its path or track; it must provide a resilient support for the car and its load, as well as accommodating the means of propulsion and for braking. Double or "bogie" trucks (as opposed to single four-wheel trucks) must additionally incorporate a means of swivelling under the carbody as the vehicle negotiates curves. More sophisticated designs also incorporate a means of horizontal alignment as well. All of the trucks in use on the MER represent the technology of the first fifteen years or so of electric traction development, ranging from the original elementary plate frame

CURRENT FLEET LIST

Car No.	Year	Builder	Type	Seats	Trucks	Motors	Latest O'haul
1	1893	Milnes	Unvestibuled saloon	34	Brush Type D	SEHC 4 x 25 hp	1978
2	1893	Milnes	Unvestibuled saloon	34	Brush Type D	SEHC 4 x 25 hp	1980
5	1894	Milnes	Saloon	32	Brush Type D	SEHC 4 x 25 hp	1980
6	1894	Milnes	Saloon	36	Brush Type D	SEHC 4 x 25 hp	1981
7	1894	Milnes	Saloon	36	Brush Type D	SEHC 4 x 25 hp	1984
9	1894	Milnes	Saloon	56	Brush Type D	ECC 4 x 25 hp	1993
14	1898	Milnes	Crossbench	56	Milnes S.3	ECC 4 x 25 hp	1956
15	1898	Milnes	Crossbench	56	Milnes S.3	ECC 4 x 25 hp	1976
16	1898	Milnes	Crossbench	56	Brush Type D	SEHC 4 x 25 hp	1957
17	1898	Milnes	Crossbench	56	Milnes S.3	ECC 4 x 20 hp	1957
18	1898	Milnes	Crossbench	56	Milnes S.3	ECC 4 x 20 hp	1960
19	1899	Milnes	Saloon	48	Brill 27Cx	SEHC 4 x 25 hp	1979
20	1899	Milnes	Saloon	48	Brill 27Cx	SEHC 4 x 25 hp	1986
21	1899	Milnes	Saloon	48	Brill 27Cx	SEHC 4 x 25 hp	1987
22	1899	Milnes	Saloon	48	Brill 27Cx	SEHC 4 x 25 hp	1985
23	1925	MER Co.	Locomotive				1979
25	1898	Milnes	Crossbench	56	Brush Type D	SEHC 4 x 25 hp	1975
26	1898	Milnes	Crossbench	56	Brush Type D	SEHC 4 x 25 hp	1964
27	1898	Milnes	Crossbench	56	Brush Type D	SEHC 4 x 25 hp	1960
28	1904	ER&TCC	Crossbench	56	Milnes S3 1899	ECC 4 x 20 hp	1957
29	1904	ER&TCC	Crossbench	56	Milnes S3 1899	ECC 4 x 20 hp	1959
30	1904	ER&TCC	Crossbench	56	Milnes S3 1899	ECC 4 x 20 hp	1950
31	1904	ER&TCC	Crossbench	56	Milnes S3 1899	ECC 4 x 20 hp	1966
32	1906	UEC	Crossbench	56	Brill 27Cx	GE60 4 x 27 hp	1981
33	1906	UEC	Crossbench	56	Brill 27Cx	GE60 4 x 27 hp	1978
36	1894	Milnes	Crossbench	44	Milnes S.2		
37	1894	Milnes	Crossbench	44	Milnes S.2		
40	1930	Eng Elec	Crossbench	44	Milnes S.1		
41	1930	Eng Elec	Crossbench	44	Milnes S.1		
42	1903	Milnes	Crossbench	44	Milnes S.3		
43	1903	Milnes	Crossbench	44	Milnes S.3		
44	1930	Eng Elec	Crossbench	44	Milnes S.2		
45	1899	Milnes	Crossbench	44	Milnes S.1		
46	1899	Milnes	Crossbench	44	Milnes S.2		
47	1899	Milnes	Crossbench	44	Milnes S.1		
48	1899	Milnes	Crossbench	44	Milnes S.1		
49	1893	Milnes	Crossbench	44	Milnes S.1		
50	1893	Milnes	Crossbench	44	Milnes S.1		Renumbered 13, 1987
51	1893	Milnes	Crossbench	44	Milnes S.1		Converted to bogie flat. Engineer's Dept
52	1893	Milnes	Crossbench	44	Milnes S.1		No trucks
53	1893	Milnes	Crossbench	44	Milnes S.1		
54	1893	Milnes	Crossbench	44	Milnes S.1		
55	1904	ER&TCC	Crossbench	44	Brill 27CxT		
56	1904	ER&TCC	Crossbench	44	Brill 27CxT		
57	1904	ER&TCC	Crossbench	44	Brill 27CxT		
58	1904	ER&TCC	UnV Saloon	32	Brill 27CxT		
59	1895	Milnes	UnV Saloon	32	Brill 27CxT		
60	1896	Milnes	UnV Saloon	18	Milnes S.2		
61	1906	UEC	Crossbench	44	Milnes S.1		
62	1906	UEC	Crossbench	44	Brill 27CxT		

Trailer No. 51 was rebuilt to 1894 condition in 1987 and renumbered 13.

Trailer No. 52 was used, with seats and roof removed, as an Engineer's bogie flat wagon each winter for many years, but re-assembled for seasonal use.

With the general availability of Trailer No. 59 for service purposes after about 1940, trailer 52 was no longer needed to make up the total of 25 trailers and became permanently allocated to engineering duties.

Trailers Nos. 36 and 54 have not operated at all for several years.

FREIGHT ROLLING STOCK

No	Type	Year	Maker	Notes
1	6 ton open wagon	1894	Milnes	Overhauled 1957-8
2	6 ton open wagon	1894	Milnes	Overhauled 1957-8
3	4 w van with platforms	1895	Milnes	Overhauled 1957-8
4	4 w van with platforms	1895	Milnes	Rebuilt 1993 (Royal Mail van)
5	6 ton open wagon	1896	Milnes	Overhauled 1957-8
6	6 ton open wagon	1897-8	Milnes	
7	6 ton open wagon	1897-8	Milnes	Overhauled 1957-8
8	6 ton open wagon	1897-8	Milnes	Overhauled 1957-8
9	6 ton open wagon	1897-8	Milnes	
10	6 ton open wagon	1897-8	Milnes	Platforms removed; serviceable.
11	6 ton Van	1899	Milnes	
12	6 ton Van	1899	Milnes	Platforms removed; no brakes.
13	5 ton Van	1904	Milnes	Overhauled 1979. Serviceable.
14	5 ton Van	1904	Milnes	
15	5 ton Van	1908	Milnes	Wrecked Ballaglass. 1944.
16	Large mail van	1908	MER	Converted to Tower Wagon/Mobile Workshop 1977
17	6 ton open wagon	1912	MER	
18	6 ton open wagon	1912		
19	12 ton Dreadnought	1912		Engineer's Dept. "Challenger"
20	12 ton Dreadnought	1912		Ex-car 12. Scrapped 3/1927.
21	Bogie flat wagon	1926		Rebuilt from 10-13 class car in 1918.
22	Bogie cattle car			Rebuilt 1926 as 12 ton Dreadnought flat wagon.
2S	Bogie freight van			Rebuilt 1926 as 12 ton Dreadnought flat wagon.
24	Bogie cattle car			Rebuilt 1926 as 12 ton Dreadnought flat wagon.
25	Bogie cattle car			Rebuilt from 10-13 class car*
26	Bogie freight van			

NOTE: Van No. 16 lost its roof en route from Ramsey to Douglas somewhere near Ballafayle in a severe winter storm in 1967. It was then given a replacement pitched roof as a replacement. The van was later converted into a Tower Wagon and mobile "Poles & Wires" workshop in 1976-7.

* Fitted air brake equipment 1/1920. Stored Laxey until 1979 then painted up for Ramsey museum.

KEY TO MANUFACTURERS

Brill	The J.G. Brill Company, Philadelphia, Pennsylvania, USA.
Brush	Brush Electrical Engineering Co.Ltd., Falcon Works, Loughborough, England.
ECC	Electric Construction Co. Ltd., Wolverhampton, England.
Eng Elec	English Electric Company Ltd., Dick, Kerr Works, Preston, Lancs., England.
ER&TCC	Electric Railway & Tramway Carriage Co. Ltd., Dick, Kerr Works, Preston, Lancs., England. (Later became part of UEC.)
GE	General Electric Company, Schenectady, New York, USA. (Never to be confused with similarly entitled UK-based firm.) UK Agents: British Thomson-Houston, Rugby, England.
Milnes	George F. Milnes & Co. Ltd., Cleveland Street Works, Birkenhead to 4/1902, then at Hadley Castle, Shropshire, England.
SEHC	Société l'Electricité et l'Hydraulique, Charleroi, Belgium, later and nowadays Ateliers de Constructions Electriques de Charleroi SA. (ACEC) and part of the Westinghouse Electric & Manufacturing Group, Pittsburg, Pennsylvania, USA.
UEC	United Electric Car Co. Ltd., Dick, Kerr Works, Preston, Lancs., England. (Later became part of English Electric Co.).

trucks, to the more developed and refined productions of the giant American manufacturer, J.G. Brill of Philadelphia.

Milnes Trucks

Of the motored tramcar trucks in the Manx Electric fleet, all of the early cars delivered up to 1899 were supplied with plate frame bogie trucks designed and assembled by G.F. Milnes of Birkenhead, a car and truck builder of considerable historic importance in the United Kingdom at the time. George F. Milnes purchased Starbuck, an old-established horse car builder in Birkenhead, in 1886 and thereafter the business traded as G.F. Milnes & Co. It duly expanded into a significant manufacturer of horse, cable and steam tram trailer cars. The firm built its first (battery) electric car to Reckenzaun's design in 1888 for the Sandhurst & Eaglehawk line. With the growth of the electric tramcar, Milnes usually turned to American-built trucks and equipment, but also designed and produced a limited range of plate frame trucks of their own, all of which clearly showed their direct lineage from their cable or steam tram trailer ancestry. Truck side-frames and other structural components were beyond the capacity of the Cleveland Street Works, and were sub-contracted to Cochran & Co, of Birkenhead.

In 1898, W.C.F. Busch of Bautzen, Saxony, (one of the constituents of the present German tramway and rapid transit equipment manufacturers, Linke Hoffman Busch GmbH) took over G.F. Milnes & Co., and in April 1902 the Birkenhead plant was closed and the business moved to extensive new premises at Hadley Castle, Shropshire (where MER Trailers Nos 40 and 41, lost at Laxey, and the existing Cars Nos. 42–3 were built), but in the trade depression that developed in 1904, the works was closed and the Busch interest withdrawn. The Hadley Castle plant was sold off (and ultimately formed part of the present GKN-Sankey works), and the Milnes car-building interests were acquired by the United Electric Car Co, of Preston, (a forerunner of English Electric) in 1905. The G.F. Milnes company was not directly involved in the G.C. Milnes, Voss & Co. tramcar manufacturer of Birkenhead. This was formed in 1902 at the time that G.F. Milnes was moving down to Salop, and in fact G.C. Milnes was the son of G.F. Milnes. Milnes, Voss was incorporated in 1906 and liquidated in 1913.

The trucks supplied by G.F. Milnes to the MER were broadly existing designs modified as necessary to incorporate electric traction motors, the trailer car trucks being virtually identical to antique designs for cable cars and steam tram trailers. The MER's Milnes trucks can be divided into three sub-types as there are some detail differences. The first group (Series 1) represent the 1893 and 1894 trailer car trucks, which are outwardly identifiable by the five rivets fastening the transoms to the sideframes. These are presently fitted to Trailer Cars Nos. 40, 41, 44, 46, 47, 48, 49, 50 and 51 (now renumbered 13), Nos. 53, 54 and 60. The second series (S.2) are similar in outward appearance but have only four snap-head rivets at the centre of the sideframes. This type is fitted to Trailers Nos. 36, 37, 45, 46, 47, 48 and 59. The trucks of the first and second series are regarded as interchangeable.

The third series (S.3) is the powered truck design which first made its appearance in 1893 under Cars Nos. 1–3. The design was subject to some detail revision as time went on, and trucks of this group are fitted to Cars Nos. 14, 15, 17 and 18 of 1898, and under Cars Nos. 28–31 of 1899. All are now fitted with axle-hung nose-suspended 20-horsepower traction motors supplied by the Electric Construction Company of Wolverhampton, and driving through open spur gearing. The trucks fitted to the two groups of cars may also be regarded as interchangeable. Between 1900 and 1914 Car No. 17's trucks were usually in use underneath the Loco (No. 23) each winter. The re-equipment programme of 1902–4 replaced a number of Milnes trucks with new Brush trucks, and some spare Milnes trucks of the third series, but without their motors, are fitted to Trailer Cars Nos. 42 and 43, and are readily identifiable by their much deeper side frames.

Overall the Milnes trucks are relatively crude and incorporate only one stage of suspension. Even this is somewhat limited in its deflection under load, presumably because of the absence of a traction motor nose suspension that would allow the the motor to follow the relative rise and fall of the wheelset when running. The truck frames were built up from ordinary structural steel sections and plate, and are extremely simple. For their weight they have great strength, but feature no separate bolster at all. This in turn has a considerable effect on the car-bodies when running, as the superelevation of the track at curves is instantly transmitted to the carbody, which is racked and twisted to suit the contour of the track. Since the cars to which these trucks are fitted run for at most a few weeks of each year (and in some cases not at all), the process may be capable of being indefinitely extended.

As already mentioned, the MER paid heavily for being an electric traction pioneer and by 1900, only a matter of seven years since the opening of the line between Douglas and Groudle, much of the equipment of both the cars and the line itself was obsolete, as a result of the rapid strides that had been taken in electric tramway technology during these years.

Brush Trucks

In the re-equipment programme launched by the MER Co. after it took over in 1902, new trucks, traction motors, control gear, power station and distribution equipments were essential to bring the line up to the then current mechanical and electrical standards, and to procure reliable and economic operation. Despite the significant part played by Britain's electric traction pioneers by that time, and due in no small measure to the Westminster governments' interference, the United States had far overtaken contemporary British manufacturers in innovation, development, production and marketing, and this state of affairs was quite naturally reflected in Manx Electric purchasing. New controllers were bought from the mighty General Electric Company of Schenectady New York, NY., (originally Edison-General Electric, and never to be confused with a similarly entitled firm operating in Britain, and based in London), some trucks from the world's greatest truck manufacturer, the J.G. Brill Company of Philadelphia, Pennsylvania, as well as replacement traction motors from the Belgian Societe l'Electricite et l'Hydraulique, Charleroi. This particular firm later became the present Ateliers de Construction Electriques de Charleroi, (ACEC), a subsidiary of the Westinghouse Electric & Manufacturing Company of Pittsburgh, Pennsylvania.

Not all of the Manx Electric's new equipment was foreign, and the first new truck order was for thirteen car sets of Brush Type D equal-wheel two-motor trucks. It was not necessarily a happy choice when contemporary options are fully considered, but the MER could have finished up with something much worse. Other truck options considered included the stately Peckham 14B, and equal wheel design available in 48' and 54' wheelbases and which in the event was imported from Kingston New York for use in Blackburn and Birkenhead only; the third consisted of the 'Empire State Radial Truck' manufactured by the Taylor Electric Truck Co of Troy, New York. This did not feature any radial axle gear and was in effect only a modified diamond frame design. The only Taylor trucks imported into the UK by their agents the Electric Construction Co of Wolverhampton, was for Hartlepools in 1898. It is of interest that all of the above trucks were usually supplied as monotraction trucks, i.e. with only one motor powering one axle. It has been said many times that Brush trucks of this period generally sold well only to "captive" customers within the British Electric Traction group, or those tramways in which the BET had an interest. The MER was no exception here, for the BET was a substantial stockholder for many years and had been one of the unsuccessful tenderers for the undertaking when it was in receivership. The British Electric Traction group also owned the Brush Electrical Company, and this inter-relationship is of some historical interest.

In 1849 Charles Francis Brush was born in Cleveland, Ohio, and ultimately became a noted physicist. In 1887 he invented and took out patents on several improvements relating to dynamos and electric lighting apparatus. The American manufacturing rights for this equipment were handled by the Brush Electrical Company, USA., but sales in the rest of the world were dealt with by the Anglo-American Brush Electric Light Corporation Ltd., formed in 1879 and with premises at Belvedere Road, Lambeth, London.

In 1883, Emile Garcke then aged 27, joined the Anglo-American Brush Company first as Secretary, and from 1887 became the manager. The boom in electric lighting rapidly outstripped the capacity of the Lambeth premises, and since by then Garcke intended to launch into electric traction as well, the Brush concern acquired Hughes's Falcon Works at Loughborough in August 1889. The works premises had originally been established by Henry Hughes in 1865 to build steam locomotives, steam tram engines and trailers, horse bus bodies and other road vehicles, being re-organised as "Falcon Engineering & Car Works" in 1883. With the move to Loughborough, the Anglo-American Brush Company was also re-organised as the Brush Electrical Engineering Co. Ltd. The original American Brush concern in the United States was eventually acquired by General Electric in 1892.

Garcke became Brush's managing director in 1891 and in 1895 formed the British Electric Traction (Pioneer) Co. Ltd., with the objects of financing and equipping electric traction, power and light facilities on a national scale. In October 1896 this concern was reformed as the British Electric Traction Co., Ltd., which specifically intended to promote and build electric tramways and light railways throughout the Kingdom (and certain other countries as well) in the wake of the legislative changes brought about by the Light Railways Act of 1896. For these purposes the Brush plant with its manufacturing facilities

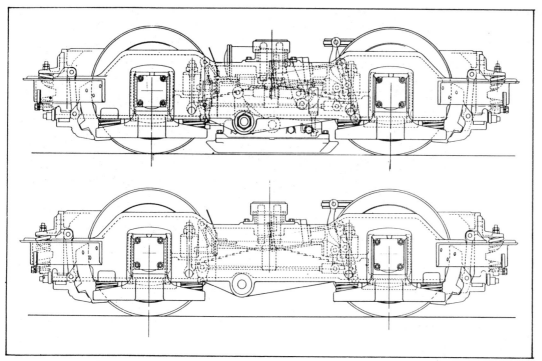

Left: Maley & Taunton swing-link equal-wheel bogie truck 4' 9" wheelbase, 27" or 28" diameter wheels. Upper drawing shows standard production truck with air wheel, air track and electromagnetic track brake equipment. Lower drawing shows projected MER variant with air wheel brake equipment only.

Below: Brush Type D equal-wheel truck on Car No. 6, showing the extended coil axlebox springs and hydraulic bolster dampers as fitted in the early 1960s to improve riding qualities.

W. P. Cubbon

was essential for the group's success.

Leaving aside the adventures of the BET Group*, which had many of its aspirations frustrated by mis-application of the new legislation and the very parochial outlooks of many local authorities, the Brush company built its first electric tramcar trucks for Hartlepools and the Dudley & Stourbridge line in 1899. The Dudley trucks were at least a fair copy of an American Peckham product and perhaps augured ill for things to come. Wholesale truck manufacture is reputed to have commenced at Loughborough in September 1900, but the initial range was far from successful and met with an icy reception from the traction industry in general, on account of poor design and inadequate construction. These shortcomings could not be ignored, and in order to put truck design and production on some sort of proper footing, Brush imported two American car truck designers, Mr T.C. Elder and Mr. Elmar E. Cook, on three-year contracts. Mr. Cook came from McGuire of Chicago, a large and successful truck manufacturer, and evidently brought with him at least the memorised details of some McGuire products. McGuire itself had, at this time, its own British subsidiary, the European McGuire Manufacturing Co. Ltd., based at Elton Fold Works, Bury, Lancashire, – premises that were in turn to house their successors, Mountain & Gibson Ltd. The range of new designs that evolved was noteworthy for its lack of originality and finally led to Brush producing clandestine copies of Brill trucks in order to retain customers. Of the entire range, perhaps the 'D' type equal-wheel bogie truck, introduced in 1902, was the best of the range. In most respects it was a fair copy of the McGuire No. 37 truck, except that the Brush version had poorer suspension and even worse braking characteristics. It was offered with wheelbases (distance between the axles) of 4' 6" and 5' 0" and the latter was selected by the MER. Brush

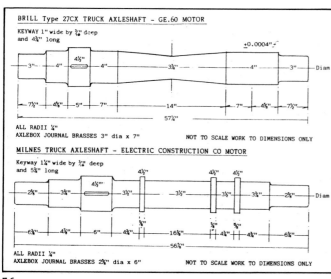

Type D trucks were also fitted to the "Cradley Bogies" of the Dudley, Stourbridge & District, Cars Nos. 178–188 of the City of Birmingham Tramways, and further batches were sold to Rochdale Corporation, Auckland, Perth (Western Australia) and the far-flung Scottish line, the Rothesay & Ettrick Bay Electric Railway. The basic truck was offered in two versions, featuring either one or both axles driven in each truck. There is a very real possibility that the original pair of Brush Type D trucks supplied to the MER had only their outer axles powered; there exists a faded picture of one of the Nos. 4–9 Class cars in 1903 with no motor or gear case visible on the inner wheelsets. These presumably provided insufficient traction and modifications or replacements ensued with all axles powered.

The basic Brush Type D truck was arranged appropriately for either one or two motor operation, with the bolster assembly offset towards the powered axle and with a central bolster respectively. Brush records show only one car set of the single-motored "maximum traction" trucks was ever sold. By the middle of 1904 the Brush Type D truck was no longer available, having been superceded by the improved and stronger 'DD' design, which enjoyed a slightly greater success. Serious complaints had certainly been received from some users of the Type D, in that they had occasionally shown a distressing propensity for disintegrating whilst out on the road.

The Brush Type D trucks delivered to the Manx Electric were serially numbered from 974 to 999, and these were fitted to Cars Nos. 1–3, 4–9, 16 and 25–27, of which Nos. 1, 2, 5, 6, 7, 9, 16 and 25–27 still exist. Of the trucks salvaged from the cars destroyed at Laxey in 1930, one de-motored set was used under works trailer No.21, whilst others survived for cannibalisation over the years. One spare Brush truck side-frame member was cut up about 1966 in order to make a singularly

* The BET Group went on to own over half of Britain's buses amongst other things and is today one of Britain's most successful and elegant investment groups.

Right: One of the 1893 trailer trucks supplied by G.F. Milnes, being used by the Engineer's Department in 1979. These Series 1 plate-frame trucks retain their chilled iron wheels and roller-type transom side-gearings. *W P Cubbon*

Right: A pair of slightly later Milnes plate-frame trucks, modified for use as accommodation bogies under Snaefell cars on their journeys to and from Douglas which necessitates the removal of their 3′ 6″ gauge trucks and the fitting of these 3′ 0″ gauge trucks instead. *W. P. Cubbon*

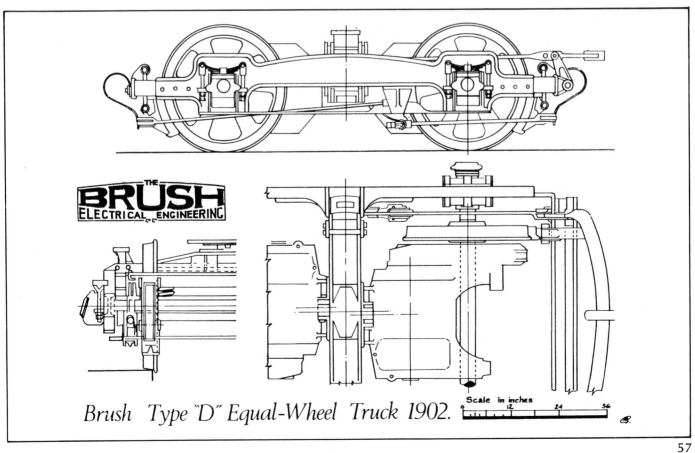

Brush Type "D" Equal-Wheel Truck 1902.

Scale in inches

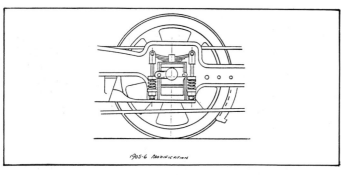

1905-6 MODIFICATION

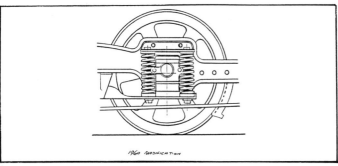

1960 MODIFICATION

unsuccessful Fell rail bending machine for use on Snaefell Mountain. One bare frame is stored against the back wall in Laxey Depot.

As originally delivered, the Manx Electric's Brush trucks had axlebox suspension comprising an ultra-short (and therefore almost useless) semi-elliptic leaf spring spread across the axlebox crowns, and coupled direct to suspension links attached to solid brackets on the truck side-frame. The spring leaves were so short that the assembly could only have reasonably been expected to act as a spring plank, but since there were no other springs for the plank to work in conjunction with, the assembly came close to being useless. Springs and suspension gear alone made it possible for vehicles to run at speed, and this cardinal fact was largely ignored in the early Brush truck designs. By the end of 1906 all of the MER's Brush trucks had been fitted with coil springs on suitably lengthened suspension links, and this at least ensured far fewer derailments. In addition, it had been necessary to heavily modify the traction motor suspension gear within twelve months of delivery, in order to permit the motor to rise and fall (relative to the truck frame) with the wheelsets. It might seem that at the time Brush produced only one type of axlebox cover; the ones fitted have lettering proclaiming the 'Maximum Traction Truck' which it may or may not have been and is certainly not now.

In just the same way as everywhere else, the MER's Brush trucks established a reputation for poor riding on anything other than absolutely first-class trackwork, and for inconsistent braking. There were problems of weight transfer under conditions of acceleration and brak-

ing, and the bolster assemblies have undergone several modifications to reduce or contain the wild lateral swing. The trucks were equipped with a wheelbrake linkage that was notorious for transmitting an unequal pull on the respective brake beams, with the result that one wheelset would lock up and skid, whilst the other continued to rotate, transmitting little or no braking effort. This linkage was improved by the MER, but to this day the trucks are regarded as "sensitive" to both rail and load conditions. If a choice exists, a Brill-trucked car would normally be taken in preference to a Brush-trucked one. In more recent times, trouble was experienced with one particular car, on which one wheelset not only locked up when the brakes were applied, but the same truck's other wheelset would slowly rotate in the opposite direction as the car came to a dead stand. The trouble was believed to be the result of residual eddy currents in the motors, or of magnetically-charged motor cases, and was solved by replacing the motors in a different order.

During the early 1960s, Mr. L.E. Gale (Rolling Stock Superintendent), and Mr. A.R. Cannell (Chief Assistant Engineer), carried out considerable work on the Brush trucks and heavily modified the suspension gear on Cars Nos. 1, 2, 5, 6, 7 and 9. This involved new and much longer axlebox coil springs with coupled hydraulic shock absorbers to either axleboxes or bolsters, resulting in an improvement in riding qualities. Cars Nos. 25–27 remain unchanged from 1906–7.

The Brush Electrical Company's trucks were not the best in contemporary British practice; the Manx Electric realised this and bought no more, insisting on genuine J.G. Brill products thereafter. Mr. Elmar E. Cook returned to America in 1906, trying to sell the "Cook Radial" truck, the memorised details of which he had clearly taken with him from the Brush plant. The Brush truck range was in time superceded by copies of Brill products, and from 1910 by increasing numbers of British Peckham designs, built under legitimate licence from the Peckham Truck & Engineering Co. Ltd., which was later absorbed by Brush. The Brush Company still exists at Falcon Works, Loughborough, as part of the Hawker Siddeley Group.

The Brill Trucks

Early in 1904 the MER Co. placed an order for four more open crossbench power cars and four trailers, with the Electric Railway & Tramway Carriage Co. Ltd., of Preston. This batch became Nos. 28–31 and Trailers Nos. 55–56 and 57–58. All were fitted with equal-wheel bogie trucks supplied by the world's largest truck manufacturer, the J.G. Brill Company of Philadelphia, Pennsylvania, USA.

These cars were delivered by the early summer of 1904 and entered service as soon as they were placed on the rails. They proved to be an enormous success, and their performance was far better than anything previously seen on the line, with smooth, easy and comfortable riding, consistent braking and comparatively minimal maintenance. The Manx Electric's management was so impressed by the Brill trucks under these new cars that it was decided to switch them from the original Cars Nos. 28–31 and fit them instead to the heavily-used Winter Saloon class, Nos. 19–22, which had been delivered in 1899 with Milnes plate frame trucks. This work was carried out dur-

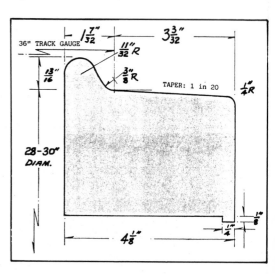

Left: The J.G. Brill Type 27Cx truck, as used by the Manx Electric. Shown here is one of Car No. 21's trucks with SEHC traction motors, after general overhaul at Derby Castle Carworks in 1970.

E. S. Johnson

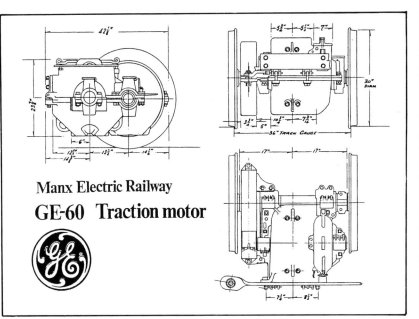

Manx Electric Railway

GE-60 Traction motor

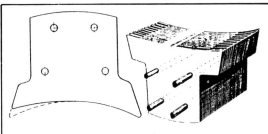

The General Electric (USA) GE.60 motors fitted to Cars Nos. 32–33, have asymmetrical field pole laminations, which are alternately reversed during assembly. The pole face is therefore solid at the centre, but has only half that area at the edges. This produces a "fringed" magnetic field under the horns, preventing distortion of the magnetic field and providing a proper field for reversing the current in the armature coils passing under the brushes with minimal sparking and low heat losses.

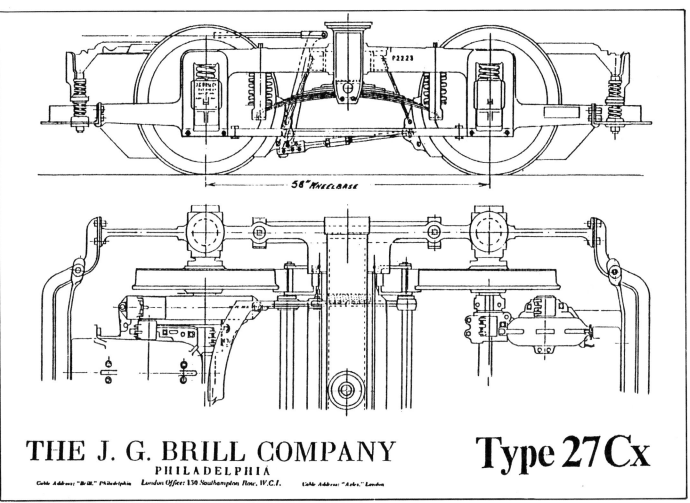

THE J. G. BRILL COMPANY
PHILADELPHIA

Cable Address: "Brill," Philadelphia   London Office: 110 Southampton Row, W.C.1.   Cable Address: "Axles," London

Type 27Cx

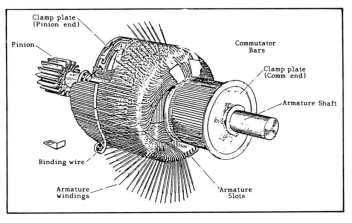

ing the winter of 1904–5 and also involved the removal of the air brake equipment (supplied by Christensen of Milwaukee) from the new cars to the saloons. Passengers tended to initially notice the increase in platform height of the re-equipped saloons, whilst the crossbench Cars Nos. 28–31 were commensurately reduced in stature. All subsequent car trucks delivered to the MER were to be of the same Brill type and design.

The truck itself was a special variant of the Brill Type 27C, originally introduced in 1896. The standard 27C wheelbase options were for 4' 0" and 4' 6" but in order to meet the special requirements of the MER, J.G. Brill produced a special design variant of 4' 10" wheelbase. In its original form, the 27C truck was a monotraction (only one axle powered) design, but the new MER trucks were equipped with two 25-horsepower traction motors per truck. The motors were "outside-hung" (i.e. outside the wheelbase) and were axle-hung and nose-suspended in the normal way, driving through spur wheel and pinion

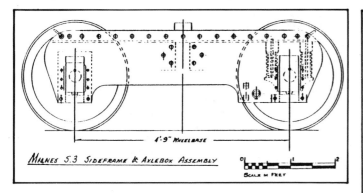

MILNES S.3 SIDEFRAME & AXLEBOX ASSEMBLY

4'9" WHEELBASE

SCALE IN FEET

CURRENT MER TRUCK ALLOCATION

Truck type	Cars Nos.
Motor Cars	
Milnes plate frame Series 3	14, 15, 17, 18, 28, 30, 31
Brush type D	1, 2, 5–7, 9, 16, 25–27
Brill 27Cx	19–22, 32–33
Trailer Cars	
Milnes plate frame Series 1	40, 41, 44, 46, 47, 49–50, 51 (now 13), 53, 54, 60
Milnes plate frame Series 2	36, 37, 45, 48, 49
Milnes plate frame Series 3	42, 43
Brill 27CxT	55–58, 61, 62

MER MOTOR TYPES

	General Elec.	SEHC	ECC
Manufacturer			
British Agents	BTH	Witting Eborall	
Type number	GE.60 (4-T)	EH.2	
Year	1905	1903	1898
Fitted to car Nos:	32 – 33	1, 2, 5 – 7, 9, 16, 19 – 22 25 – 27	14 – 17 28 – 31
Voltage	550 V	500 V	500 V
1-Hour rating (h.p.)	27 ½	25	20
Axle dia. at bearings	4''	3¾''/4''	3¾''
Type of bearings (motor)	roller	plain/roller*	plain
Wheel diameter (new)	30/32''	28/30''	28/30''
Wt in lbs. (incl pinion)	1,665	1,324	
Case or frame type	split	split	split
No. of poles	4	4	4
No. of compoles /interpoles	none	none	none
No. of field coils	4	4	4
No. of field turns	151.5	127	270
No. of Bands	4	5	5
No. of armature slots	37	33	63
Conductors per slot	12	24	8
No. of commutator bars	111	131	125
Armature diameter	13¾''	11⅞''	13¼''
Armature length	11¼''	13¾''	12¼''
No. of brush holders	2	2	2
Brushes per holder	1	2	2
Brush size	2½'' x 2½''	2¾'' x 1½''	1 15/16'' x 1½''
Air gap minimum	⅛''	⅛''	¾''
Field coil wire size	0.180''	0.176''	0.147''
Armature wire size	0.104''	0.096''	0.104''
No. of gearwheel teeth	67	68	67
No. of pinion teeth	14	14	16
Gear ratio	1:4.78	1:4.86	1:4.19
Brush span	26 bars	30 bars	29 bars

Roller bearings have been fitted to the armature shafts of cars Nos. 5. 6. 7. 9. 19. 20. 21 and 22.

gearing, fitted with oil-bath lubrication in enclosed gear casings. The motors were made by SEHC, Belgium. Since Brill's truck design designations used a suffix 'x' to denote special variants, the correct nomenclature for the MER's Brill trucks is '27Cx' in the case of trucks equipped with motors; Brill added the suffix 'T' at one stage in their rather confused numbering and classification system to denote a trailer truck. Thus the unpowered Brill trailer trucks are officially '27CxT'. Brill's numbering system was amended at several stages in their long history, and at a fairly early date the numbering began to refer to classes, not individual designs, but this too is not consistent. Suffix letters originally denoted a variant of a basic design or its later development, i.e. 22A, 22B, 22C and so on. The suffix 'E' at first indicated a solid-forged frame and an additional code (E.l, E.2 etc) denoted the carry-ing capacity. The 'x' after the suffixes, denoting a special variant, might indicate either the design or equipment, and for example a Brill 79Ex would have been a standard 79E truck but fitted with non-standard large diameter wheels. It is quite incongruous to assume a similarity between the members of certain numbered groups: the 27 class embraced several totally different and distinct types, including, as it happens, the 27MCB, which was an extremely heavy equalised truck design. Some of the MER's Brill trucks still carry their plates, most referring to 'Type 27 Truck' although one spectacular specimen proclaims the designation '27D' which it is not.

The J.G. Brill Company was for many years the greatest electric railway and tramway vehicle and truck manufacturer in the world. Founded in 1868 by John G. Brill (previously employed by an earlier Philadelphia horse tramcar builder, established in 1889) and his son, Martin Brill. The J.G. Brill Company rapidly established itself as America's leading horse and cable car builders, and with the advent of the electric traction, commenced production of a "patent Independent Rigid Car Truck" in 1887. This formed the basis for a long and comprehensive range of electric car trucks; by 1899 the total was no less than 9,000 trucks built and sold, as well as 2,000 complete cars.

Two car sets of Brill 22E and nine 21E single trucks comprised Brill's first British electric car truck order in 1899, although they had been supplying horse and cable car equipment in the United Kingdom since 1890. Brill truck and equipment sales in Britain were handled until April 1898 by Messrs Martin and Breckenridge, then for a short time by Laing, Wharton & Downs, and from April 1899 by the Dick, Kerr Company which, as part of what was eventually to become the English Electric group, carried large stocks of current American-built Brill trucks and parts.

J.G. Brill continued to build streetcars and trucks until 1941 when production at the Philadelphia plant switched to petrol-engined buses. For reasons unknown the Brill company flatly refused to build any diesel-engined buses, and closed its plant in 1954. The company was wound up in 1956.

The MER's Brill 27Cx trucks, with their inside-hung brakes have proved to be consistently reliable for over eighty years, and no modifications have ever been attempted. About twenty-five years ago the bolster spring gear of the trucks under the 19–22 class was altered, when new

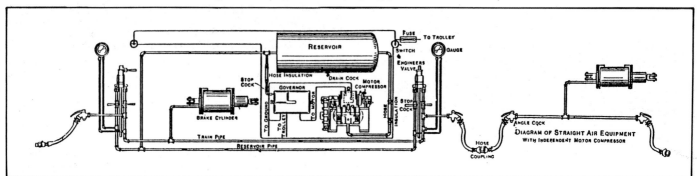

RESERVOIR — FUSE — TO TROLLEY — SWITCH — GAUGE — ENGINEERS VALVE — STOP COCK — HOSE INSULATION — DRAIN COCK — GOVERNOR — MOTOR COMPRESSOR — TO GROUND — TO TROLLEY — TO MOTOR — STOP COCK — INSULATION — BRAKE CYLINDER — TRAIN PIPE — RESERVOIR PIPE — ANGLE COCK — HOSE COUPLING — DIAGRAM OF STRAIGHT AIR EQUIPMENT WITH INDEPENDENT MOTOR COMPRESSOR

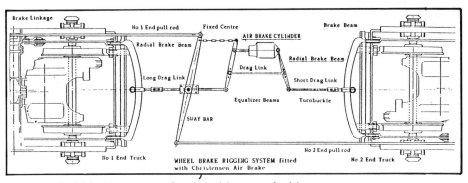

WHEEL BRAKE RIGGING SYSTEM fitted
with Christensen Air Brake

Below: Two types of air brake application valve. The upper one is one supplied by Christensen, Milwaukee, U.S.A., during the re-equipment programme of 1902–4, whilst the lower one is a Westinghouse self-lapping air brake application valves, as fitted to Car Nos. 21 and 22 after World War II.
Alex Townsend

springs with thicker leaves were fitted, and have resulted in poorer riding. The MER's Brill motor and trailer trucks are essentially identical save only for the difference in the headstocks needed to accommodate the motor gear.

Since the delivery of the MER's latest 3' 0" gauge car trucks in 1906, various newer designs have been considered. The Maley & Taunton Co. Ltd. of Wolverhampton was one of Britain's most famous truck manufacturers, and its founder, Mr Alfred Walter Maley, had originally been born in Athol Street, Douglas, on 7th November 1880. By 1932 Maley & Taunton were in the process of producing large numbers of their legendary Swing Link bogie truck for Leeds, Liverpool, Glasgow, Johannesburg, Lisbon and elsewhere, and Mr Maley was quite prepared to arrange a most favourable "over-run" price for a variant suitable for the MER. The new trucks could have either the motors out of the old trucks or be fitted (then or later) with new 35-horsepower Metropolitan-Vickers MV109 traction motors. The use of this remarkable truck design on the MER would have led to substantial savings in the costs of truck, carbody and track maintenance as well as providing a superbly comfortable ride. The MER, however, beset with the problem of trying to meet the costs of its inherent over-capitalisation, the liability for the great Laxey Flood of 1930, the residual losses incurred in the Laxey Depot fire of the same year, and the destruction of the Dhoon Glen Hotel in 1932, were unable to meet any further expenditure at the time.

BRAKE EQUIPMENT

Electric tramcars are invariably fitted with a multiplicity of brakes, any or all of which may be selected and applied by the motorman (or the conductor) according to circumstances, and the cars of the Manx Electric are no exception.

All of the Line's cars have at least two separate and distinct means of braking and all are equipped with traditional hand wheel brakes; on the majority of power cars, application may also be by compressed air. In addition, many cars are also fitted with a Milnes patent scotch brake, applied by a hand wheel on the platform (to the left of the ordinary wheel brake handle). All of the power cars are additionally capable of being braked electrically, by reversing the controller, although the retardation may be savage, and its effect on the mechanism and equipment equally so.

The open crossbench trailer cars are also fitted with an unusual emergency mechanical brake, operated by a chain attached to a fixed point on the power car. In the event of a breakaway, the chain is designed to apply the scotch brake rigging on the trailer (and which is held

Above: Whilst local craft techniques, such as armature winding, were seriously jeopardised by the use of outside contractors in 1977–87, Derby Castle Carworks has once again reverted to a high level of self-sufficiency. Here, an SEHC traction motor armature has been freshly rewound in 1989 using local skills.
Alex Townsend

Left: One of the excellent 12 Cubic feet per minute motor-compressor sets built by Maley & Taunton Ltd. of Wolverhampton, and purchased second-hand from Glasgow and Sheffield Corporation Transport Departments. *Maley & Taunton Ltd.*

on by a ratchet lock) and then part at a specially annealed "weak link" which ensures that the car's rigging incurs no damage. The Milnes patent scotch brake applies a wedge or triangular-shaped friction block to the wheels, and this brake is (usually) quite separate from the trailer's normal wheel brakes, operated by handwheels on either of the platforms. Certain trailer cars are equipped with air brakes.

The system of levers and rods used to apply the mechanical brakes are divided into two groups: the first consists of the "rigging" which is attached to the underside of the carbody, and consisting of a sway bar and its associated rods which transfer the effort from the means of application (hand or power) equally to each truck. In order to equalise this effort, particularly on curves, this rigging is often of considerable complexity and the accompanying diagram shows a typical layout. The second group of levers and rods consist of the "linkage" which is incorporated entirely within the truck itself, and transmits the movement and effort of the rigging to the brake shoes.

The Manx Electric Company was quick to appreciate the advantages of power braking, using compressed air, and in the re-equipment programme of 1902–4, eighteen car sets of air brake equipment were purchased and ultimately ended up on Cars Nos. 1–3, 5–9, 16, 19–22 and 23. Subsequent deliveries of new cars such as Nos. 32–33, were delivered already fitted.

The "straight" air brake (as opposed to the automatic air brake commonly found in full-scale railway practice with trains of rolling stock) was and remains ideal for only one or two trailers. Apart from the pipework, coupling hoses and so on, the straight air brake system fitted to tramcars consists of a motor-driven air compressor which is switched on and off by an automatic governor as required; the automatic governor usually consists of a small pressurised air cylinder, with a piston fitted or attached to electrical contacts. The stroke of the piston in or out of its cylinder automatically makes or breaks the electrical contact which feeds or isolates the compressor motor. The position of the piston is dependent on the pressure of air in the system. The pressures at which the automatic governor switches the motor on or off is adjustable.

The compressed air is stored ready for use in a Reservoir or tank(s) and fed through pipework to the motorman's air brake application valve, a rather complex tap, which allows compressed air to enter or leave the brake cylinder. The piston of the actuating cylinder is forced outwards by air pressure to apply the brakes. Brakes are released by the appropriate setting of the motorman's application valve, which cuts off the supply from the reservoir, and connects the brake pipe to an exhaust port, which allows the used air to escape to atmosphere. The air brake application valve handle is removable. Three types are in use: the original Christensen; the Westinghouse No.7 (a close relative of the Christensen but featuring an evil slit in the segment plate which can and does tear gloves and fingers) and the Westinghouse self lapping type W valve fitted to cars 21 and 22.

All of the Manx Electric cars involved with the air brake programme of 1902–1904 were fitted with air brake application valves, automatic governors, switchgear, actuating cylinders and Type A.5 motor compressors, running at 200 rpm., manufactured by the Christensen Engineering Co. Inc., of Milwaukee, Wisconsin, USA., and supplied by their UK Agents, R W Blackwell & Co. Ltd. The working pressure was between 75 and 90 lbs per square inch. The Christensen system originally featured "duplex" type pressure gauges, with two needles on a single dial, showing both the air reservoir pressure and also the pressure in at the brake pipe. None of these gauges remain in use, if indeed all the cars were ever fitted with this type. The Christensen system has never featured unloader or safety valves or low-pressure alarms, although unloader valves are now fitted to cars 22 and 32.

Four car sets of new Westinghouse motor compressors replaced the aging Christensen units on Cars Nos. 19 and 20 in 1947, and 21–22 in 1951; two sets of Westinghouse self-lapping application valves were also fitted at this time to Cars 21–22. The impending closure of Sheffield's tramways resulted in the purchase of twelve almost-new Maley & Taunton motor compressor sets in 1959, and a further four similar units followed from Glasgow in 1961. All these were used to replace the original Christensen sets, and none of these now remain in use.

CONTROL EQUIPMENT

Most electric tramcar passengers are familiar with the external appearance of the drum controller on the car's platforms, with its large handle for speed control, and a smaller handle or key to control the direction of running. Underneath the casing, however, the tramcar controller is far more than just a series of switches; it is in fact a compact and clever mechanism comprising not only the switchgear by which it regulates the speed and direction of the car, but also a series of in-

AIR BRAKE EQUIPMENT ROSTER

Car	AV	MC	AG	SG	Cyl	TAC
1	W 7	M&T ex-S	M&T	M&T	W	No
2	Chr	M&T ex-S	M&T	M&T	Chr	No
3	Chr	Car destroyed by fire, Laxey, 1930				
4	Chr	Car destroyed by fire, Laxey, 1930				
5	Chr	M&T ex-S	W	M&T	Chr	Yes
6	Chr	M&T ex-S	M&T	M&T	Chr	Yes
7	Chr	M&T ex-S	M&T	M&T	Chr	Yes
8	Car destroyed by fire, Laxey, 1930					
9	Chr	M&T ex-S	M&T		Chr	
16	W 7	M&T ex-S	W			No
19	W 7	M&T ex-G	W	M&T	W	Yes
20	W 7	M&T ex-G	W	M&T	W	Yes
21	W W	M&T ex-G	W	M&T	W	Yes
22	W W	M&T ex-G	W	M&T	W	Yes
23	Chr	Chr				
24	Car destroyed by fire, Laxey, 1930					
25	Chr	M&T ex-S	M&T	M&T	Chr	No
26	Chr	M&T ex-S	M&T	M&T	Chr	No
27	Chr	M&T ex-S	M&T	M&T	Chr	No
28–31	Equipment removed 1904 and transferred to cars Nos. 19–22.					
32	Chr	M&T ex-S	M&T	Chr	Chr	No
33	Chr	M&T ex-S	M&T	Chr	Chr	No

AV   Application valves
MC   Motor compressor
AG   Automatic governor
SG   Switchgear
Cyl   Cylinder
TAC Trailer air cocks

M&T   Maley & Taunton Ltd. Wolverhampton
ex-G   ex-Glasgow Corporation Transport Department
ex-S   ex-Sheffield City Transport Dept
Chr   Christensen
W   Westinghouse

terlocks and other provisions to guard against irregular manipulation or mishandling. It additionally incorporates means by which a defective motor or circuit can be cut out, so that the car can still make its way back home. The actual power contacts are provided with the means to extinguish (and therefore minimise damage by burning) the electric arcs that are created when a circuit is opened or switched off, under load, by using the magnetism that surrounds any current-carrying conductor. Additionally, the controller has the ability to provide electric braking in one or more of several forms.

Disregarding the original and rather experimental control gear manufactured by Mather & Platt and originally fitted to Cars Nos. 1–13, all of the Manx Electric's later deliveries featured the products of the American General Electric Company, never to be confused with a similarly entitled firm based in the United Kingdom and commonly known as GEC. It was a choice of excellence that has stood the test of time, and remains in constant use to this day, over ninety years since its despatch from GE's Schenectady plant outside New York.

Ever since the 1898–9 deliveries of rolling stock, the Isle of Man Tramways & Electric Power Co. had chosen the GE K.11 type drum controller, and in the re-equipment programme of 1902–4 by the new Manx Electric Railway Company, it was wisely decided to standardise this excellent unit throughout the fleet and the earlier Mather & Platt controllers were replaced. All types of orthodox traction controllers provide a series of steps by which the starting rheostat or resistances in the power circuit are progressively cut out as the motors are brought up to speed. The very earliest electric tramcars, even before the MER, usually had only one motor, but when two or four motor equipments began to come into use it was found that if the motors were connected in pairs to start off with, in series with one another, and later reconnected in parallel, with all motors or motor groups taking full line voltage, this required much less hardware in the rheostats and was far more economical in terms of electrical consumption through reduced resistance losses. It is to be remembered that any power fed to the rheostats is wastefully burned off as heat, so that the more power fed to the rheostats, the higher the electricity bill. The 'series parallel' system of traction control also meant that there were two economic running notches on the controller, namely top series and top parallel, where none of the power is diverted into the rheostats. All of the other positions on the power notches of a controller are referred to as

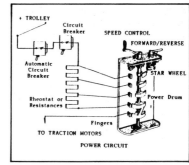

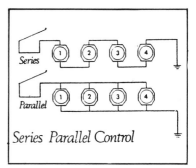

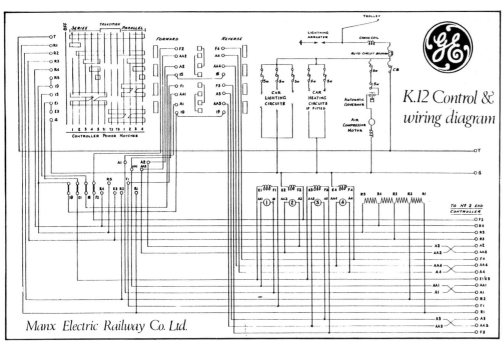

Series Parallel Control

Manx Electric Railway Co. Ltd.

"rheostat positions" and may not be used for sustained running.

Controller Operation

On the General Electric K.11 or K.12 controller, there are nine power notches or "points" of which the first five, clockwise from the "Off" position, are series connections and marked as such. The last four notches are the parallel connections. Between the end of the series notches and the beginning of the parallel ones, there are three unmarked notches which come into play when the controller switches go through the steps of the "shunt" transition between series and parallel connection.

To start a car away, and assuming the trolley is on and the circuit breakers "in" to give power at the controller, the Motorman fits a key into the reversing drum on the right-hand side of the controller top plate, and turns it forward or backward, according to the required direction of running. Due to a mechanical interlock underneath the top plate, the key cannot be removed from the controller unless both it and the speed control handle, on the left of the controller, are in the "Off" positions. This provision is to guard against any attempt to use the controllers at both ends of the same car simultaneously, and there have been some formidable accidents in faraway places when, for some reason or another, a deluded motorman could not retrieve his key from the top of the controller at one end, and successfully butchered the drum at the other end with a wrench or spanner.

Having selected the direction of movement with the controller key, the Motorman then moves the speed control handle clockwise to the first or "Series 1" position to start the car away, assuming that the mechanical brakes are off. At this point the motors are connected in series with the whole of the rheostat in circuit. The second, third and fourth notches maintain the connections in series, but progressively cut out sections of the rheostat so that more power is fed to the motors as speed builds up, until the fifth or top Series notch is reached, where all of the rheostat is cut out, and the power from the overhead wire is being shared between the motors, producing approximately half the top speed of the car. The first Parallel notch brings most of the rheostat into the circuit again, but with the power now being connected to each motor; the succeeding two parallel notches again cut out parts of the rheostat until, on the fourth and final parallel notch, it is cut out altogether and the motors are receiving full line voltage, bringing the car up to full speed.

The transition between series and parallel is a sequence of some complexity and maintains some motor torque to prevent a major jerk or surge as the transition into parallel connection is completed, whilst disconnecting the series motoring connections altogether. Transition from series to parallel can be effected in two ways, either by "bridge" transition (more usually associated with heavy electric railway practice, but notably fitted to Leeds railcar No. 601 of 1953 by Metropolitan Vickers) which enables the normal accelerating torque to be available from both motors or motor groups during the entire period of acceleration, (but is relatively complicated) or by the earlier and simpler expedient of "shunt" transition, as featured in the MER's controllers.

In this case, shunt transition consists of three steps, made as the handle of the controller is moved between the top series and first parallel

notches. At the first step, a part of the rheostat is reinserted into the motor circuit, with the motors still joined in series. The value of this resistance is supposed to be such that the current input on the second transition notch, at the point where one of the motors or motor groups is shorted out, is roughly equal to the upper limit of the current during starting. The short-circuiting of the motor or motor group at the second step is done by connecting the negative terminal of the machine to the negative wire; at the third and final transition step, the series connections between the motors is broken so that the second motor or motor group is ready to be connected in parallel with the other motor or group, thus completing the transition. Nevertheless, the surge of motor torque as the controller is moved up to the first parallel notch is usually discernible by the average passenger. Tramcar riders of old knew from experience, particularly as standing passengers, that there were two distinct phases of acceleration, and in association with antique "maximum traction" type trucks (bogie trucks featuring a large driving wheel and a small pony wheel) which clearly had only one motor per truck, this led to the curious and quite unfounded notion that only one motor was used for starting away, and with the other motor brought in as speed built up. From a scientific point of view, the notion ignored the most essential characteristics of d.c. traction motors, where the maximum torque or starting effort is produced when the motor is running very slowly. As the speed of the motor rises, the torque diminishes, and this is obviously ideal for the purposes of traction.

Controller Mechanism

The General Electric K-type controller consists of two vertical drums or barrels inside the outer casing, with the left hand drum providing the speed control and the right hand drum making the forward and reverse connections. Segments of copper fixed to the drums make and break contact with spring-loaded copper-tipped fingers on the frame at the side of the drums; the fingers are connected directly to the traction wiring, which is led in through a hole in the bottom of the controller from the car's wiring harness. As the drums are rotated, either by the handle or the key, they make and break contact with the circuit fingers as shown in the diagram.

The controller case or frame of the K.11 or K.12 controller (identical except for the internal wiring and connections) is 33⅛" high from the car deck to the top of the controller; the height from the deck to the top of the speed control handle is 42¼" whilst the width of the casing is 16⅝" and 17½" wide over the tip of the reversing key. The unit is 8⅛" deep, The top of the controller consists of a heavy brass casting through which the spindles of the two drums project to receive the handle and key caps. The coverplate is waterproof, and the semi-ornamental top is suitably grooved to allow rainwater to run off quite harmlessly – a major point with an open crossbench car caught in a cloudburst!

The controller's sheet steel outer case is usually fixed to the frame by two of the four wing nut studs. The case is quite readily removable to reveal the moulded asbestos arc-shield, which can be unlocked and swung round out of the way to reveal the power barrels and contact fingers. A magnetic blow-out coil is fitted and is a vital component in the extinguishing of arcs. Any d.c. circuit breaker or switch is, of

Left: Motorman's eye view of the General Electric K.11 Controller. To the right is the Christensen, Milwaukee, air brake application valve; the piece of wood on the front window ledge is a carefully shaped wedge to jam the platform door shut and keep out the winter draughts.
Alex Townsend

SYNOPSIS OF CONTROL GEAR

Car No	Original control	1904 control	Present control
1	M&P	GE K.11	Modified to K.12 in October 1947
2	M&P	GE K.11	Modified to K.12 in November 1947
3	M&P	GE K.11	Destroyed Laxey fire, 1930
4	M&P	GE K.11	Destroyed Laxey fire, 1930
5	M&P	GE K.11	Received K.12 off Car No.14, 1963
6	M&P	GE K.11	Modified to K.12, January 1946
7	M&P	GE K.11	Modified to K.12, (?) 1946
8	M&P	GE K.11	Destroyed Laxey fire, 1930
9	M&P	GE K.11	Modified to K.12 before February 1948
10	M&P	Withdrawn 1902	
11	M&P	Conv. to Motor freight car, controllers unknown	
12	M&P	Converted to Motor cattle car, believed K.11	
13	M&P	Withdrawn 1902	
14	GE K.11	Same	Modified to K.12, controllers to Car 5, 1963, now K.11
15	GE K.11	Same	Given K.12 controllers off Car 25 in 1936
16	GE K.11	Same	Modified to K.12 by 1946
17	GE K.11	Same	Modified to K.12 by 1946
18	GE K.11	Same	Modified to K.12 by 1945
19	GE K.11	Same	Modified to K.12 1936
20	GE K.11	Same	Modified to K.12 1936
21	GE K.11	Same	Modified to K.12 1936
22	GE K.11	Same	Modified to K.12 1936
23	GE K.11	Same	
24	GE K.11	Same	Destroyed Laxey fire, 1930
25	GE K.11	Same	Modified to K.12 1935, controllers to No. 15, 1936
26	GE K.11	Same	Modified to K.12, (?) 1948
27	GE K.11	Same	Modified to K.12 by 1939
28	GE K.11	Same	Modified to K.12 by 1954
29	GE K.11	Same	Unaltered, still K.11
30	GE K.11	Same	Unaltered, still K.11
31	GE K.11	Same	Unaltered, still K.11
32	GE K.11		Modified to K.12 before February 1948
33	GE K.11		Modified to K.12, date unknown

necessity, designed to feature a quick-break action on account of the arcing propensities of direct current. Any attempt to break or rupture a 550 V d.c. supply at well over 200 amps is quite certain to produce an arc, and it is essential to quench it instantly, since not only does it burn, pit and damage the contact tips and segments but, if sustained, might flashover to the nearest earth or ground wire. Fortunately for electric traction, nature provided the laws of magnetism, and the most fundamental law of magnetism states that a current-carrying conductor situated in a magnetic field (the direction of which is always perpendicular to the conductor's axis) is acted upon by tending to move the conductor out of the magnetic field. In a controller of this type, this magnetic field is augmented by a powerful "blow-out" coil, excited by the main current and aimed exactly at the space where arcing is likely to occur, by the pole pieces of the coil. The magnitude of this force is always proportional to the product of the current and the density of the magnetic flux. In order to prevent an arc reaching any adjacent contact fingers or ground or earthed components, fireproof arc deflectors are inserted horizontally and are incorporated in the moulded asbestos arc shute or shield, referred to above.

For reasons connected with the arc-quenching properties of the blow-out coil, it was the practice of most tramway operators to insist that motormen must switch the controller off, from whatever position they had reached, by a single anti-clockwise movement of the handle. If the motorman wished to continue motoring in top series instead of top parallel, he was invariably trained and required to switch off altogether, and then notch up again to the desired point.

Only the main speed control drum assembly is designed for rupturing traction current; the reversing barrel cannot do so, and indeed, movement of that drum is physically prevented by mechanical interlock if the speed control handle is not in its "Off" position. If for any reason a controller should jam on a power notch, the power can be taken off either by knocking out either of the main circuit breakers, or having the trolley removed from the overhead wire.

Underneath the controller top-plate, both drum spindles are equipped with "star wheels" which in conjunction with spring-loaded rollers, provide the positive "feel" of notches, whilst ensuring that a motorman cannot hold the barrel in an improper intermediate position, i.e. in between one notch and another. Inside the controller there is a series of hand operated switches which enable a motorman to isolate motors or circuits in the event of a defect arising.

The controller itself does not directly guard against the overloading of the motors. If a motorman notches up too quickly for the load and speed, the automatic circuit breaker will trip the circuit. The automatic circuit breaker is at the south or Douglas end of all MER cars with the exception of Nos. 32–33 which for some reason are wired to the Ramsey end; one is tempted to suspect that the cars were placed on the rails the wrong way round when they were delivered in 1906, but there may have been some other obscure reason that is now beyond human recall.

Finally, it might be mentioned that the GE K-type controller frames feature feet specifically designed to permit some slight rocking movement, with the spring of the dash panel, to which they are also attached, as the car's platforms deflect slightly when running.

Many British and foreign electric tramcar controllers also feature braking notches, normally engaged by turning the power handle backwards from the "Off" position. These were common in Britain and Europe, but definitely unusual in contemporary American traction practice, and since the technology of the MER tended towards a Transatlantic bias, the choice of controllers with power notches only was entirely in keeping with that philosophy.

The MER's General Electric controllers have been in service ever since their delivery with little modification, although most (but not all) of the circuits have been altered to the later K.12 pattern. With the original arrangement of the K.11 circuit, load sharing between motors could (and did) become unbalanced by a variety of factors, the most common being wheels of a slightly unequal diameter, since wheel tyres rarely tend to wear at exactly uniform rates throughout a set of eight wheels on four axles. If uncorrected, this condition will lead to the traction motor on the wheelset with the largest diameter wheels trying to do most of the work, with consequent overheating and other troubles. This could also be exacerbated by other practical defects, such as a serious voltage drop in the supply. A glance at the power feeder arrangements on the MER, particularly north of Laxey, shows the relative distance from sub-stations, and the hardest sustained climbing (from either direction) occurs at the summit of the line at Bulgham top, places as far away as possible from any sub-station. In years gone by, extreme conditions in the Ballaragh district was occasionally known to produce a drop to 370 volts, instead of the official 550 volts. In this instance, there were other factors involved too.

Whilst the correct and equal diameter of wheels is still significant with the K.12 control circuit, it is not as vital as with the earlier arrangement. The MER fully appreciated the advantages of the K.12 system, and began a lengthy programme of conversion in 1935, commencing with Car No. 25. This was followed by the four Winter

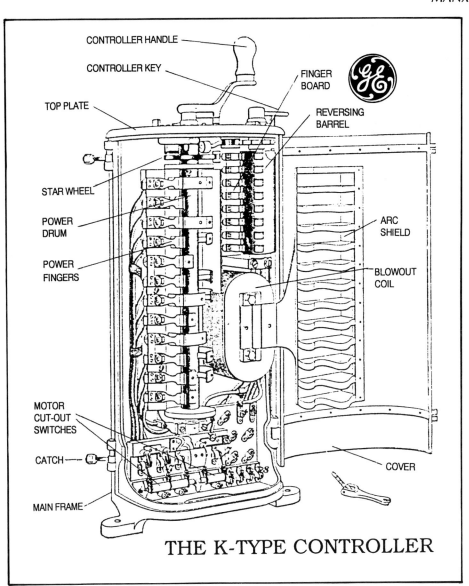

THE K-TYPE CONTROLLER

Saloons, Nos. 19–22, and thereafter the new wiring was usually carried out whenever a car came into Derby Castle Carworks for major overhaul. The process continued throughout World War II and afterwards, and between October 1947 and February 1948 Cars Nos. 1, 9, 26 and 32 were dealt with and received K.12 circuits. Car No.5 was given the K.12 control gear off Car No. 14 in 1963. It must be assumed that Cars Nos. 14, 29, 30 and 31 still have their original K.11 wiring circuits.

Whilst general maintenance of controllers amounts to keeping the units very clean and lubricated and free from copper dust, segments and finger tips are replaced as and when necessary. For many years these items were supplied by the Colton Electrical Co., Upminster, Essex, but since this firm ceased to make tramway electrical equipment, the items have been produced by the MER at Derby Castle. The self-sufficiency of the undertaking is nothing short of remarkable.

CHAR-A-BANC & MOTOR COACHES

The Manx Electric Railway Co. Ltd. was the first operator of motor coaches in the Isle of Man, opening a service from the Bungalow, on Snaefell Mountain, down to Tholt-y-Will in Sulby Glen, where the company had erected an hotel and extensive tea gardens. The two original Argus 16-seat char-a-banc were augmented by a new de Dion in 1914, but services were suspended on the outbreak of the First World War, and the motor vehicles sold off. The old service was reinstated in 1920 when two new 27-seat Caledon motor coaches arrived, and which lasted until June 1926 when three new Ford Model "T" chassis with 14-seat bodies took over. The Second War also resulted in the cessation of services, and the Fords were disposed of in April 1942, although the MER Co. retained two Bedford WLB 20-seater coaches which had been acquired in 1939. The Bungalow-Tholt-y-Will service was reinstated after the war, and continued until the end of 1952. Both Bedfords were sold off early the following year. The nationalised MER Board of Tynwald of 1957 boldly reinstated the service, using two elderly ex-Douglas Leyland Cubs, in 1957 and 1958, with little or no commercial success. The last public appearance of the two MER buses was on 7th August 1959, when they operated a shuttle service between Ramsey (Plaza) and the Royal Manx Agricultural Showground on Lezayre Road. The vehicles were broken up in 1961.

Reg.No.	Year New	Acqd	Chassis	Body	Type	Withdrn
MN 67	1907	New	Argus	?	Ch16	1914
MN 68	1907	New	Argus	?	Ch16	1914
MN 475	1914	New	De Dion	?	Ch18	1914
MN 1053	1920	New	Caledon	?	Ch27	6/1926
MN 1054	1920	New	Caledon	?	Ch27	6/1926 *
MN 4416	1926	New	Ford "T"	?	Ch14	4/1942
MN 4417	1926	New	Ford "T"	?	Ch14	4/1942
MN 4418	1926	New	Ford "T"	?	Ch14	4/1942
MN 8685	1933	1939	Bedford WLB	?	C20F	5/1953
MN 8874	1933	1939	Bedford WLB	Duple	C20F	5/1953 §
CMN 709	1938	1957	Leyland KPZ1	Pk Ryl	B20F	5/1960
DMN 585	1939	1957	Leyland KPZ1	Pk Ryl	B20F	5/1960

* Sold for use as lorry to Corlett, Sons & Cowley Ltd, Douglas.
§ Converted to MER Co. lorry; Withdrawn 1957, scrap 6/1962.
Pk Ryl = Park Royal Vehicles Ltd.
Body Types:

Ch = Char-a-banc, C = Coach, B = Bus, F = Front or forward entrance.

Above: Car No 7, a crossbench trailer and a freight van, a typical MER make-up or "consist" for over 85 years, at Derby Castle Station in 1904, shortly after the Cars of the 4–9 Class were re-equipped with Brush Type D equal-wheel bogie trucks and Belgian-built SEHC traction motors. Note the original chilled-iron wheels.

Left Crossbench Cars Nos 27, 25 and 32 awaiting service at Derby Castle Car Depot in 1977.   *W.P. Cubbon*

Below The nearest the MER came to street tramway practice: Car No 20 and Trailer 41 heads south for Douglas on the short section in Walpole Avenue, Ramsey, equipped with grooved tramway rail, side poles and bracket arms, complete with ornamental ironwork and finials, in August 1978.   *J.G.Fenton*

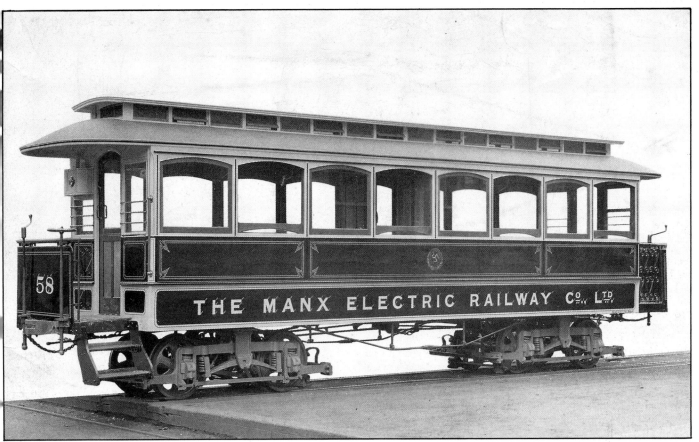

Above: Maker's photograph of Trailer Car No 58, the second of two such winter trailers delivered by the ER&TC Works, Preston, in 1904. The Brill trucks were equipped with Milnes-type scotch brakes. Note also the manager's name inscribed on the rocker panel – "Harold Brown, Gen. Manager" under the "Ltd" of the main title. *MER Collection*

Below: Cars Nos 3 and 6 posed in the "hospital roads" at Derby Castle Depot in 1894. The spacing of tracks in the depots suited the requirements of Hopkinson bow collectors, but creates some difficulties in turning trolley poles. Note the alarm bell hanging from the cantrail of Car No 3; these were later replaced by traditional foot-operated gongs. *Mather & Platt Ltd*

CHAPTER FIVE

OVERHEAD EQUIPMENT

THE Manx Electric's overhead line and current collection equipment is of great interest to traction engineers, historians and technology students since no attempt has been made to dilute antiquity by adopting modern techniques and recent innovation. The present equipment is effectively unchanged from the early days of the present century. Since the Island does not have to comply with the British Board of Trade (later Ministry of Transport and now the Health & Safety Executive) requirements, it has led to some interesting deviations from orthodox British tramway practice.

In the beginning, tramway electrification proposals led to considerable discussion on the relative merits of the systems then available. For simplicity, reliability and low costs in capital and maintenance, the overhead conductor wire was by far the system of choice. In localities where unusual preconditions existed, the alternatives to overhead wires consisted of either underground conduit collection, such as was used in London, Paris, Washington, New York, etc., or of some form of surface contact equipment, such as the Griffiths-Bedall, Lorain or similar systems. Both of these main alternatives were either notoriously expensive or unreliable. Pure electric railways on their own right of way had the additional option of a live third rail on the track, but this was conditional on the total enclosure of the line by fencing, and few grade

ALBERT & J. M. ANDERSON MFG. CO.

crossings and so on. In the case of the original Douglas–Groudle line of 1893, the overhead conductor wire electrification system was selected from the start. This choice is of some significance in that the only British lines to have overhead wires at that time consisted of the demonstration line at the Edinburgh Exhibition of 1890, and the Roundhay Park line at Leeds, which opened for service on 11th November 1891. In addition there had also been a little-known line at the Cork Exhibition of 1889, which can claim to have been the first electric tramway in the British Isles to use an overhead conductor wire.

The purpose of a tramway's overhead line equipment is to distribute electric power to the cars, and comprises the means by which a tramcar makes contact with its power supply. An overhead conductor wire is also required to function as a feeder and must be fully able to withstand the mechanical stresses due both to operation and temperature variation and any other factors. The means by which the tramcar made contact with the wire led to persistent and lengthy experiment to produce a reliable form of current collection gear. The early American traction pioneer, Charles van DePoele is credited with the invention of the under-running trolleywheel collector, which he successfully applied to his own experimental tramcars in 1882. Van DePoele's electric line at the Toronto Exposition of 1884 was thus equipped and proved to be highly successful. After a brief flirtation with other forms of less successful "trollers" or "travellers" at Scranton, Pennsylvania, Appleton, Wisconsin, and at Lima, Ohio, van DePoele reverted to his original design for his line at Montgomery, Alabama which opened in 1886. Van DePoele was originally born in Belgium in 1846 and is also to be remembered as the inventor of carbon brushes for electric motor commutators. The more famous American inventor, Frank J. Sprague, also conceived the idea of an under-running trolley collector in 1882, but the American Patent Office upheld Van DePoele's prior claim.

Since almost all of the electric tramways or street railways in the United States depended upon the overhead conductor wire, it is not surprising to find that a very large and comprehensive range of overhead line equipment and fittings became readily available from American manufacturers, who were already well established by the time British tramways were considering electrification. One particularly prominent manufacturer was the Albert & J.M. Anderson Manufacturing Co. of Boston, Mass., established in 1877; their brand name "Aetna" and their trade mark of a capital 'A' in a circle, was to become very familiar to most overhead line gangs in Britain for many years. Another major

Left: Often seen but rarely recorded, the MER's trolley-rope knot tightens instantly when pulled by the trolley, and must be learned by every conductor before being allowed out in charge of a car.
Alex Townsend

American manufacturer was the Ohio Brass Co. of Mansfield, Ohio, established about 1894, and happily still very much in business.

COLLECTION SYSTEMS

Whilst the Douglas and Groudle line was equipped with overhead wires, the promoters stopped short of using the already-proven under-running trolleywheel collector and instead chose to use Dr John Hopkinson's patent bow collector, not dissimilar to the present-day equipment retained on the Snaefell Mountain cars. Two large sliding or under-running bows were fitted on the roof of each tramcar, approximately over each bogie truck centre; the collector bar was set to run fractionally below the height of the wire at poles, so that it was only touching the wire where the line sagged between supports. As one of the bow collectors lost contact as it neared a pole, the other one would (or should) be in mid-span and therefore in contact. The object of this arrangement was to avoid hammer blows at the wire supports as the collector passed underneath it. The need to align the overhead wire within close tolerances necessitated the use of considerably more poles than would otherwise have been the case.

There can be little doubt that the original choice of the Hopkinson bow collector was the cause of serious and expensive problems; whilst the Groudle line was really ready to open by 8th August 1893, it was not finally opened for passenger traffic until 7th September, by which time the holiday season was almost over. This costly delay was almost entirely due to difficulties with the current collection gear. During the following winter of 1893–4, the original rigid collector was modified by John Hopkinson's brother, Dr Edward, who added spring gear hopefully in order to ''provide greater wire height range and flexibility''. Much of the task of getting the bow collector system to work at all was the responsibility of the legendary (but at the time youthful) Mr. Josua Shaw, who had originally arrived in the Island with Mather & Platt's staff. In 1894 he took up employment with the Isle of Man Tramways & Electric Power Co. Ltd., as their ''Overhead Specialist.'' He was concerned with the lack of reliability of the Hopkinson bow collectors, which could be made to work well on one day, but foul the wire or fail to reach it at all the following day if there were major differences in the ambient temperature. He was also cognizant of a further disadvantage of the type of bow, that of being unable to quickly remove if from the contact with the wire in an emergency. Nevertheless, the bows managed to struggle on but in 1897 Mr. Shaw, together with Mr. J. Aldworth, the manager, carried out a study of various European electric tramway installations and also sought the advice of the City of Birmingham Electric Tramways Co. Ltd. on contemporary overhead equipment. This resulted in a decision to re-equip the entire Douglas–Laxey section for trolleypole operation using the fixed-head type trolleywheel. This conversion, which cost £2,800 at 1898 prices, involved far more than just the roof-top equipment of the cars, for the original suspension of the wire had been by means of direct bracket arm suspension hangers. These comprised a split clamp fitting onto the bracket arm, with an insulating sleeve between the arm and the hanger, and with a double insulation provided by the normal insulated bolts onto which the ear that held the wire was screwed. Suspension of this sort was highly rigid and quite unacceptable for relatively high-

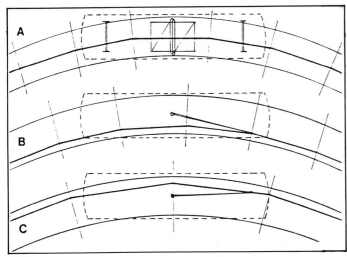

Below: Diagram showing route of overhead line through curves. Fig.A shows the position required for bow or pantograph collectors (and which needed more poles and pull-offs); Fig.B shows the wire arranged for ''fixed head'' trolleys, as used on the MER from 1897, and Fig.C shows the wire arranged for ''swivel-head'' trolley operation.

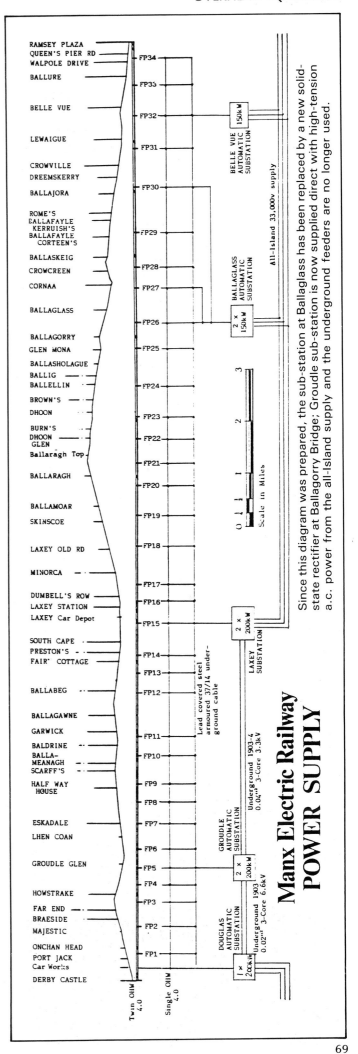

THE
Electric Construction Co., Ltd.,
LONDON AND WOLVERHAMPTON.

CONTRACTORS FOR
Central Stations, Railways, Tramways,
and Transmission of Power Plant.

HEAD OFFICE:
Dashwood House,
9, New Broad Street,
LONDON, E.C.

Telegraphic Address:
"CONCORDANCE, LONDON."

Telegraphic Address:
"ELECTRIC, WOLVERHAMPTON."

WORKS:
WOLVERHAMPTON.

Direct-Driven Multipolar Tramway Generators.
As supplied to the Isle of Man Tramways Company,
525=550 volts., 230 amps., 175 revs.

Left: An advertisement from TRAMWAY & RAILWAY WORLD, April 5, 1900, showing the ECC equipment at Ballaglass Power Station. *Harley McKnight*

Below: Tower wagon No. 3 in 1977, since dismantled. *Mike Goodwyn*

speed trolleywheel operation, and new line fittings throughout were necessary to provide resilience. Most if not all of the overhead line fittings came from Albert & J.M. Anderson, together with their "Boston Pivotal" type trolley bases and trolleyheads or harps. This particular trolleyhead was (and is) perhaps the lightest unit ever made, weighing just under 3 lbs, without its wheel. The 4¾" diameter trolleywheel is approximately 2 lbs. in weight. Anderson's "Boston Pivotal" type trolleybase weighed 80 lbs, without its pole and trolleyhead, and was designed to produce a fairly constant pressure, irrespective of the angle of the pole.

The choice of a "fixed" type trolleyhead was in keeping with general American traction practice, and was preferred to the "swivelling" type trolleyhead on the basis of its more reliable high-speed operation. The fixed head was never generally adopted in British practice, and indeed only thirteen other places in the United Kingdom used it. The fixed head required a high degree of accuracy in the hanging of the overhead wire. In traction practice, the wire is strung out above the centreline or middle ordinate of the permanent way on straight sections (with certain exceptions noted later) but at curves, the wires for fixed or swivel heads take entirely different routes. Fixed heads need a wire that takes what is termed the "line of pursuit" on the inside of the curve; the wire route for swivel heads describes an arc outside the curve's middle ordinate. The two are not compatible and for this reason alone the 1973 Transmark recommendation that the Douglas–Ramsey line should be converted to swivel heads was a total nonsense on two counts: firstly it would have resulted in less reliable operation and secondly it would have necessitated the rehanging of much of the 35 miles of overhead wire and equipment, to no useful purpose.

The hardware of electric tramway overhead equipment is divisible into three groups of components: the traction poles or supports for the overhead; the suspension and insulated fittings used to suspend the wire, and the conductor wire itself, with its own fittings.

TRACTION POLES

Traction poles are required to support the overhead above the tracks, and may be of timber, reinforced concrete or steel. Steel poles came in tubular, lattice and girder types, whilst tubular poles may be further sub-divided into the tapered or jointed types, the latter having two or more concentric tubes joined by telescoping the sections together, usually providing an overlap of about 18". The Manx Electric has steel poles of innumerable types, and some timber poles can be found, notably at Dhoon Quarry sidings and on part of the Snaefell section. The original poles on the Douglas–Groudle line were 25 ft long, with a ground depth of 5 ft., and of a neat tapering design in

two sizes. The normal duty pole was 6" diameter at the base, tapering to only 3" diameter at the top; for heavy duty, a pole with a base of 7" diameter, tapering to 4" diameter, was used. The extension to Ramsey, which was designed from the start for trolleypole operation, saw the use of a new type of stepped or jointed pole, supplied by R.W. Blackwell Ltd. These poles came in two sizes, according to requirements, with a standard pole of 6" base diameter and 4" diameter at the top, and 7" base diameter, again with a 4" diameter top. Special extra-length poles of up to 31 ft. (the later British standard) were used for special locations where the pole had to be sited some distance below the track level, as for "pull-off" purposes on curves. Converse-

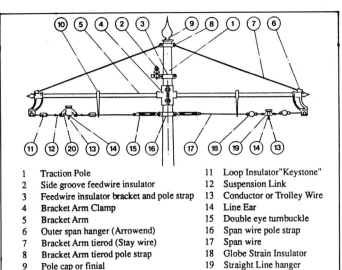

1	Traction Pole	11	Loop Insulator"Keystone"
2	Side groove feedwire insulator	12	Suspension Link
3	Feedwire insulator bracket and pole strap	13	Conductor or Trolley Wire
4	Bracket Arm Clamp	14	Line Ear
5	Bracket Arm	15	Double eye turnbuckle
6	Outer span hanger (Arrowend)	16	Span wire pole strap
7	Bracket Arm tierod (Stay wire)	17	Span wire
8	Bracket Arm tierod pole strap	18	Globe Strain Insulator
9	Pole cap or finial	19	Straight Line hanger
10	Guide casting or Carrier Bracket	20	Double curve hanger

M E R   Traction pole fittings

ly, a small number of special "dwarf" or short-length poles were similarly used on the banks of cuttings or embankments. No rosettes or wall-fixing devices were used anywhere on the system, although a convenient tree at the entrance to Groudle south curve has been used for many years to secure a pull-off wire.

Pole holes were (and are) hand-bored by means of augers and "spoon" shovels, with the depth of the hole in the ground depending on the duty requirements of the pole and its location. About 5 ft. is the normal depth, but many examples are to be found of increased or decreased depth, largely depending on the nature of the ground. The pole is theoretically planted on a concrete "biscuit" about 6" thick, under its base, but later MER practice has favoured a selection of large flat stones of suitable size. After inserting the pole into its hole, the surrounding space was usually filled with concrete and "plumbs" consisting of clean stones and pebbles. The concrete extends for 6–9" around the pole at its base, but this procedure is now rated as necessary only in areas of soft or unreliable ground.

Traction pole support systems generally comprise of span wires strung between the poles on either side of the roadway or tracks, bracket arm poles, situated between the tracks, with arms on either side and commonly referred to as "centre poles" and bracket arm poles with a bracket arm on one side only, and extending over one or more tracks from the side of the line. The distance between poles is usually 90–105ft, on straight track, with a British statutory maximum of 120 ft. The spacing of poles on curves is dictated by the radius of the bend, operating speeds and the types of overhead construction and componentry. Limits are imposed on the maximum length of bracket arms; the old Board of Trade maximum permitted length was 16 ft. Similarly, where a span wire strung between parallel poles would exceed 40 ft., the stated preference was for the operator to go to the trouble and expense of two side bracket arm poles instead. The generally accepted criteria in British street tramway practice was that single side bracket arm poles were suitable for streets up to 26 ft. wide. cross span-wire construction for streets between 27 and 40 ft. wide, and twin side bracket arm poles at both sides for widths over 40 ft. Centre poles in street tramway work were severely discouraged by the Board of Trade at an early date, and by the late 1920s it had become virtually mandatory to replace them with some other form of construction that would leave the thoroughfare clear of any obstruction.

Traction pole placement is (or should be) dictated by mathematical computation of the layout, loads and stresses involved. Poles may be erected with a slant or rake away from the load, so that the pole is pulled almost to the vertical under tension; a pole that is leaning away from the direction of pull from the wires is said to have a "positive rake" whilst poles so deranged as to lean forward towards the pull, are said to have a "negative rake."

Whilst examples of almost all types of original pole are still be seen on the Manx Electric, the past thirty years or so has also seen the introduction of a large number of poles purchased second-hand. The majority of these are ex-Douglas Head Marine Drive and can be readily identified by their distinctive collars. These particular poles were originally supplied by the Morris Tasker Co. of Philadelphia, a firm originally founded in 1821 and an important pioneer manufacturer of pipes and boiler tubes. In 1893 they introduced a range of traction poles which were notable, not only for the high-grade steel used, but

also for their methods of heavy hot zinc galvanisation of the top sections. How successful this has proved can be discerned by the lack of corrosion on these poles even after ninety years. Morris Tasker also supplied similar poles to Norwich and Bristol, and this particular type was known as the "SSS" for reasons not now known. More recently cut-down poles purchased from the Douglas Corporation Electricity Department, after service as lamp-posts on Douglas Promenade, have been used as random replacements.

As every MER passenger can see at a glance, pole corrosion has been (and is) a serious problem and various means have been tried to extend the useful life of a pole. The corrosion is often concentrated just above ground level and has been countered to some extent by the use of cast iron split collars, clamped on the worst affected area. Poles have also frequently been given ferro-concrete reinforcement, using 12–15 ft. lengths of angle iron as the "re-bar" and bedded in concrete, which is poured in from the top. Poles thus treated were the earliest to lose their cast iron finials, which were a fairly tight fit inside the top of the pole, and which when corroded could not be got out again. Certain other poles received wooden plug tops, others acquired an almost flat cap, whilst the majority now have none at all.

CONDUCTOR WIRE AND FITTINGS

The Manx Electric's trolley wire height above rail level is normally taken as 16' 0" to 16' 6" although the later British regulations required a minimum wire height of 17' 0" and a normal mid-span height of 20' 0". In earlier years the height of the MER's conductor wire was of interest to nobody except the Railway but just after the Second World War, the Isle of Man Road Services introduced highbridge type double deck buses on the Promenades and Onchan routes, and the upper deck ventilators of these vehicles were apt to get caught up in the trolley and backbone wires at the compound inclines of the Port Jack crossing. A lengthy correspondence between the late Mr. A.M. Sheard, Manager of the Road Services (and the IMR) and the MER's manager, the late Mr. Barnes, ensued. After a series of site meetings, it was Mr. Sheard, not Mr. Barnes, who produced the detailed adjustments for the modifications needed to raise the landward side trolley wire suffi-

ANDERSON BOSTON TROLLEY BASE

Component Parts

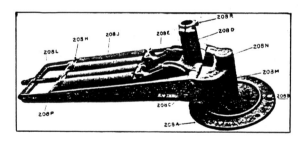

Cat. No. 208

Trolley Base complete without pole, harp or wheel, weight 80 lbs.

208A	Stand or feet with terminal binding screw and washer
208B	Terminal binding screw and washer
208C	Pole socket axle pin with cotters
208D	Pole socket complete with link plates and spring washers
208E	Link plate (4 required)
208H	Spring holder and pin (4 required)
208J	Tension spring with hooks (8 required)
208L	Adjusting bolt
208M	Swivel frame without bushing
208N	Swivel pin collar and cotter
208P	Adjusting crosshead
208R	Bolt for clamp (2 required)
208S	Brass bushing for same

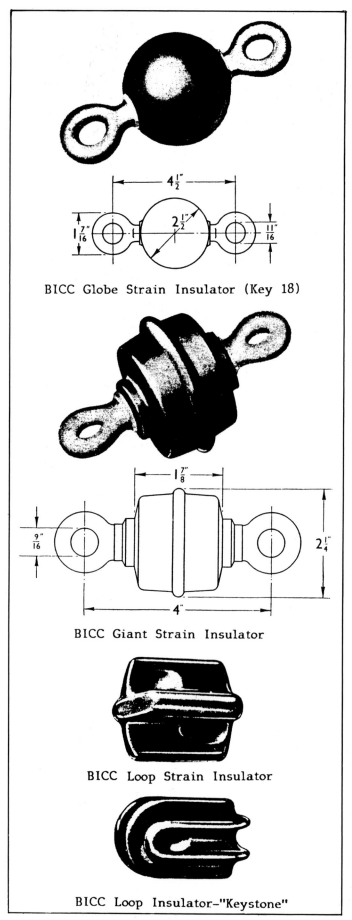

BICC Globe Strain Insulator (Key 18)

BICC Giant Strain Insulator

BICC Loop Strain Insulator

BICC Loop Insulator–"Keystone"

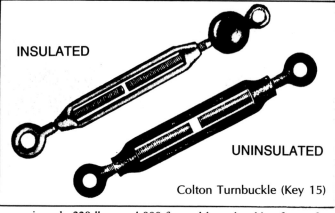

INSULATED

UNINSULATED

Colton Turnbuckle (Key 15)

approximately 320 lbs. per 1,000 ft., and has a breaking force of approximately 4,517 lbf. Trolley wire is normally available in either half-mile or one-mile lengths but the financial stringency of the MER meant that only half-mile drums were bought. It was the practice to always hold a new drum of wire in stock against emergencies. With the spool or drum, a half-mile length of trolley wire weighs about 1,580 lbs. New wire is strung at a tension of about 750 lbf., or "as tight as possible" although wire tensioning by dynomometer is not used on the MER. Tension is equalised as far as possible by always stringing new wire in late May or early June, when the ambient temperature helps. Wire wear is regularly gauged, but splicing ears in the line immediately after a pole are sure signs of badly worn wire, as this area tends to get the most wear.

The trolley wire is suspended by means of "ears" of various types and sizes. Ears are manufactured for a large variety of wire sections, with round, "figure 8" and grooved sections in general use around the world. Each type requires its own fittings. The earliest form of trolley wire was the round section, still in use on the MER, as is the early form of "clinch" ear. These have extended lips which are hammered closed or clinched around the wire, using a forming block. After the lips are closed, the original fitting procedure called for finally soldering the ear to the wire. This process involved the use of "come-along" clamps on the wire on either side of the ear, so that the heat of the soldering did not cause the wire to stretch as it was annealed. Nowadays clinch ears are only soldered on the MER on tight radius curves, or where the wire is so badly worn that it is not possible to close the ear's lips around the wire.

The major drawback with this form of suspension ear is that it is quite expensive in labour cost and the nature of the fitting is such that an ear can properly be used only once, whilst lengthwise adjustment after assembly is not possible. Additionally, since the lips of the ear almost surround the wire, they do not provide a perfectly smooth path for the trolleywheel, and there is an inevitable hammer-blow effect as the trolleywheel hits each ear. Apart from the physical wear, the electrical contact between the trolleywheel and the wire can be compromised, and is usually seen in the form of a flash or spark as the wheel passes each ear (although this can also be the result of a worn trolleywheel). All of these problems were solved many years ago by the use of irregular-shaped wire sections. The most commonly used of these is "grooved" wire, where the appropriate fittings do not impinge on the contact surface at all, and the wheel or slipper is provided with a completely smooth path. Other benefits accrue from "mechanical ears" which are screwed together with the wire clamped in the jaws of the fitting. These ears can be re-used time and time again, as well as slackened and tightened repeatedly to equalise or adjust line tension. Whilst the development of newer technology has largely been ignored, it is of interest to note that the MER still uses a very early and unusual form of mechanical ear on the Snaefell Mountain line between the North Shoulder and the Summit, where the wire is normally taken down each winter to avoid damage by snow and ice. The only exceptions to this ritual occurred in 1954–5 when the Ministry of Civil Aviation radio station was being built, and again in 1978–9, when the then "chief

ciently to provide clearance, and the work was carried out. The trolleywire height at the major road crossings near Halfway House, at Ballabeg and Ballure was occasionally discovered by visiting lorries who found that amidst the plethora of road signs, there was no mention about the height of the wire above the road at the time. The rehanging of wires damaged through any cause is unusually rapid.

The hard-drawn copper trolley wire was (and is) American Wire Gauge (AWG) 'O' round section, having a nominal diameter of 0.325" and an actual diameter of 0.3249." The new weight of this wire is

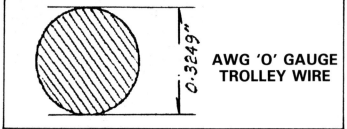

AWG 'O' GAUGE TROLLEY WIRE

ALBERT & J. M. ANDERSON MFG. CO.

WEST END STRAIGHT LINE SUSPENSIONS
750 Volts

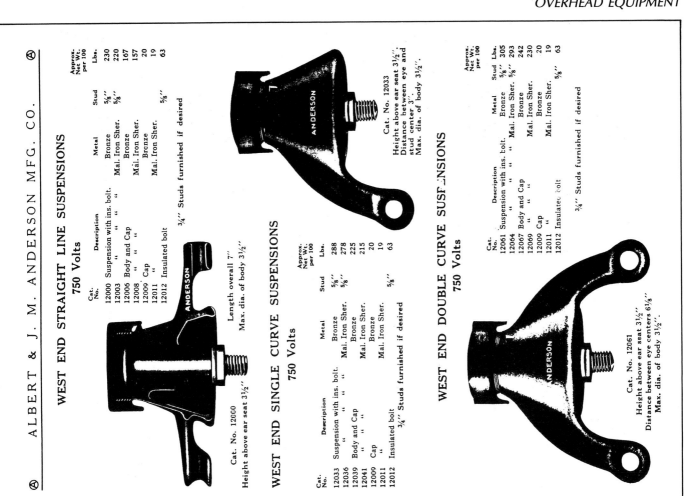

Cat. No. 12000
Height above ear seat 3½"
Length overall 7". Max. dia. of body 3½"

Cat. No.	Description	Metal	Stud	Approx. Net Wt. per 100 Lbs.
12000	Suspension with ins. bolt.	Bronze	5/8"	230
12003	"	Mal. Iron Sher.	5/8"	220
12006	Body and Cap	Bronze		167
12008	"	Mal. Iron Sher.		157
12009	Cap	Bronze		20
12011	"	Mal. Iron Sher.		19
12012	Insulated bolt		5/8"	63

¾" Studs furnished if desired

WEST END SINGLE CURVE SUSPENSIONS
750 Volts

Cat. No. 12033
Height above ear seat 3½"
Distance between eye and stud center 3". Max. dia. of body 3½".

Cat. No.	Description	Metal	Stud	Approx. Net Wt. per 100 Lbs.
12033	Suspension with ins. bolt.	Bronze	5/8"	288
12036	"	Mal. Iron Sher.	5/8"	278
12039	Body and Cap	Bronze		225
12041	"	Mal. Iron Sher.		215
12009	Cap	Bronze		20
12011	"	Mal. Iron Sher.		19
12012	Insulated bolt		5/8"	63

¾" Studs furnished if desired

WEST END DOUBLE CURVE SUSPENSIONS
750 Volts

Cat. No. 12061
Height above ear seat 3½"
Distance between eye centers 6⅛". Max. dia. of body 3½".

Cat. No.	Description	Metal	Stud	Approx. Net Wt. per 100 Lbs.
12061	Suspension with ins. bolt.	Bronze	5/8"	305
12064	"	Mal. Iron Sher.	5/8"	293
12067	Body and Cap	Bronze		242
12069	"	Mal. Iron Sher.		230
12009	Cap	Bronze		20
12011	"	Mal. Iron Sher.		19
12012	Insulated bolt		5/8"	63

¾" Studs furnished if desired

ALBERT & J. M. ANDERSON MFG. CO.

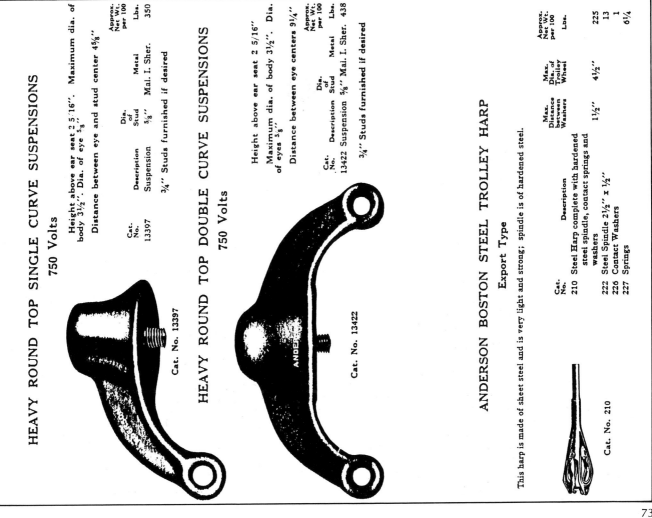

HEAVY ROUND TOP SINGLE CURVE SUSPENSIONS
750 Volts

Cat. No. 13397

Height above ear seat 2 5/16". Maximum dia. of body 3½". Dia. of eye 5/8".

Distance between eye and stud center 4 5/8"

Cat. No.	Description	Dia. of Stud	Metal	Approx. Net Wt. per 100 Lbs.
13397	Suspension	5/8"	Mal. I. Sher.	350

¾" Studs furnished if desired

HEAVY ROUND TOP DOUBLE CURVE SUSPENSIONS
750 Volts

Cat. No. 13422

Height above ear seat 2 5/16". Maximum dia. of body 3½". Dia. of eyes 5/8".

Distance between eye centers 9¼"

Cat. No.	Description	Dia. of Stud	Metal	Approx. Net Wt. per 100 Lbs.
13422	Suspension	5/8"	Mal. I. Sher.	438

¾" Studs furnished if desired

ANDERSON BOSTON STEEL TROLLEY HARP
Export Type

Cat. No. 210

This harp is made of sheet steel and is very light and strong; spindle is of hardened steel.

Cat. No.	Description	Max. Distance between Washers	Max. Dia. of Trolley Wheel	Approx. Net Wt. per 100 Lbs.
210	Steel Harp complete with hardened steel spindle, contact springs and washers	1½"	4½"	225
222	Steel Spindle 2½" x ½"			13
226	Contact Washers			1
227	Springs			6¼

Left: Onslaught on Overhead: Car No.2 and Tower Wagon 1, and Car No.29 and Tower Wagon 3, at Ballafayle during the rehabilitation of the Northern Line between Laxey and Ramsey in 1977.
Mike Goodwyn

Below: The air-gap section insulator used on the MER and believed to have been supplied by Brecknell, Munro of Chard in the 1930s. *Alex Townsend*

executive" insisted on finding out whether the process was really necessary, and costly and widespread damage ensued. The standard clinch ear comes in a range of sizes, and on the MER 7", 9", 12" and 15" lengths are commonly used. Other types of ear include special splicing ears, used to join together two lengths of wire, or to repair a break; splicing tubes at joints are used on the Snaefell section. Feeder ears with a connection for the supply feeder cable are found in conjunction with section insulators, as are half-strain ears. Orthodox ears are manufactured from a grade of bronze selected for great tensile strength with a high elastic limit, but ductile enough to prevent fracture as the ear is bent or hit by the trolleywheel. Ears are cast in solid form and milled to provide the groove for the wire, whilst the boss is drilled and (usually) tapped for a ⅝" BSW thread, into which the insulated bolt of the hanger is screwed.

Hangers also come in a wide variety of types. When the Douglas–Laxey section was converted to trolleypole operation, the Isle of Man Tramways & Electric Power Co. standardised on Anderson's Aetna brand "West End" fittings, which consisted of straight line, single and double curve suspensions; the cap of all West End type fittings can be unscrewed with a key to get at the insulated bolt inside. Another feature is that all Aetna insulated bolts have milled faces just above the threaded portion, so that they can be held with a spanner when screwing the bolt into the ear. Straight line hangers are, as the name implies, used where the line is straight and has no curve torque. Such a torque results in the wire twisting towards the inner radius as it attempts to follow the line of least resistance. In some cases this would result in the hanger and its ear lying sideways, resulting at best in a diabolical rate of wear, and at worst in perpetual dewirements. The double curve suspension is used wherever there is a curve torque, and is designed so that the line of force lies through the point of attachment, thus countering the twisting moment involved. The small single curve suspension is used for pull-off purposes on curves, where a high degree of accuracy in alignment is needed.

The most complex overhead fittings are section insulators, usually in conjunction with supply feeder points. The old British Board of Trade required every positive conductor to be divided into electrical sections of not more than 880 yards or half-mile lengths. Leaving aside the problems posed by some hopeful tramway undertakings that wired their track as the positive conductor, the Douglas–Groudle section opened before the Board thought up its regulations, and this route was divided into electrical sections of about 1.16 mile lengths, with six sections altogether between Douglas and Laxey. The Northern Line to Ramsey followed the Board's requirements rather more closely, with sections of just over half a mile. At all these points the wires could be isolated from the supply by operating the knife switches inside the cast-iron pedestal boxes at the base of the pole. For many years now these arrangements have been revised, and the line is treated as two electrical sections.

Early Aetna section insulators had renewable wooden runners, requiring considerable maintenance, and about 1934 the MER Co. purchased new "air-gap" section insulator assemblies, thought to have been manufactured by Brecknell, Munro & Rogers, which remain in use. The hanger is connected to a span wire by means of links or loops

of wire, to strain insulators. Two main types of these exist: the "Loop" type or "Keystone" in MER parlance, and the "globe" or round type. The glazed porcelain loop insulator has surface grooves for the wires, which are fed through holes in the casting. This type measures about 4⅜" by 2⅜" and has an average tensile strength of 10,000 lbf., with a dry flashover breakdown at around 30,000 volts. The corresponding values in double-eyed globe strain insulators are typically 9,000 lbf. and 14,000 volts. The globe insulators, specifically known as "tee and basket" type, consist of two bronze or malleable iron castings, one being compressed over the other over a mica interface insulation. Moulded composition surrounds the components to protect and waterproof it, as well as increasing the surface area. For many years the Manx Electric has preferred this design to the loop type on the basis of its increased surface, whereas the distance between the two wires on a loop insulator is much less, and these fittings are therefore never normally used in locations where they might be covered by sea spray, such as the section between Douglas and Onchan Head.

The Manx Electric tends to suffer from electrical leakage, largely as a result of its geographical location, but also due to other factors. Insulator flashover is always reduced by dirt or damp on the insulator's surface, and the MER is perhaps the world's only electric railway that actually covers its overhead fittings and insulators with layers of paint. Cracks in the composition surface of some insulators were at one time even filled up with multiple coats of paint and then refitted into the line. Tests carried out many years ago showed that once the insulator surface begins to deteriorate, or is smeared with something, electrical breakdown can occur at under 15% of the value for a new, clean and unpainted insulator. A broken-down insulator that has flashed over usually burns brightly like an incandescent lamp bulb for up to half an hour, before extinguishing itself, leaving a smoking, whitened and leaking pebble. After such a breakdown, leakage on the line is increased and can normally be spotted by an experienced sub-station attendant. Formal leakage test procedures are carried out on a regular basis, one morning each week at Groudle, Laxey and Ballaglass, and the

ALBERT & J. M. ANDERSON MFG. CO.

ANDERSON BRONZE EARS

STRAIGHT LINE EARS FOR ROUND WIRE

For use with all types of Suspensions

This ear has an exceptionally deep groove and the lips are not tapered, so that when it is cinched completely around the wire, a uniform, generous thickness of tough, durable metal is formed which takes up wear. The approaches are tapered at a specific angle, to a knife edge, so that when the ear is in place "knocking" is eliminated and an unusually smooth approach is presented for the passage of the wheel.

Cat. No. 17075

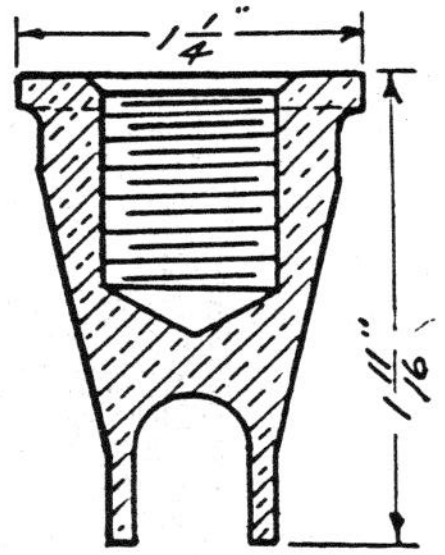

Cat. No.	Length	Wire	Stud	Metal	Approx. Net Wt. per 100 Lbs.
17075	9"	0	5/8"	Bronze	85
17079	12"	0	5/8"	"	100
17083	15"	0	5/8"	"	116

STRAIGHT LINE EARS FOR ROUND WIRE

Clinch or Deep Groove Type. Universal Center
For use with all types of suspensions

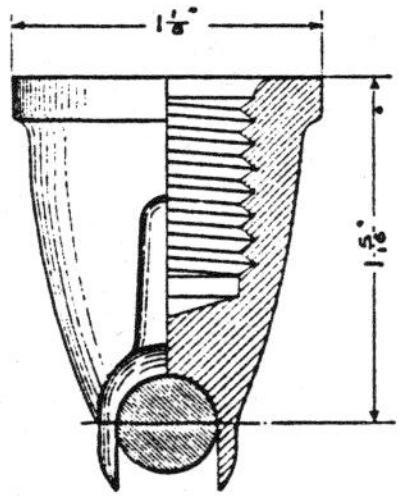

Cat. No. 17023

Cat. No.	Length	Wire	Stud	Metal	Approx. Net Wt. per 100 Lbs.
17023	7"	0	5/8"	Bronze	41
17024	9"	0	5/8"	"	50
17028	12"	0	5/8"	"	63

Clinch or Deep Groove Type. High Center
For use with all suspensions except insulated bolt type

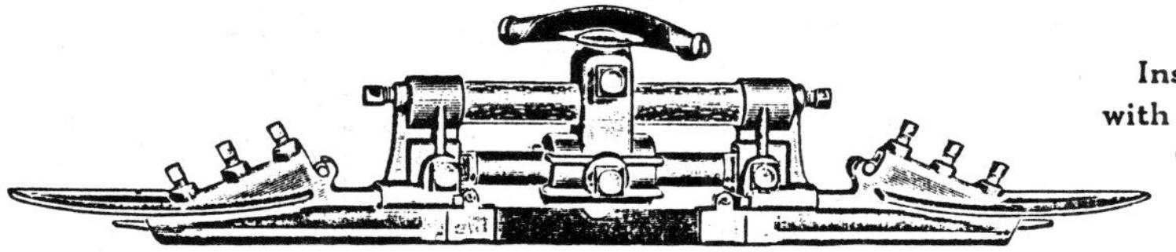

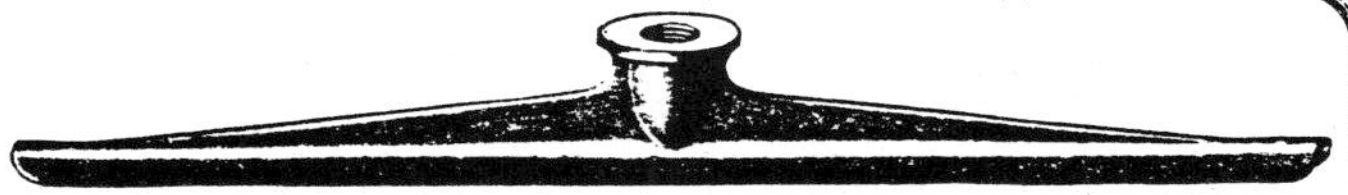

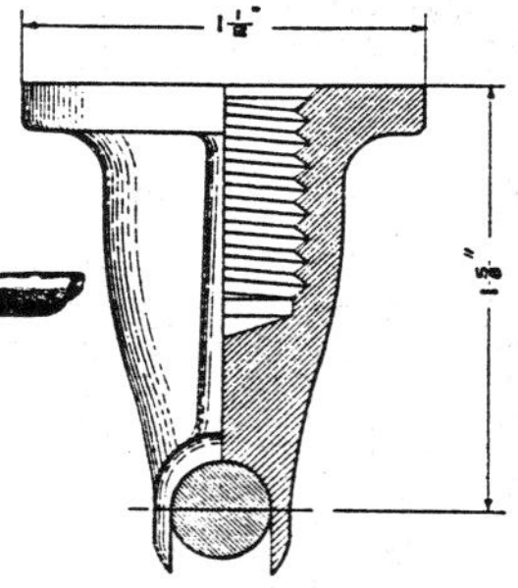

Cat. No. 17052

Cat. No.	Length	Wire	Stud	Metal	Approx. Net Wt. per 100 Lbs.
17052	7"	0	5/8"	Bronze	56
17054	9"	0	5/8"	"	63
17061	12"	0	5/8"	"	88
17067	15"	0	5/8"	"	100

ALBERT & J. M. ANDERSON MFG. CO.

TROLLEY WIRE SPLICING EARS

For Round and Grooved Wire

For use with all types of suspensions
Can be supplied without Boss

Cat. No. 17811

Cat. No.	Length	Round	Wire	Stud	Center of Wire to Top of Boss	Metal	Approx. Net Wt. per 100 Lbs.
17811	15"	0	0	5/8"	2"	Bronze	188

Clinch or Deep Groove Type
Reinforced Centre
For use with all types of suspensions
Round Wire

Cat. No. 17456

Cat. No.	Length	Round	Wire	Grooved	Stud	Center of Wire to Top of Boss	Metal	Approx. Net Wt. per 100 Lbs.
17456	15"	0	0	00	5/8"	2"	Bronze	238
17457	15"	00	000	00	5/8"	2"	"	238

SINGLE BEAM SECTION INSULATORS

Insulated Bolt Type
With Renewable Wooden Center Runner

Cat. No. 15722

Cat. No.	Round	Wire	Grooved	Length Overall	Extreme Width	Metal	Approx. Net Wt. per 100 Lbs.
15722	0	00	0	32½"	7"	Bronze	1400
15723	000	0000	000	32½"	7"	"	1400
15724	0	00	00	32½"	7"	Malleable Iron Sherardized	1325
15725	000	0000	0000	32½"	7"	"	1325
15726	Extra center runner						
150	Insulated bolt						

Insulated Bolt Type
with Renewable Wooden
Center Runner

Cat. No. 15746

Cat. No.	Round	Wire	Grooved	Length Overall	Extreme Width	Metal	Approx. Net Wt. per 100 Lbs.
15746	0	00	00	35½"	6"	Bronze	1425
15747	0	00	00	35½"	6"	Malleable Iron Sherardized	1425
15748	Extra center runner						
150	Insulated bolt						

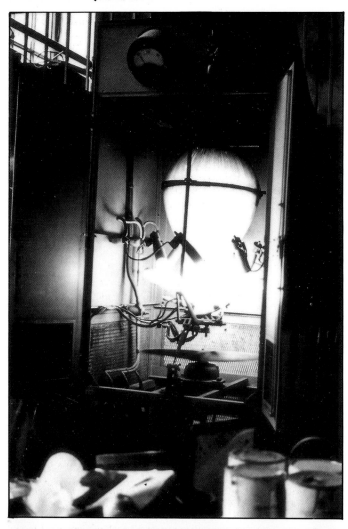

Above Left: The 200 kW Hewittic mercury-arc glass bulb rectifier at Derby Castle, which rectifies a.c. to d.c. current by electronic emission from a hotspot on the cathode (a pool of mercury) in a high vacuum; the anodes consist of six graphite elements. The cathodic hotspot reaches 3,000 degrees C, and the upper part of the pear-shaped bulb forms a condensing chamber for the hot mercury vapour. This and the anodes are kept cool by the airstream created by a propeller fan, mounted under the bulb in the cubicle. These rectifiers are now being replaced as necessary by new and more efficient solid-state units (below left). *W.P. Cubbon*

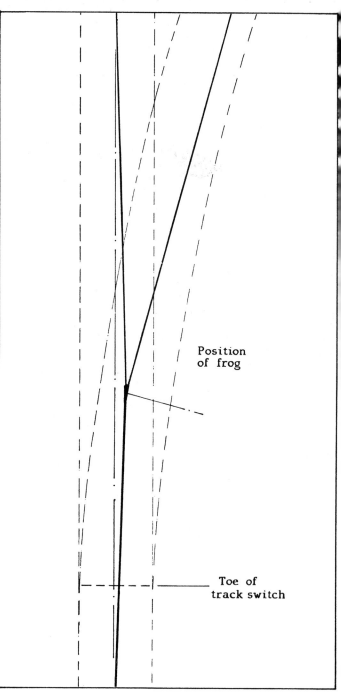

Position
of frog

Toe of
track switch

readings entered on the statutory form. To physically locate a failed insulator, the "Wire Car" is despatched to test each traction pole in the suspect area. The leaking insulator can often be seen but otherwise tests are made with a wooden stick wired up with a 5 amp fuse and earthed to the car. As the car runs past each pole, the "Poles and Wires" man on the platform swipes at it with the stick; the leaking insulator is located by the rupture of the fuse on the stick, and repairs can then be effected.

The insulators, placed on each side of the hanger, may be single or in multiple, depending on the location and the likelihood of leakage. A span wire of 7/14 galvanised iron (not steel) wire runs from the outer eye of the turnbuckle to the "arrowend" fitting at the outer end of the bracket arm, and is attached to the spool insulator inside the fitting. The original bracket arms were tapered, but most of the arrowend fittings have been bored out over the years to receive standard

1½" diameter pipe. The outer span wire is known as the "short fitting" whilst the length between the turnbuckle and inner insulator, passed through the guide or carrier bracket, is termed the "long fitting." The purpose of the double-eyed turnbuckles is to provide a means for limited tension and alignment adjustment.

The fittings for a typical pole are completed by a pole strap and bracket for a side-groove insulator carrying a "00" gauge AWG (0.365" diameter.) feeder cable, which extends from Douglas through to the most northerly Feeder Post, (No. 34) at Queen's Drive, Ramsey. It is augmented in part as indicated in the power supply diagram.

Overhead frogs are provided over all points or switches in the trackwork in order to permit the trolleywheel to follow the wire appropriate for the track. In general, overhead frogs come in two main types: those that are fixed, and have no moving parts whatever, and those equipped with a movable blade of some sort to direct the trolleywheel onto the appropriate wire; these are essential when using swivel head trolleys. The MER has always used the fixed-type frog, which requires no maintenance but demands very high precision in its location. The accompanying diagram shows the layout of trolley wires and the approximate position of the fixed frog in relation to the track switch. It will be noted that the layout features a very slight offset from the middle ordinate for the trolley wire, so as to produce a slight drag against the trolleywheel's cheeks as it runs up to the frog, and ensuring that the wheel will follow the required direction when it actually gets to the frog.

The actual positioning of the frog in relation to the trackwork layout is very critical if consistent performance is to be guaranteed. There is a mathematical formula for this which provides an invaluable guide, but the amount of "lead" (i.e. the distance from the toe of the switch blades to the overhead frog) depends on whether the main track is straight or curved, the radii of those curves, the superelevation, the height of the car and wires, and the length of the trolleypole itself. It is therefore often necessary to set out the wires and determine the position of the frog for optimum performance by trial. Overhead frogs are commonly equipped with two or four eyes on the sides of the casting for guy wires, which can be anchored off to pull the frog into its precise lateral position.

Whilst there are only two facing frogs on the MER's main line, with all of the others being arranged as trailing connections (unless the line is being temporarily worked in the wrong direction) it is always necessary to run cars through frogs with some caution, since quite apart from any considerations of the trackwork, the weight of the overhead frog represents a rigid spot in the conductor wire, and if run through at great speed, can cause the trolleywheel to bounce downwards as it hits it, possibly resulting in dewirement.

For very many years during the present century, trolley wire and some overhead fittings were supplied by British Insulated Callender's Cables Ltd., but when this firm announced that it was ceasing production of components for which there was very little demand, many items were thenceforth supplied by the Colton Electrical Co. Ltd. This old established manufacturer had the singular distinction of being the British Agents for Albert & J M Anderson of Boston, Mass., for many years and their "Aetna Works" at Upminster, Essex, reflected that connection. Colton's also supplied the MER trolleywheels for some decades. These are 4¼" diameter with a ½" diam. spindle bored through a ⅞" diameter graphite bush 1¼" long. The bush was distinctive in having a diamond pattern grease groove cut into its surface.

The trolleywheels, which necessarily rotate at very high speed, and become very hot in the process, can often last up to a week on a good, well-polished wire, but its life may be cut down to as little as a single trip under particularly adverse conditions. All of the MER's trolleywheels tend to wear slightly heavier on one side, and at one time it was the practice to reverse the wheels at about half-life. Until 1977 all of the Winter Saloon cars always carried a "Sleet Wheel" in their toolboxes. This was a special trolleywheel with slits machined in the cheeks, and used to cut through ice on the overhead wire. The presence of air frost on the wire is indicated by an intense blue arc at the trolleywheel. For some considerable time the MER had old trolleywheels melted down at a local foundry and made into truck bearing pads and other useful components, as well as being recast into trolleywheels. Colton's ceased to manufacture tramway equipment in the early 1980s, leaving the MER with a series of problems. The Engineer's Department, in collaboration with Douglas Plastics Ltd., have developed a successful form of insulated bolt, which is now being used in considerable numbers.

TRACK

The return circuit from the positive overhead trolleywire is made by means of the track. The Manx Electric's permanent way consists of 3' 0" gauge double track throughout its route length. The original flat-bottomed rails used on the Douglas–Groudle section in 1893 consisted of 56 lbs. per yard rail, dogspiked to timber sleepers measuring 72" by 7" by 3½". The sleeper size was later increased to 72" by 9" by 4½" on the Groudle–Laxey section, and is currently 74" by 9" by 4½". The Laxey–Ramsey section was laid throughout in 62½ lbs. per yard flat-bottomed rail in lengths of 31' 6" laid on sleepers at 36" centres, except for eleven lengths of Belgian grooved tramway rail, laid along Walpole Avenue in Ramsey at the behest of the Ramsey Commissioners, who intended to surface the roadway in 1899.

All rail joints are fishplated, using four-bolt pattern straight or angle type fishplates, except for a lengthy stretch from South Cape to Laxey Car Depot, where the rail ends were cropped and Thermit-welded most successfully in the 1950s.

Renewals of running rail in the 1960s and onwards have been carried out in 60 lbs. per yard BS11 section flat-bottomed rail, although 50 lbs. section was later recommended by the Ryan Report. A 200-yard length of track north from Ballagawne (just north of Garwick) was laid in 1960 using elastic spikes and with the rails laid on rubber sole-pads supplied by the Clyde Rubber Works Co., of Porterfield Road, Renfrew, near Glasgow. These pads, which are still in use, were available in hard or soft grades for use with timber or concrete sleepers respectively. Both types were moulded to provide a rail seat inclination of 1 in 20, which eliminated the need to adze the sleeper to receive the foot of the rail.

Every rail joint is (or ought to be) electrically bonded to ensure the return of the current flowing through the track, and this traditionally consists of a braided copper bond, approximately 15" long and fitted with brass ferrules at each end for insertion into a small hole drilled and reamed in the web of the rails, clear of the fishplate itself. The ferrule is expanded into its hole by a press. A number of other types of bond have been and are being tried on the line. Cross-bonds between the rails and between each track are also provided at irregular intervals.

CHAPTER SIX

BUILDINGS AND PREMISES

Even to those familiar with most aspects of the Manx Electric, it is not always apparent that the Board's properties extend, even now, to over seventy buildings, ranging from car depots to wayside shelters. Little has been chronicled on the distinctive design of many of these structures, and individual site histories can be extremely difficult to determine with accuracy.

Some of the buildings were (and are) of timber construction, and often provided with a curious "rustic" appearance, produced by fixing pieces of split log onto the external walls. The finished result presented a formidable painting problem (and over the years some of the rustic logs have fallen off) but the overall result was aesthetically pleasant, and often blended well into the sylvan surroundings. Elsewhere, steel or timber-framed and corrugated iron-clad buildings were erected, and usually painted dark green. Various unusual hues appeared on certain buildings during the 1977–87 era, when a significant number of structures ceased to exist at all. The MER possessed a considerable amount of property, in Douglas and Laxey in particular, some of which was disposed of over the years as needs and requirements changed. Certain buildings which were regarded as an essential part of the MER infrastructure, such as the great Canopy at Derby Castle, or some of the wayside shelters, were never owned by the MER, but have been included for the sake of completeness. In the following schedule, the serial numbers are provided only for the purposes of reference, and do not have any other significance.

DOUGLAS:

0.1 No. 1 Strathallan Crescent.
Sold off, 1978.

0.2 No. 2 Strathallan Crescent.
Sold off. 1978.
The IoMT&EP Co. purchased these two semi-detached villas in June 1891, using the house, garden and stables of No. 1 as offices, temporary horse car storage and tram-horse stables respectively, prior to the completion of their new depot. No. 2 was used as the Manager's residence, and there were (private) communicating doors between the two buildings. The premises passed through the Liquidator in 1902 to MER Co. ownership, leaving Douglas Corporation to build an office for their own administration at the east end of the horse tram depot. The original garden and stables of No. 1 were later cleared and made into a memorial garden, Nos. 1 and 2 remaining in use for their original purposes until 1978, when the MER Board administration moved into leased accommodation in the Douglas Corporation Transport offices. The old premises were sold off by public tender, and No. 1 became the present Craig-A-Dell holiday apartments.

0.3 No. 13 Strathallan Crescent.
0.4 No. 14 Strathallan Crescent.
Sold off, 1944–5
From about 1895 the IoMT&EP Co. acquired the two terraced houses nearest the horse tram depot for their own staff purposes. They were occupied for many years by senior management officials of the MER Co. after passing into its ownership in 1902. Mr Frank Edmondson lived for some time in No. 14, before moving into the Manager's Residence. Mr Barnes, during his time as Chief Assistant Engineer lived at No. 13, with Mr Legg, the Hotels and Catering Manager, at No. 14. The properties were finally disposed of during World War II.

0.5 Calvary Glen
Sold off. 1934. At the rear of the present horse tram depot there is a steep hillside with a pathway and waterfall, approached from either Summer Hill Road, or by the passageway down the west side of the

horse tram depot. Incapable of being built upon, it was sold to Mr Robert Cubbon in January 1934, and became known as "Calvary Glen" when holy statues were erected. Whilst the sale involved the land, it specifically excluded the boundary wall along Summer Hill Road; this was retained either because the MER intended to use the wall for posters (and never did) or because it represented too much of a liability to the new owner of the Glen. It is still a liability.

0.6 The Great Canopy, Derby Castle
1896, Demolished 1980. This was never owned by the MER Co., but served as part of the Derby Castle terminal for over eighty years. Erected by the IoMT&EP Co. in 1896, the canopy was 82 ft. long, 18 ft.high to the eaves, and 29 ft. high at the apex of the roof, with a width of 35 ft. It was intended not only to shelter passengers but also spanned the four (later three) terminal horse tram tracks. The canopy was an elaborate and ornate cast-iron structure with ornamental gables, fanlight windows and had a 13 ft.-high clock tower on the roof. The structure passed from the Liquidator to Douglas Corporation. Over the years, the gables, fanlights and clock tower were dismantled. The seaward side of the roof featured a deep eavesboard hoarding, rented by the MER Co. (later Board) to carry the words: "Laxey-Ramsey Electric Railway Station" until the hoarding was taken down about 1974. The entire structure was suddenly and surprisingly declared unsafe and razed to the ground in 1980.

0.7 Booking Office. Derby Castle, 1897. Extant.
The IoMT&EP Co. erected a wooden, rustic-style booking office near the south-west corner of the Canopy and sandwiched between the MER terminal tracks and the southbound line of the horse tramway. Measuring 12' 6" by 8' 0" the building was completed in 1897 and is now notable in being the last remaining example of an original IoMT&EP structure at Derby Castle. It is provided with two ticket window positions and accommodation for the Station Master. Lighting and heating is provided from the traction supply. An antique notice inside insists that "Motormen & Conductors Must Not Loiter In This Office." The exterior was liberally equipped with racks and clip or hook-boards for handbills and posters.

0.8 Strathallan Hotel, Derby Castle, c.1890. Sold off. 6/1957
The building originated as Strathallan Lodge, part of the manorial residence of the Pollock family at Derby Castle. The estate was sold and many of the buildings converted into a tourist attraction in 1877, with a theatre and ballroom and other facilities, under the Derby Castle Co., later the Palace & Derby Castle Co. Ltd. The lodge was converted into a public house and passes into IoMT&EP Co. ownership. Part of the premises at the north-east end was converted and enlarged to form a waiting room for MER passengers, with adjacent toilet facilities. The hotel was sold off in June 1957 as part of the nationalisation arrangements and has subsequently been restyled "Terminus Tavern." The sale included the old waiting room, but not the toilets.

1.0 DERBY CASTLE CAR DEPOT & WORKS (See sketch map on page A.12)

1.1 Yard Office, 1924
Formerly Rolling Stock Superintendant's office, now used for Traffic purposes.

1.2 Engine House, 1893
Converted into Machine Shop, 1904–date, equipped with sub-station gear in north west corner.

1.3 Boiler House, 1893
Partly demolished and rebuilt to form Goods Shed, 1908. Became Store after 1966 until 1988 when converted to form new Paint Shop.

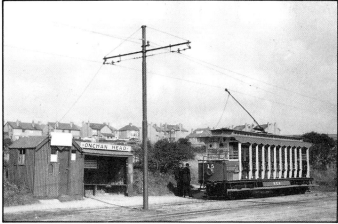

Left: The last remaining original IoMT&EP Co. building at Derby Castle: the Booking Office, built in 1897. The tasteless pole-mounted sign with its plastic stick-on letters was a 1979 addition. Note the "rustic" split-log finish, somewhat abbreviated in parts. For many years a weighing machine was sited at the north-west (right) corner of the building. *R. Dodge*

Below: The Shelter, booking office and Inspector's hut at Onchan Head, which once handled very intensive local short-stage traffic. The buildings were completely demolished in 1978. *Dr. C.C. Thornburn*

MAIN LINE

2.1 ONCHAN HEAD: Shelter, 1899
Demolished and site cleared 1978.

2.2 Booking Office,1899
Demolished and site cleared 1978.

2.3 HOWSTRAKE: Shelter, c1910
Extant. Arched portico stone shelter, built and maintained by Howstrake Holiday Camp.

2.4 GROUDLE: Shelter, 1894
Buildings erected on land not owned by the MER.

2.5 Booking Office, 1894, MER.
Extant.

2.6 Battery House, 1893
Demolished between 1929-35.

2.7 Sub-Station, 1903
Extant.

2.8 Toll House,1893
Sold off c1926, demolished 1988.

3.0 HALFWAY: Shelter, c1900
Demolished and site cleared.

3.1 BALDRINE: Shelter
Extant.Substantially rebuilt 1991-2.

3.2 GARWICK: Shelter,1895
Buildings erected on land not owned by MER. Demolished 1979.

3.3 Booking Office, 1895
Demolished, 1979.

3.4 Kiosk
Demolished c1968.

1.4 No. 1 Car Shed, 1893
Extant. Smithy at rear rebuilt and substantially enlarged 1992. Referred to as "hospital roads" as all heavy repairs to cars are carried out in this depot. Pits are provided in the two south side roads.

1.5 Main Stores
Extant. Small store to rear now termed "Aachen Store" containing German spares.

1.6 No. 6 Car Shed, 1924
Converted into new Joiners' shop, 1989.

1.7 Joiners' Shop
Premises vacated 1983, demolished 1986.

1.8 Crews' Mess Room, pre-1900
Demolished 1988 and replaced by the new building almost on same site.

1.9 Paint Store
Demolished.

1.10 No. 2 Car Shed, 1894-5
Extant. Incorporates existing paintshop

1.11 No. 3 Car Shed, 1895-6
Extant.

1.12 No. 4 Car Shed, 1895-6
Extant.

1.13 No. 5 Car Shed, 1924
Extant.

1.14 Works Office & Mess Room, 1988
New, Rolling Stock Supt's office at the north-west side of building.

1.15 Oil & Paint Store, 1988
Rebuilt and converted from original toilet block.

1.16 Toilets/Washroom, 1988
New building.

Above: The Derby Castle Yard Hut. It is here that the motorman signs on each morning before commencing his duties. On completion of duty, he meticulously records details of his journeys, cars and trailers and any faults observed on them.
Alex Townsend

Right: The wayside shelter at Baldrine, built about 1899, on the east side of the tracks, and with its GPO Letterbox (cleared by MER staff) at the north end. *Manx Electric Railway*

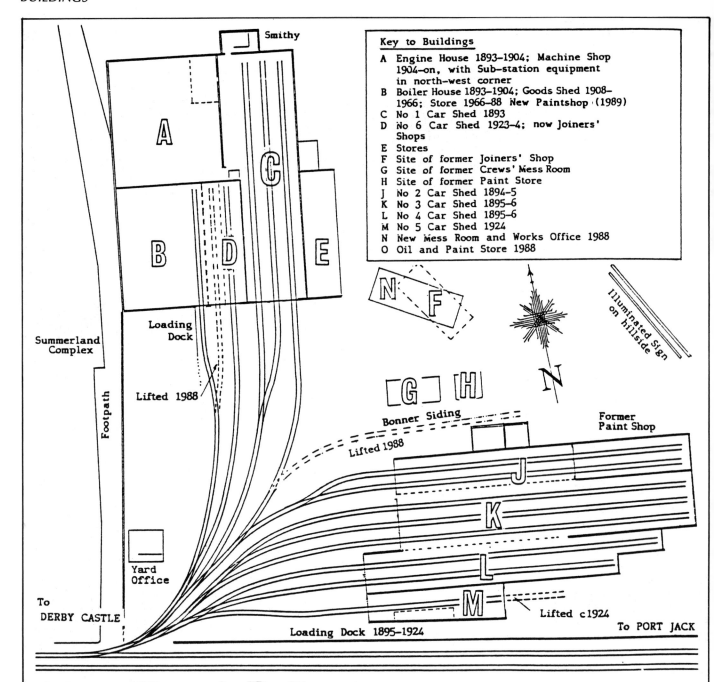

Key to Buildings

A Engine House 1893–1904; Machine Shop 1904–on, with Sub-station equipment in north-west corner
B Boiler House 1893–1904; Goods Shed 1908–1966; Store 1966–88 New Paintshop (1989)
C No 1 Car Shed 1893
D No 6 Car Shed 1923-4; now Joiners' Shops
E Stores
F Site of former Joiners' Shop
G Site of former Crews' Mess Room
H Site of former Paint Store
J No 2 Car Shed 1894-5
K No 3 Car Shed 1895-6
L No 4 Car Shed 1895-6
M No 5 Car Shed 1924
N New Mess Room and Works Office 1988
O Oil and Paint Store 1988

Manx Electric Railway
Derby Castle Carworks & Depôt

3.5 BALLABEG: Shelter
Extant.Substantially rebuilt 1992.

3.6 FAIRY COTTAGE: Shelter
Extant.Substantially rebuilt 1992.

3.7 SOUTH CAPE: Shelter
Extant.

4.0 LAXEY SOUTH

4.1 Distillation House, 1895
Extant. Stone structure in ruins. Used originally to supply distilled water to barrels for Battery Houses.

4.2 Car Depot, 1894
Destroyed by fire, 1930. Car Depot, 1930. Extant.

4.3 Sub-Station, 1934
Extant.

4.4 Store Cottage, c1860
Extant. Known as "Granny's House".

4.5 Office
PW Supt's Office, using one of two huts acquired by MER Co from the Isolation Hospital, White Hoe, near Douglas. This building re-sited at Bungalow, 1985.

LAXEY STATION

4.6 Station Hotel
Sold off by MER Co, June 1957. Building was originally Mine Captain's dwelling; stables to rear accommodated horses for Glen Road horse freight tramway (Great Laxey Mines). Now called "Mines Tavern".

4.7 Booking Office/Waiting room, 1899
Extant.

Right: Garwick Glen in its heyday, with thatched kiosk, flagpoles, and a station building not dissimilar to Groudle; it comprised a waiting room, booking office, station master's room and toilets. This is one of the postcards (Reference L.08) of the MER's official series.
Manx Electric Railway

Below: The shelter at South Cape, on the descent into Laxey. *R. Dodge*

Above: The shelter at Ballabeg, dating from 1905; it formerly featured a GPO Letterbox to the left of the shelter. *R. Dodge*

Left: The large double-fronted shelter at Dhoon Glen, thought to date from 1899, prior to its demolition in 1985. The building also had a toilet at the rear.
Manx Electric Railway

Left: Car No.21 leaving the Ramsey Goods Shed in 1979. The conversion of Ramsey Car Depot into a "museum" in 1979 resulted in all of the pit-roads being filled in; an inadequate hollow was scraped out from between the rails in the Goods Shed but this persistently floods.

W.P. Cubbon

Below: Derby Castle terminus, Douglas, with a cast of thousands, waiting for MER cars in the late 1920s. Note the complete IoMT&EP Co. ornamental iron canopy, with its gables, fanlights and clock tower. The entire structure was razed to the ground in 1980.

Manx Electric Railway

4.8 Refreshment Rooms, 1899
Destroyed by fire, 24th September 1917.

4.9 Refreshment Stall
Extant.

4.10 Despatcher's Cabin
Demolished, 1987.

4.11 Kiosks (3)
One demolished date unknown, two extant.

4.12 Goods Shed, 1903
Extant.

4.13 Snaefell Line shelter, 1963
Extant.

4.14 Laxey Power Station, 1899
Sold off by MER Co in 1935; industrial Glen Rd, Laxey premises. Extant.

4.15 Turbine House,1899. Sold off by MER Co, use unknown.
Old Laxey. Extant.

4.16 Test House, 1899
Ruinous structure from 1935; demolished for building stone, c1968.

5.1 MINORCA: Shelter
Extant. Building was formerly at Half-way House.

5.2 BALLARAGH: Shelter
Demolished 1973.

5.3 DHOON GLEN: Shelter
Demolished 1985; new one erected 1987.

5.4 Hotel & Refreshment Room
Destroyed by fire, 3rd April 1932.

5.5 Kiosk-Cafe
Extant; leased from Forestry Board.

5.6 DHOON QUARRY: Shelter
Extant. Not owned by MER, but built by local quarrymen, date unknown.

5.7 Sawmill/Sleeper depot
Demolished 1973; SEHC traction motor used to power sawmill salvaged.

5.8 Store Cottage
Known as "Creosote Cottage," demolished and site cleared, 1979–80.

5.9 Store Building
Extant. Leased off until 1992. Now p.w. department store.

5.10 Weighbridge
Extant.

6.1 GLEN MONA: Shelter
Demolished 1987 and new one erected 1988.

6.2 BALLAGORRY: Sub-Station, 1989
New building underneath footbridge, to replace facilities formerly housed at Ballaglass Power Station.

6.3 BALLAGLASS: Shelter
Demolished,1985. New building 1989.

6.4 Kiosk
Demolished, 1944–5.

6.5 Power Station, 1899
Sold off 1968 to a Mr. Briggs for use as industrial premises, with sub-station area leased back to MER until 1989. Now owned by Mr. E. Martin of Cambar Ltd.

6.6 CORNAA: Shelter
Extant.

6.7 BALLASKIEG: Shelter
Extant.

7.1 BALLAFAYLE-CORTEEN: Shelter
Not owned by MER, but built by local farmer. Demolished 1979.

7.2 ROME'S CROSSING: Shelter
Not owned by MER, but erected by local people. Structure fell over onto track in storm, but was put back up again by MER.

7.3 BALLAJORA: Shelter
Extant.

7.4 DREEMSKERRY: Shelter
Extant.

7.5 LEWAIGUE: Shelter
Demolished after vandalism 1986, and replaced by new structure.

7.6 PORT-E-VULLEN (Belle Vue) Sub-Station, 1934
Extant.

7.7 Shelter
Extant.

8.0 RAMSEY TOWN

8.1 Car Depot, 1899
Extant.

8.2 Goods Shed, 1903
Extant.

8.3 Palace Concert Hall
Purchased 1897; original MER station staff facilities were housed at rear of building. Palace was leased to the concert hall operator, later converted into Plaza Cinema, and sold off by MER Co in 1938. Demolished 1991. Now car park.

8.4 Toilets
Demolished 1964.

8.5 Station Building, 1964
New construction incorporating toilets, Station Master's office/booking office etc. Extant.

9.0 SNAEFELL SECTION

9.1 Laxey Car Depot, 1895
Extant.

9.2 Battery House, 1895
Moved from car depot approach nearer to Dumbell's Row. Demolished, 1934.

9.3 Store Shed (Depot), 1895
Consists of part of original station.

9.4 CAA Railcar Shed No. 1, 1951
Extant.

9.5 CAA Railcar Shed No. 2, 1954
Extant.

9.6 Snaefell Power Station, 1895
Converted to sub-station. Extant.

9.7 Bungalow Hotel, 1895
Demolished,1958.

9.8 Bungalow Booking Office, 1895
Demolished,1984. The TT Race Marshals' hut is used when Races are not on.

9.9 Traffic Office
See 4.5

9.10 Snaefell Summit Hotel
Leased off from 1982. Burned out, 5–6th August 1982; rebuilt 1983; re-opened May 1984. Extant.

9.11 Tholt-y-Will Hotel, 1897
Sold off by MER Co. c1940.

CHAPTER SEVEN

TRAINING OF MOTORMEN

Most boys of an earlier generation, wished at some stage to become engine drivers but many of the boys who grew up to become members of the MER Society and readers of this journal may well have harboured a more sophisticated ambition to become electric tramcar motormen. Some never got the opportunity, but each year a very fortunate few are selected for training as MER motormen, and following a rigorous medical examination, finally make their way to Derby Castle Car Depot, Douglas, on the appointed day.

In general, most MER employees "sign-on" at 8.00 a.m., although there are numerous exceptions: by 8.00 a.m. the Rolling Stock Superintendent and some other Engineering staff will already have completed part of their morning's work; others will arrive later and finish accordingly. A particularly dim view is taken of anyone who lacks punctuality. In earlier times it is said that an employee only had the opportunity to arrive late for work twice. After that he was looking for other employment.

On the novitiate's first morning at the MER, he will usually be introduced to the other staff, and provided with a conducted tour of the Car Depot and Works, with the different functions and responsibilities of each department explained. In the course of this expedition the location of first-aid and fire-fighting equipment will be pointed out, together with the potential hazards that inevitably exist, in the shape of open pit roads, moving tramcars, belt driven and self-starting machinery, the possible perils of the 600 V d.c. traction supply and other sources of danger. He will also be shown the whereabouts and procedures for signing on and off, the official notices board, duty roster lists and the provisions for reporting faults and accidents of any kind.

The bulk of trainee motormen come to the MER with at least some prior knowledge of the line or a developed interest in the technology of the tramcar. To anyone devoid of these attributes, the way ahead may well be tortuous, difficult and prolonged. A few might arrive with the happy notion that tram driving skills can be acquired almost overnight. And so they can, perhaps, but the whole essence of the MER's training is not only to instil the basic art, but to familiarise the learner with precisely what to do on those occasions when everything seems to be going wrong – misfortune is rarely a solitary traveller. A few never complete the training, one side or the other recognising that the difficulties are too many or the aptitude or attitude inappropriate. Those who also pictured the motorman's job as consisting of parading at the helm of a tramcar on the open road, also find that the preconception is not wholly appropriate, for the traditional tramway motorman has much more to do than his motor bus counterpart.

Having been shown the car depot and works, if time permits, the trainee is then provide with a close-quarters introduction to the anatomy of the electric tramcar, with the different types of carbody, trucks, traction equipment and componentry explained and demonstrated, and its maintenance needs defined. He will be shown how to oil the different types of traction motor without getting oil inside the motor casing, and the three types of axlebox, and how to detect the possible presence of water in the axlebox packing by poking a finger in it. The couplers, hand, air and emergency brake systems and sanding gear will also be shown and explained, together with the path of the traction current, from the trolleywheel through automatic circuit breaker and canopy switch, controller barrels, wiring harness and resistances to the motors. The action of the controllers will be demonstrated with the controller cover off and the arc-shute swung back, and the importance of always moving the controller handle correctly will be emphasised.

Throughout this initiation, the pupil will be clearly told not only the right and proper ways of effecting any given action but it will also be made clear what the results of any transgression are likely to be. He is also given the opportunity to ask appropriate questions as the tour proceeds.

By this time the trainee will have had every opportunity to have read his copy of the current rule book, which does not differ to any enormous extent from the earlier, 1926, edition. The MER's Rules are remarkably detailed and well repay intensive study. They have to be read, and read very thoroughly; staff are not necessarily expected to be able to recite the content in parrot fashion but they will normally be required to know them sufficiently well to quote the rule nnmber that is likely to be applicable to any given set of circumstances. It is often useful to learn why a particular rule exists or was first introduced. All platform staff are required to know very intimately the rules and procedures to be followed in single-line operation, the use of flags, the significance of the Warning Boards at certain curves along the Douglas–Laxey section, the special requirements at the three traffic-light-controlled crossings at Halfway, Ballabeg and Ballure, and the procedure to be followed in the event of any untoward occurrence.

The Rules also cover the internal bell signals between conductor and motorman and vice versa; one bell to the motorman is to indicate a need to stop the car at the next orthodox stopping place; two bells indicate the orthodox "go-ahead" and three bells indicates the need to stop at once. From the front platform, a single bell from the motorman means that he wishes the conductor to come to the front platform; two bells to the back platform indicates the need to apply the trailer brakes, and so on. No car may move at all until the motorman receives two bells and the motorman has also received permission for the movement intended from the Station Master at Douglas, Laxey or Ramsey, or the Yard Master at Derby Castle.

Before even attempting to move, the motorman will have completed what might be termed a "pre-flight" check list, easily remembered by the mnemonic "FEAST", standing for:

F – Flags: One red and one yellow flag must be aboard the car; in the saloons are invariably clipped inside the vestibules, but on the open crossbench cars they may be clipped under the canopy or inside the locker underneath either of the platform seats. A red flag cannot be run past under any circumstances; the yellow indicates a requirement to proceed with extreme caution and be ready to stop at once.

E – Extinguishers: all MER cars are equipped with fire extinguishers, which must be physically checked before starting out. "E" also stands for electric lights, which must be checked and tested.

A – Air: No car is normally permitted to move before the gauge of the compressed air system shows that 60 pounds per square inch is available. The air brakes and air whistles must be checked and tested.

S – Sand: No car may move without sand in the hoppers, under the

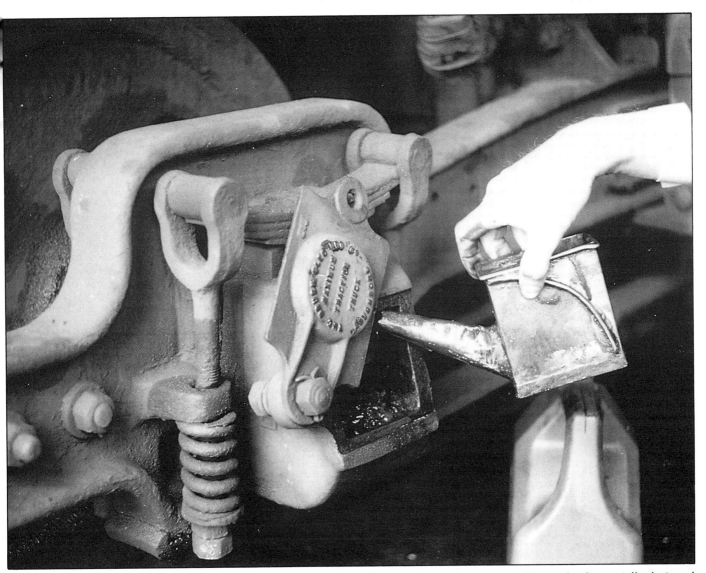

A sprung cover must be raised to gain access to the axlebox of a Brush Type D Truck. Oil is poured from a kettle specially designed for the purpose. Judicious poking with the fingers can establish the condition of the tweed packing, and detect the presence of water.
Alex Townsend

Right The axlebox cover of a Brill 27Cx Truck is removed after releasing a securing pin. *Alex Townsend*

Left The sand hoppers should be checked regularly for adequate supplies. The efficient operation of the sanding gear should likewise be discerned. *Alex Townsend*

seats, and the sand tramp or foot pedal must always be in position at the appropriate end of the car.

T – Trolley: The trolleyhead, wheel and rope must be checked, and it is also a mandatory requirement that a spare trolley rope is aboard the car since this can have a number of uses in addition to the obvious one.

The process of the induction of a trainee can and is modified according to the individual. Some people can seemingly gobble up and readily assimilate great chunks of knowledge at once; others need to have the information spread gradually over a period.

Initial motorman-training on the line is always carried out between Douglas and Laxey, interposed between Service cars and driver training is often carried out on Car No. 5 which is virtually always maintained in near idyllic condition. The instruction of the trainee is almost always carried out by the yard master and chief motorman, Mr. J.B. Matthews whose skills in both handling tramcars and in teaching has produced many successful graduates from the MER "Motor School" over the years.

On the first trip out from Douglas, the pupil is given a demonstration run, usually as far as Groudle, with every action, sequence and movement being explained in detail. Then comes the magic moment (for some) when the pupil steps behind the controls and makes his first essay into trying to drive a tramcar. Suddenly the smooth nonchalance of the experienced motorman seems light-years away. For a start there is a particular knack to be acquired in almost (but not) simultaneously releasing the air brake and applying the first Series notch of power in order to start away without a jerk. It tends to be forgotten in the excitement of the moment that the single notch movement

brings in 100-horsepowers-worth of traction motor power. The need to notch up according to the load, gradient, curve, weather and so on is inculcated as too is the requirement never to stay on any of the resistance notches for longer that is absolutely necessary. The trainee is taught the necessity for switching off cleanly, in the same single movement of the hand. A peculiarity of the MER technique that has often baffled close observers is the practice of switching back from top parallel notch to top series when running whereas orthodox street tramway practice would be to switch off completely, and then pick up again to the top series position. The explanation lies in the widespread use of trailer cars, where no matter how meticulously the working parts of the draftgear and couplers is maintained, there is bound to be some free movement (otherwise the cars and trailers could never be coupled or uncoupled) and the process of switching off and then picking up power notches again would often result in at least one and possibly two distinct jerks, most noticeable to the passengers aboard the trailer car.

The pupil is also taught how far a tramcar will coast along after the power has been switched off, slowing down as tractive and rotational resistance (and other factors such as curves) eats into the kinetic energy stored in the moving car. The use of brakes, and the air brake in particular, demands good judgement. On the MER there are three air brake application valves in use: the original Christensen, the Westinghouse Type 7 (virtually identical to the Christensen) and the sophisticated self-lapping Westinghouse Type W, fitted only to Cars 21 and 22. On the Christensen and Westinghouse Type 7, the air is "nibbled" off from the high pressure reservoir pipeline to the brake pipe by an acquired (and sometimes painful) supple wrist action, until the required

Facing Page Top A small valve allows condensation to be blown off from the air reservoir on a daily basis, another necessary Motorman skill.   *Alex Townsend*

Left Twentieth century technology in the shape of a "Fairy" liquid bottle, used to squirt oil into the tiny holes provided in the ancient Milnes trailer axleboxes. Where the oil goes to, nobody knows. You just keep squirting until you think its had enough.
    Alex Townsend

Right The anatomy of the inside of the tramcar controller is essential knowledge for any Motorman. Here, switches are pulled to isolate motor groups in the event of a breakdown or failure.   *Alex Townsend*

Left The polished brass top plate of a G.E. controller. Getting to grips with this must surely be every budding Motorman's aim?
    Alex Townsend

amount of air (and retardation) is obtained. Because the co-efficient of sliding friction is not constant, the braking effect will increase as the wheels slow down, and to prevent a violent stop or the possibility of a lock-up and skid, the pressure must be judiciously bled off to exhaust as the car slows to a standstill. Once the car is at a dead stand, the brake is reapplied to guard against any movement during loading or unloading. The correct "running" position of the handle is in the centre of its quadrant, but inevitably some valve face wear takes place from time to time, and it is regarded as good practice to move the valve handle from the centre to the exhaust position and back again from time to time when running.

The Westinghouse Type W valve is a mechanism of transcending complexity and exquisite performance. The infinitely variable braking effect is dependent upon the position of the handle; any normal leakage that takes place at the cylinder is automatically made good by a special internal valve arrangement. The farther to the right the handle is moved, the greater the braking effect. In all cases the air brake is released by moving the handle to the left or clockwise.

It is obviously of critical importance to know, virtually all of the time, what the reservoir pressure is, as indicated by the air gauge. No low-pressure alarms are fitted and nor should they ever be necessary. In practice it quickly becomes second-nature to "know" what the pressure is at any given time, and close observers will have noticed how the average motorman's eyes tend to almost unconsciously "brush" across the gauge at intervals, and almost always whenever a brake application is contemplated.

The electric tramcar has always been an inherently safe vehicle, and should compressed air not be available, or for parking purposes, all MER cars (and trailers) possess very powerful handbrakes, applied either by wheel (as on Nos 1, 2, 16, 26 etc) or by traditional goose-neck handle, such as 19–22. 32–3 etc. The use of the handbrake is preferred by a few motormen, despite the physical effort, on the grounds that it is virtually impossible to jerk or snatch a car and its occupants by its use, and by virtue of the fact that the motorman can "feel" (through the palm of his hand) just how much brake he is applying. Releasing the handbrake by simply kicking the dog or pawl out after a stop is never recommended, and nor is leaving any part of the human anatomy within range of a flying handle. The traction motors too can be used

as an emergency brake by putting the forward/reverse barrel of the controller into the opposite direction of travel. This is a formidable and sometimes highly expensive way of stopping a car dead, but is to be used only in the last resort. The procedure is demonstrated to trainee motormen with the car just rolling, and even then the howl of protest from the car is an adequate indication of the mechanical and electrical agony that is being inflicted on the machine.

In the course of a series of training runs to and from Laxey the pupil motorman will also be forcefully introduced to the geography of the line itself. Most railways and many tramways were occasionally in the habit of expressing curved or graded track as a percentage of the whole; on the MER things are different, for a glance at either a map of the line or the gradient profile shows that in the 17¾ miles between Douglas and Ramsey, there is barely half a mile of dead straight and level track. The line abounds with curves down to 90 ft radius, whilst the gradient profile has been likened to a cross-section of the Swiss Alps with inclines (some of them very lengthy) of anywhere between 1 in 23.5 and 1 in 550. Each curve and incline possesses an optimum speed of approach and transition. In addition there are countless unguarded level crossings where a moment's inattentiveness or lack of judgement could have the most serious consequences. On top of everything else, there is a total of no less than 63 possible stopping places in addition to the obvious ones at Douglas, Laxey and Ramsey. True, a large number are infrequently used, but they have to be learned.

By the time that the trainee has completed around a dozen closely-supervised trips to Laxey and back, and depending upon aptitude, he will be capable of driving at least by rote, and will be competent to apply power appropriately and brake reasonably smoothly. At this stage he is then transferred for further training to a Service car on the main Douglas–Ramsey run, usually under the expert tutelage of Mr. Tony Gilett, who, apart from a lengthy railway career in the UK and on the MER, also happens to be a qualified professional teacher as well. For two, three or more weeks, the trainee motorman will be required to drive on the service, with the instructor initially calling out the notches as required, explaining when and where to start braking, where to release, and where to coast. Since the bulk of training work is carried out before the beginning of the season, when major engineering works are still being finished off, there is a likelihood that this period will involve single line working, and if any doubts existed beforehand about the procedures to be followed, the repeated experiences will engrave themselves on the trainee's heart.

If by this stage the trainee motorman has become deluded into thinking that he now knows more than something about driving an MER tramcar, the experience of being at least partly responsible for the safety and comfort of real passengers, and trying to run to time under all kinds of varying conditions, is usually sufficient to enforce a realisation of just how far he has yet to go.

This period also sees a growing familiarity with detail: the precise positioning of the car at stopping places, and the observance of the various stop lines painted against the track at Douglas, Laxey and Ramsey, and the fouling of clearance points used when shunting. The close-shunting to couple-up trailers is easier said than done, but can be acquired with practice. The coupler bar is always fitted to the trailer, and the motor car run up to it. The aim is to land the end of the bar inside the mouth of the coupler, which requires a degree of skill and precision but seemingly presents not the slightest problem to other experienced men. If the car lands just short, the practice is to inch in on the first power notch against the brake, something that is not enjoyed by either the controller or the motorman. The shunting of trailers is generally done by hand, aided by a favouring gradient. However,

some trailers are noticeably less inclined to roll easily than others and in some cases a considerable physical effort is needed. In the last resort, the layout of double crossovers makes it possible to run the motor car around the trailer, but this is a procedure to be seen perhaps once or twice a season. The trainee is also taught to examine the car before and after a journey for possible defects, how to isolate motors or motor groups, the procedures to be followed to cover any sort of contingency, and the thousand and one other things that come only with practice, such as braking whilst motoring on top series power notch in order to get out of a skid on slippery rails, and how and when to apply sand. The trainee quickly learns that there is little to be feared from rail conditions in a downpour when everything is soaking wet; it is the period as the rain starts, or the early morning dew, or during what the Irish would term a "soft" or misty day, that can be fraught with peril. Since the construction of the Douglas Breakwater, it seems that tidal patterns in the Bay have changed considerably, and it is by no means unusual for an on-shore wind to lift green sea-water across the promenades. Similarly the exposed MER line past Derby Castle Depot and up to Port Jack is quite frequently lashed by flying sea-spray, making rail conditions very bad indeed. It is often said that the Isle of Man is one of the few places on earth where it is possible to find all four seasons of the year all in the same day, and sometimes all in the course of one trip from Douglas to Ramsey, but the weather, in all its forms, inevitably plays a very direct and important part on driving conditions on the MER.

There are no speedometers on the cars, and nor should they be necessary. All MER motormen estimate their speeds fairly accurately by timing themselves between points of distance. The bulk of MER rails are 30 ft in length so by counting the number of rail joints passed over in 10 seconds and multiplying by two, the result is the number of miles per hour. For those of a mathematical turn of mind, the constant is $0.682\,L$, where L is the length of the rail in feet.

By the end of this training period, the pupil motorman will have been assessed by internal process, and if his grasp of the fundamental art of safely driving a tramcar is considered sufficient, a likely examination date will be fixed for his test. A few, however, will not have sustained either their hopes or their efforts, and will have departed for pastures new, for the motorman's Examination is not to be regarded as anything less than a formidable ordeal.

The Examination of motormen can be undertaken by a certain few of the Line's most senior officials, and are usually conducted by Mr. Maurice Faragher, the Engineering Superintendent, in person. Whilst those concerned undoubtedly do all in their power to put the applicant at ease, there is no question in most people's minds that they are on trial for their lives. The test usually starts off on board the 10.00 a.m. Service car from Douglas, meeting the southbound car somewhere between Ballagorry and Cornaa, when the examiner and his aspirant will change over to return to Douglas. The test may well be extended or abbreviated according to circumstances and the satisfaction or otherwise of the examiner. The test is indeed a moment of truth, for every moment and action is carefully monitored and evaluated. If the applicant manages to pass the first part of the examination by driving acceptably, the scene is then set for the second part, which consists of a very lengthy oral examination on rules and procedures. The pass

rate is not high for first-time attempts, but assuming the applicant is successful, he will then be permitted to sign the register of motormen, and will be allowed to perform his first "solo" run on the same day. This is an experience that is never likely to be forgotten, for by then the euphoria of actually passing the examination has evaporated, to be replaced with considerable nervousness when the realisation dawns that no matter what difficulty arises, you are now very much on your own. It is also said with great justification, that only after the applicant has passed his examination, does he then really learn, notwithstanding all that has gone before.

The fundamental requirements of a motorman's performance consist of safety, comfort, economy and other factors, at least as important, including respect for the tramcars themselves, courtesy and

Left Washing the Tram. A daily ritual enjoyed by one and all. As too is ensuring brasswork is brightly polished, and windows crystal clear.   *Alex Townsend*

Below The line up of oil kettles outside the Derby Castle oil shed, is a sight the novice Motorman may not have anticipated. Neither is the oil up the sleeve resulting from the choice of the "wrong" kettle, a mistake experience will soon eliminate.
Alex Townsend

punctuality, both personal and in maintaining the Service if required to do so. There are many ways in which the various curves and gradients can be tackled, and only experience in all weathers and under all conditions of load, can produce a knowledge of the best way. As this experience grows, there comes a time when it is possible to reach a pitch of rich and immense enjoyment in the job, a state of mind not difficult to achieve since the vast bulk of the customers themselves are there to enjoy themselves and no two runs on the MER are exactly identical. There is something enormously exquisite about the MER, not least the ever-unfolding vistas, from the high rock cliffs and seascape at Groudle and Ballaragh, to the tranquil serenity of Ballaglass and Dreemskerry. As the last traces of snow melt from the hidden crevices of North Barrule, a carpet of fresh green grows daily more abundant; buds unfurl into flower with the spring; the sunlight, ever stronger, lights a blaze of gorse and a mist of bluebells. The summer sun draws the scent of pinewoods and salt air as the lineside crops ripen and haymaking begins, heralding the coming of early autumn, a time of diminishing traffic as the holiday season falters and draws to a close, the seasonal staff become thin on the ground. Finally, there is the wage packet in which there is also a note thanking you for your services, and bringing employment to an end. The withdrawal symptoms can be very traumatic, but their ought to be the realisation that a job on the MER is something quite unique, and which could almost certainly not be reproduced anywhere else in the world. The MER, unlike so many of the "preserved" railways and tramways, still fulfils its original function; it is a transport utility and used by many as such. And even after a day which ended with a sudden torrential downpour, when one

was miles from anywhere with an open crossbench car, and the rain had soaked through every stitch of clothing, and even filled up your shoes, as you squelch across the Yard at Derby Castle to sign off, you can still rest assured that there is nothing else like it on earth. One motorman, albeit given to some overstatement, when asked if he liked his job, replied that he thought he had died and gone to Heaven. Only it wasn't an overstatement at all. This is the MER.

CHAPTER EIGHT

THE SNAEFELL MOUNTAIN RAILWAY

It is said that one of Man's most basic urges is curiosity and a compulsion to explore his surroundings. A mountain is climbed not just "because it's there", but to see what can be seen from the top. As soon as a Manx tourist trade developed, there was a stream of visitors climbing to the top of Snaefell, the only Island peak that at 2,036 ft above sea level, officially qualifies as a mountain. From this lofty peak, the visitor was rewarded with a splendid vista and which, according to the advertisements embraced the Kingdoms of Mann, England, Wales, Scotland, Ireland and Heaven, on a clear day. It was the perfect place for a Mountain Railway.

THE FELL SYSTEM

With the Manx tourist industry reaching a peak of investment and development in the reign of Queen Victoria, Mr. G. Noble Fell carried out a survey for an intended steam railway line from Laxey up to the summit of Snaefell, as part of the planned Douglas, Laxey & Snaefell Railway, which received Tynwald approval in 1858, but which was never started. G. Noble Fell's father, John Barraclough Fell, had been born in London in 1815 and later became a railway contractor of some note, being involved with the Furness and Whitehaven Railway, and a number of substantial railway construction contracts in Italy under a partnership known as Brassey Jackson, Fell & Joplin. J.B. Fell was a man of considerable genius and the inventor of what was later to become known as the 'Fell Incline Railway System'. All orthodox railways depend on the coefficient of friction between the wheel and the rail for propulsion (and conventional braking) and this in turn limits the loads that can be handled. Most railways are as nearly level as possible as any gradient effectively reduces the loads that can be hauled or propelled by a given unit of motive power. If a railway is built on gradients sufficiently steep to overcome the adhesive force or tractive effort of the loco, wheelslip may very well occur, and it is necessary to resort to some additional means of assistance, such as banking or pilot locos. Where an incline is very steep and is clearly beyond the limits of normal adhesion, special arrangements are required such as haulage cables or rack and pinion gear. The Fell Incline Railway System was devised to enable gradients of up to 1 in 10 to be worked solely by adhesion, using an additional double-headed centre rail laid horizontally between the running rails and which could be used not only for additional horizontal driving wheels but also for additional friction braking as well.

J.B. Fell was not responsible for inventing the principle of a centre rail – indeed he never claimed either originality or novelty but specifically invented a means by which the centre rail system could be successfully applied. The first Patent for an additional centre-rail in conjunction with auxiliary wheels for additional adhesion and traction was granted to Mr. Charles B. Vignoles and John Ericsson in London on 30th September 1830. On 15th October 1840 another similar invention was granted by the United States Patent Office to Henry Pinkus, a character more usually associated with atmospheric and pneumatic propulsion. In France broadly the same idea was registered at the Paris Academy of Arts & Sciences on 18th December 1843 by Baron Sequir. Similar applications were lodged by Teller in America, by Kraus of Hannover

Left A pre-1914 coloured advertisement card is a reminder of the large and extensive (and profitable) range of material that was offered as souvenirs, particularly at the Snaefell Summit Hotel, and the numerous kiosks that graced the stations at Garwick, Laxey, Dhoon, Ballaglass and Ramsey.

in Germany and also by Dumery Giraud and Fedit, whilst another British Patent was granted to A.V. Newton on 13th July 1847. J.B. Fell's first British Patent was applied for on 26th January 1863 and became Patent 0227 of 1863. A second (No. 3182) was lodged on 16th December 1863. Other centre rail patent applications were made by Fell in August 1860 (No. 2174); in March 1869 (No. 899) and January 1895 (No. 762). Fell was a fairly prolific patentee, although many of his other inventions related to monorails and elevated narrow-gauge railways, with or without guide rails.

Whilst J.B. Fell was not the original inventor, he certainly was the most earnest and ardent advocate of the centre-rail system and from July 1863 to February 1864, he carried out extensive trials alongside the Cromford & High Peak Railway's Incline at Whaley Bridge in Derbyshire, where an experimental length of 3' 7½" gauge Fell rail track was laid up inclines varying from 1 in 30 to 1 in 12, and featuring curves of 2⅜ chains radius on grades of 1 in 12 and 1 in 13. In this instance, the Fell centre-rail was positioned 7½" above the level of the running rails. A 16 ton four-cylinder Fell gear equipped steam locomotive, designed by Mr. A. Alexander of Millwall Iron Works was built and used in the trials, and found to be quite capable of propelling 24 ton loads up the twisting inclines, and quite irrespective of the wintry weather conditions experienced in the Pennine foothills. The application of the idea was proved.

The French Government was particularly interested in the Fell system and promptly arranged for the laying of an experimental section (also 3' 7½" gauge) on the slopes of Mont Cenis, in conjunction with the Italian Government. This experimental section was 1¼ miles in length, and from its commencement at Lamslebourg (at 5,035 ft above sea level) it climbed to a summit of 5,820 ft on an average gradient of 1 in 13. The line was worked by the locomotive that had carried out the earlier trials in Derbyshire, but this was soon joined by another loco, the front elevation of which is shown in the accompanying drawing. The French Fell railway trials lasted for just over three months during the spring of 1865 and were closely observed by delegates and commissions from Austria, Italy and Russia and with Capt. Tyler of the Railway Inspectorate representing the Imperial Government. Of greater significance was the close and personal interest shown by the Emperor Napoleon III in the experimental line. With consistently successful results, the trials favourably impressed the French Emperor, who issued an authorisation on 4th November 1865 for the immediate construction of a Fell Railway between St. Michel and over the Italian frontier in order to provide a railway link across the mountains until the new Alpine Tunnel under Mont Cenis was completed. Building of this temporary line commenced on 1st May 1866 and the route was opened throughout for traffic from St. Michel de Maurienne to Susa in June 1868.

By all the standards commonly applied to railways, the new line was nothing short of staggering, stretching across the Alps for a distance of 48 miles, abounding in tight horseshoe curves and truly appalling gradients. The line carried both passenger and freight traffic, with a normal journey time of seven hours, or marginally under 7 miles per hour. This unique railway route was graphically described in the 1869 edition of "Scrambles through the Alps" by Edward Whimper, a noted mountaineer. A model of a Fell-equipped locomotive for this line is in the Science Museum collection, London.

The Trans-Alpine line evidently worked well enough, but finally closed in October 1871, following the completion of the Mont Cenis Tunnel from Modane to Bardonecchia and most of the trackwork and

Left New Zealand Fell Railway: the Rimutaka Incline featured a 1 in 15 gradient and was worked by 3' 6" gauge steam locos and Fell brake-equipped Brake Vans. Here a Neilson-built tank locomotive tackles the gradient. *New Zealand High Commission*

Below A train descending the Incline before the Rimutaka line was superceded by a more easily-graded deviation and a five-mile tunnel. *New Zealand High Commission*

equipment was dismantled and shipped out to Brazil, (although some went to Switzerland) where a lengthy metre-gauge Fell-equipped steam railway between Nitcroi (opposite the Harbour in Rio de Janeiro) to Novo Friburgo was built and opened as the Cantagalo Railway, later the Leopoldina system. This line was supplied with some specially designed locomotives by Manning Wardle & Co. which tested them on a specially constructed track alongside the Goathland Incline of the Whitby & Pickering Railway in 1872. The Brazilian Fell line was to survive into the 1960s

Another Fell railway of international fame was the Rimutaka Incline of the New Zealand Government Railways, and which formed a vital link in the main line from Wellington (North Island) and Masterton, and opened in 1878. This 3' 6" gauge line commenced at Cross Creek, some 34 miles from Wellington and was steam-worked by a batch of 0–4–2T locos. These had two 18" diameter by 16" stroke cylinders driving the usual coupled wheels and two 12" diameter by 16" stroke cylinders working horizontal driving wheels on the Fell centre rail. The 39 ton locos were often used in multiple, according to the total tonnage of the train, and suitably interspersed throughout the train's length. The engines were fitted with Westinghouse air brakes and quadruple Fell rail track brakes. Trains were also equipped with a suitable number of Fell-brake-equipped brake vans for descending the

Incline. Rimutaka was finally superseded by a lengthy deviation which included a five-mile tunnel in 1955, but which permitted normal methods.

A later Fell system variant, in which the centre-rail wheels were forced against it by compressed air (instead of springs) to obtain maximum tractive effort, was patented by Hanscotte and used on the Chemin de Fer du Puy de Dome, a steam-worked, Fell equipped mountain line at Clermont Ferrand, opened in 1907 and closed in 1926.

THE BUILDING OF THE SNAEFELL MOUNTAIN RAILWAY

Meanwhile, back in the Isle of Man, the advent of the 1893 electric tramway between Douglas and Groudle, and its extension to Laxey

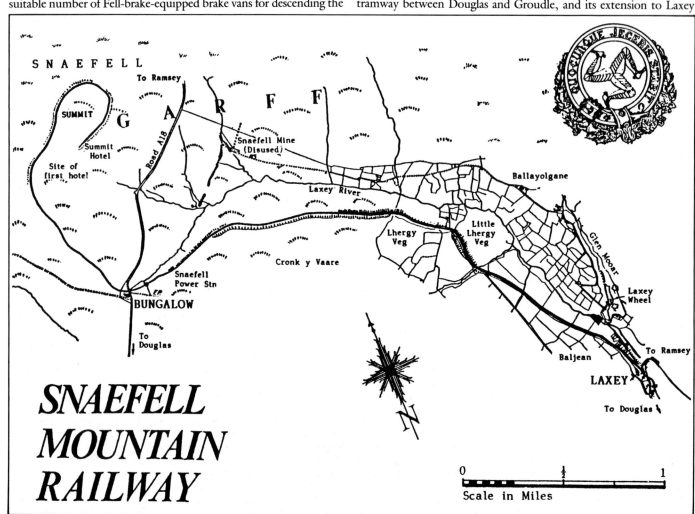

SNAEFELL MOUNTAIN RAILWAY

Scale in Miles

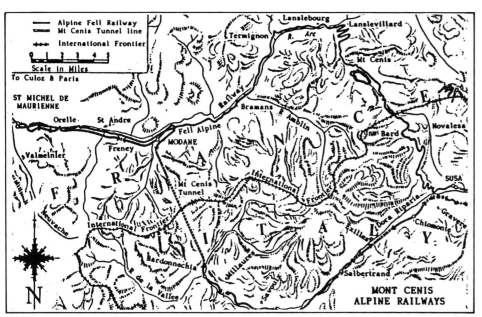

MONT CENIS
ALPINE RAILWAYS

Front elevation of a Mount Cenis loco with
Fell centre-rail gear, built in 1865.

in 1894, had produced renewed interest in G.N. Fell's earlier plans for the Douglas, Laxey & Snaefell Railway, approved in 1888 but never begun, but revived in 1891 under the Manx East Coast Railways scheme. The residual Snaefell Railway Co. maintained an office in Athol Street, Douglas. On 4th January 1895, a Snaefell Mountain Railway Association held an inaugural meeting in Laxey and announced its intention to independently revive the earlier scheme and construct a railway to the Summit; the new Association had nothing to do with the original Snaefell Railway Co., but the Syndicate included most of those who were already involved in the coastal electric line, including Mr. Alexander Bruce and other directors of what had now become the Isle of Man Tramways and Electric Power Company Limited.

The syndicate discussed various proposals relating to motive power for the new line; the early and eminent expert on electric traction, Dr. Edward Hopkinson was retained as a consultant and it was resolved to build an electric tramway up to the summit of the mountain, using the Fell Incline Railway system centre-rail in order to produce the tractive effort needed to propel a laden car up the ruling gradient of 1 in 12.

The route of the Snaefell Mountain Tramway from Laxey to the summit of Snaefell followed Fell's Survey of 1888 and since it was to be built on Crown Lands or land purchased or leased entirely under voluntary agreements there was no need for an Act of Tynwald with statutory powers, and this in turn resulted in the avoidance of the lengthy delay and costs of the usual procedure. In fact the entire 4 mile, 53 chain length of the route up to Snaefell summit, with Herd (or Hurd?) of Douglas as the main contractor G. Noble Fell as Works Superintendent and Mr. Alexander M'Kerrow as Engineer, was finished very quickly. During construction, a third rail, laid to the 3' 0" gauge was temporarily provided to enable the Manx Northern Railway steam loco 'CALEDONIA' to propel works and construction trains up the Mountain. The loco was brought by sea from Ramsey to Rowe's Pier Laxey and then pushed and hauled up Glen Road along two short lengths of track until it reached the site. The choice of a 3' 6" track gauge for the Mountain Tramway was said to result from the problems of incorporating the Fell rail gear within any gauge narrower than this although in other accounts it was claimed to stem from earlier Fell lines, which had ranged from one metre (3' 3⅜") to 3' 7½.

Somewhat later it was said that both Fell and Hopkinson insisted that the Snaefell gauge was to provide for greater stability for the rolling stock, especially under severe crosswind conditions on the exposed upper slopes of the mountain. Certainly at no stage was through-running between the Douglas–Laxey coastal line and the mountain section ever envisaged. The extra 6" of gauge was unlikely to produce a great difference in relative stability and there are innumerable stretches of the coastal tramway where the 3' 0" gauge cars are often exposed to fairly merciless crosswind conditions without being blown over. Similarly there does not seem to have been trouble with the line across Mont Cenis, where the altitude and weather conditions were more extreme.

By the time that construction of the new Mountain line was reaching completion, it had been more than adequately proved that normal electric tramcars could and would readily climb gradients of up to 1 in 9 by means of adhesion alone, and the intended Fell rail traction gear was deleted from the equipment scheme, although a technical account in "The Engineer" for 30th August 1895 states that "....the (Fell)

horizontal wheels on each car are worked by separate traction motors." This was incorrect, and no such equipment was ever fitted to the Snaefell cars. The Fell rail gear on Snaefell Mountain whilst quite superfluous for traction purposes even before the line was completed, was retained for friction braking purposes.

Construction of the Snaefell line began late in January, but the February of 1895 was notable for ferocious weather, with high winds, blizzards, frost, and snow "some several feet depth in places" and as a result nearly a full month was lost. The opening date, originally scheduled for "early July" became progressively delayed. A superhuman effort eventually resulted in the line being essentially complete by early in August. In the first week of that month, the steam loco 'CALEDONIA' hauled a trainload of visiting officials from the London & North Western Railway and the Lancashire and Yorkshire Railway from Laxey to a point just beyond the Bungalow.

The overhead equipment of the Snaefell line was the responsibility of a Mr. Willis from Mather & Platt, and who strung out and erected the overhead wire in just eight or ten (accounts differ) days. The copper overhead wire was of No. 3 BWG (British Wire Gauge) section, substantially heavier than the No. 0 BWG of the coastal line. The wire was directly suspended from centre poles approximately 110 ft apart with double bracket arms and to which the wire was attached by means of a split-clamp fitting onto the bracket arm, and with an insulating sleeve between the arm and the hanger, and with double insulation provided by an orthodox insulated bolt into which the ear that held the wire was screwed. All of the fittings carried the "Aetna" brand totem of the Albert & J.M. Anderson Manufacturing Co. of Boston Mass., USA. The nominal height of the conductor wire, 16' 0" above rail level, was critical on Snaefell in order to avoid the hammer-blow of the bow-collector at each point of suspension, where the height of the wire was adjusted to ensure that it was (and is) lifted clear of the collector as it passes the pole. Thus the leading collector looses contact and the car is fed via the trailing collector which is still in mid-span, and by the time the trailing collector loses contact the leading collector is in full contact with the next span. The relatively extreme conditions on the upper Mountain reaches led to the adoption from at least 1904 and possibly earlier, of an early form of mechanical ear on the section above the Bungalow, which held the wire in a clamp which could be unscrewed and refastened repeatedly, unlike the customary "clinch-ears" where the lips of the ears are hammered round the wire to grip it, and which can really only be used once. These fittings enabled the wire to be taken down each winter to prevent frost and gale damage. Many years later, this annual ritual was deemed unnecessary in the second winter of the MER Board's "chief executive" Mr. W. Jackson in 1978–9, when the wire was left in situ; the widespread damage that promptly ensued was repaired with new poles and wires at a sub substantial and unnecessary cost.

On 16th August 1895 the new Snaefell line was examined by Colonel J.H. Rich, RE of the Board of Trade's Railway Inspectorate and Major P. Cardew, who was described as an "electrical engineer to the Home Office". The inspectors travelled up from Douglas to Laxey in a special car, accompanied by Alexander Bruce, the IoMT&EP Co. Chairman together with Alderman Hopkinson of Manchester, of Messrs. Mather & Platt, Mr. C.B. Nelson, Dr. Farrell, Mr. J.R. Cowell MHK, Mr. W. Todhunter and Mr. F.G. Callow and Mr. J. Aldworth,

Left: Steam Mountaineer: Manx Northern Railway loco No 4 CALEDONIA, (later IMR No 15) built by Dubs & Co of Glasgow in 1885 was used on the Snaefell line during construction. *Mike Goodwyn*

Right: Engraving of Snaefell Mountain Tramway Car No 1 from 'The Engineer' Aug 30 1895.

Below: The Snaefell Mountain opening day, August 21 1895, with a line of the new electric cars at the original depot terminus. *Manx Museum Archives*

directors and manager of the owning companies. At Laxey the party then transferred to a Snaefell car, (thought to be No. 2) which slowly made its way up the mountain to the Summit, frequently stopping to allow the inspectors to examine the way and works. An account of the proceedings in the *Mona's Herald* for 21st August 1895 refers to the inspection which included a series of brake tests on the gradient and carried out with live loads consisting of the directors, managers and engineers and a balance "made up of navvies." The car was "set going at full speed and when it reached a rate that will never be approached when the car is in use for ordinary traffic the brakes were applied . . . . and In less than its own length, brought to a standstill."

At the conclusion of these adventures, the party adjourned to the Summit Hotel, where the new Hotel manager, Mr. George A. Bowling (formerly of the Groudle Hotel) provided an outstanding luncheon". The newspaper's account concluded that "both of the Inspectors expressed themselves as being thoroughly satisfied . . ." but their subsequent reports to the Governor were somewhat different.

No great fault was found by Colonel Rich save only for the provi-

posing the use of regenerative braking and Major Cardew required extensive and exhaustive testing of this equipment prior to it being approved for use.

In his Report, Colonel Rich noted that right-hand running had been adopted, and said that this was to keep ascending cars on the soft, outer-part of the formation. This was perfectly true along the lower section from Laxey to the Bungalow, but scarcely valid in respect of the upper slopes of the Mountain, where the route followed a spiral curve to the right, and where a descending car would be running on the soft part of the unconsolidated road bed.

The Snaefell Mountain Tramway opened with special cars for Members of Tynwald and other local dignitaries on 20th August, with the full public service in operation from Wednesday 21st August. With a return fare of 2s 0d (10p), the new tramway was an outstanding commercial and technical success, carrying a daily average of 900 passengers up to the end of the season. With a journey time of just under 30 minutes the fleet of six cars could provide a ten-minute headway. As originally completed, the line ran to a terminal alongside the Snaefell depot, where cars were winched across from one track to the other. The depot itself was built in brick, with a corrugated iron roof, and was 119 ft long. However its restricted width of 20' 6'' made the accommodation somewhat cramped. The track was laid in 56lbs/yard Vignole rail, bolted to sleepers measuring 7' 0'' by 9'' by 4½''with nine sleepers to each 24 ft length of rail. The Fell centre-rail, of 65lbs/yard double headed section, was mounted on steel chairs or brackets, and was 4'' (not 8'' as quoted in certain erroneous accounts) higher than the surface of the running rails. Though often cited as preventing derailments, the Fell centre-rail most certainly cannot avert derailments on track that is fractionally wide to gauge, as the events of the past seven years have so amply demonstrated. A deranged car, with its Fell gear heavily entangled with the centre-rail is certainly not a matter for jest and often presents a serious problem for the re-railing gangs. In addition, it should be noted that the Fell rail is not continuous, and there are several lengthy stretches where it was not fitted .

The Mountain Tramway climbed from its Laxey terminal at a maximum grade of 1 in 12, although there were some quite lengthy stretches on easier grades, as the gradient diagram shows. The line attained a climb totalling 1,820 ft. The minimum curvature was officially stated to be 10 chains radius, but on the final Summit spiral there is at least one curve with a radius of 5 chains. The summit of the line, at 1,992 ft is just 44 ft blow the actual mountain summit.

The contractor for the electrical equipment of the line was Mather & Platt Ltd. of Salford Ironworks, Manchester, a justly famous undertaking whose pioneer endeavours in electric traction were well rewarded by future lasting success; indeed the firm is very much active to this day. The Snaefell Power Station which generated the line's electricity, was equipped with four Galloway boilers, supplying steam at 120 lbs/square inch to any of the five Mather & Platt 120 hp horizontal compound engines, each of which was coupled to a Hopkinson dynamo rated at 60 kW. An iron chimney 60 ft high and 15 ft in diameter was erected on the south side of the line and the boilerhouse flues to it passed under the tracks; the footings and the flue can still be traced. Water supply for the Power House was provided via a 2'' diameter main from a small steam pumping station built downstream

sion of fences and lamps for the pits at the stations, and a requirement to closely monitor the settlement consolidation and drainage of the new major earthworks. Major Cardew, on the other hand, seems to have had a fit when he was told that the official line voltage was 550 V d.c. since this was 50 V more than on the coastal line. ''This is a higher pressure than has been sanctioned previously,'' he said, ''and I am very reluctant to create a precedent.'' One may be sure that he was, but he then proposed a maximum line voltage of 520 V, as if there were some sort of mystical or magical significance to this particular figure. He also gratuitously claimed that the Snaefell Power Station was, in his opinion, sited uneconomically where it had been built a short distance downhill from the Bungalow level crossing, for what were considered to be sound and obvious reasons by the line's engineers and owners. In fact the site was not ideal, but it represented roughly the mid-point of the line, and no evident alternative existed, and nor did the Major find one. In fact the remit of the Inspectorate was to determine the relative safety of the line for public traffic, not to enter into a discussion about the relative merits of the power generation site. Elsewhere it was said that the line voltage, to which the Major took exception, had been ''critically adjusted'' but there is little evidence to suggest that the line output pressure was tampered with simply to solve the problems of Major Cardew.

The Major had other misgivings as well and dwelt at considerable length on the electrical equipment of the cars. The four traction motors produced a tractive effort of 3,500 lbf, and a loaded car on a grade of 1 in 12 was held to possess a tractive resistance totalling 2,850 lbf. This meant that in Major Cardew's opinion, a single motor failure would incapacitate a car. It was evidently overlooked that the motors were all arranged in series pairs, so that would mean that the two motors on the same circuit would be out of action. In practice it was possible to move a car under these circumstances, but much of this seems to have got lost in the Major's preoccupation only with theory. Mather & Platt, the suppliers of the electrical equipment were additionally pro-

Left: Snaefell Car No 4 with saloon windows and clerestory roof, on the west shoulder above the Bungalow in 1905 and with the original SNAEFELL MOUNTAIN TRAMWAY title. *IoM Dept of Tourism*

Right: A Snaefell Car standing on the main line just short of the original 1895 terminal.
Manx Museum Archives

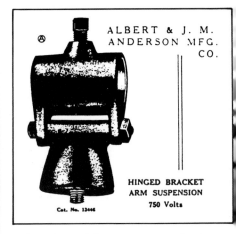

SNAEFELL MOUNTAIN RAILWAY
Section of Fell rail & Chair

Left The Snaefell Mountain Power Station Engine Room in 1895 equipped with horizontal compound steam engines and dynamo sets.   *Mather & Platt Ltd*

from Tholt-y-Will on the Sulby River, about two miles away. From the Snaefell Power Station, the supply was transmitted by underground feeder cables in both directions with individually switched feeder posts to the overhead wire at intervals of roughly one mile. An accumulator House at Laxey, a short distance from the depot, was fitted with 266 Chloride battery cells, fed directly from the main feeders, and provided a capacity of 560 Amp-hours and was used to balance the load on the Power Station.

ROLLING STOCK

The line's rolling stock consisted of six 46 seat tramcars, with carbodies 33' 9" in length and 7' 2" wide, built by G F Milnes & Co. of Birkenhead. They were finished in red, white and varnished teak, with gold "SNAEFELL MOUNTAIN TRAMWAY" side-titling.

As delivered the cars were devoid of both clerestories and saloon window glass, and these seem to have been deliberately omitted in deference to the imagined perils of wind loads on the exposed upper flanks of the Mountain, rather than initial economy. The window apertures were fitted with striped canvas roller blinds instead of glass, and were evidently not entirely popular. By April 1896 sliding glazed windows had been fitted to all the cars, but when closed in windy but sunny weather, the greenhouse effect soon brought unbearable temperatures in the saloon. As a result clerestories were added to the roofs in 1896–7. The seating capacity was increased by two to 48 with the addition of two single corner seats in the saloons against the bulkheads.

The cars were equipped with a special type of Milnes plate-frame bogie truck of 6' 9½" wheelbase at 20' 6" centres, fitted with one Mather & Platt Manchester Type 5A traction motor to each axle. Each half-line voltage motor was conservatively rated at 25 hp, making these tramcars the most powerful anywhere in the British Isles at the time of their introduction. The inner headstocks of the trucks were equip-

ped with a pair of horizontal flanged Fell rail guide wheels, and providing some lateral play or movement from the middle ordinate when negotiating some of the tighter curves. The opposite headstocks were fitted with a calliper brake acting on both faces of the Fell rail, and fitted with soft iron slipper brake shoes, ⅝" thick, measuring 14" by 2.2" and providing a frictional contact area of 70 square inches. The trucks were fitted with orthodox hand wheel brakes with one shoe to each wheel. Both types of brake were independently operated from a pair of brake masts on either platform. The Fell rail calliper brake gear coupling was later modified to reduce the stress on the platform of the car after experience had shown that the original arrangement was responsible for hogging the underframes.

The original Mather & Platt controllers provided full series/parallel motor control from the mountain end, and series-only at the Laxey or downhill end. The Summit-end controllers were superseded in 1903–4 by General Electric (USA) K.11 controllers, in turn modified to Form K.12 in 1954. The original Laxey-end controllers remained unchanged, since they were only ever used for starting away from the Summit and the Bungalow and when shunting.

The six passenger cars were augmented by Car No. 7, or "MARIA" as it was usually referred to, which consisted of a 5 ton open wagon with twin cabs, used for freight, and which borrowed trucks and control gear from one of the passenger cars (usually No. 5) each winter to carry the next season's coal supply up to the Power Station. Although the precise construction date and certain other details of the car remain unresolved, Snaefell No. 7 was definitely in use by 1898 but it may have been in existence earlier. It Is thought that the car's underframe was supplied by G.F. Milnes, but that the body was built or at least erected locally. The Snaefell roster of rolling stock was completed by a Tower Wagon of unknown origin, and a small goods wagon, built by Hurst Nelson of Motherwell, supplied in 1895 and used for the carriage of hotel supplies.

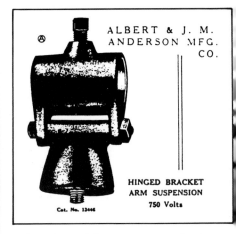

ALBERT & J. M.
ANDERSON MFG.
CO.

HINGED BRACKET
ARM SUSPENSION
750 Volts

Cat. No. 13446

Left A view of the 1895 terminal at Laxey with Car 2 running downhill. Note the Mines' heaps and the Heyman lift to the left of Dumbell's row cottages.
Manx Museum Archives

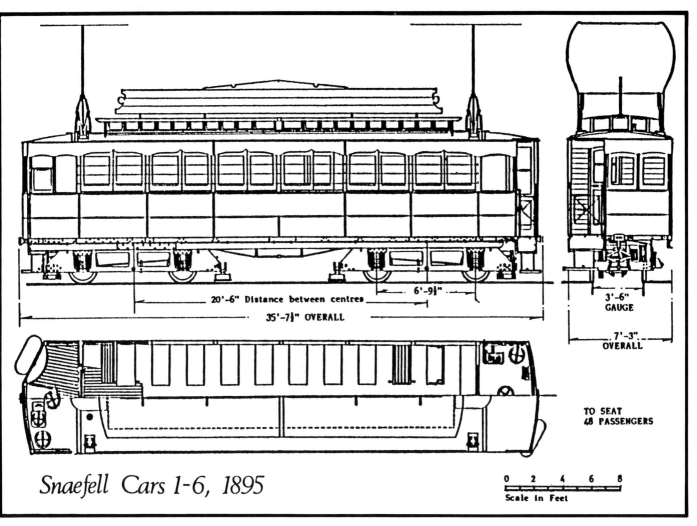

20'-6" Distance between centres

6'-9½"

35'-7½" OVERALL

3'-6" GAUGE

7'-3" OVERALL

TO SEAT 48 PASSENGERS

Snaefell Cars 1-6, 1895

0 2 4 6 8
Scale in Feet

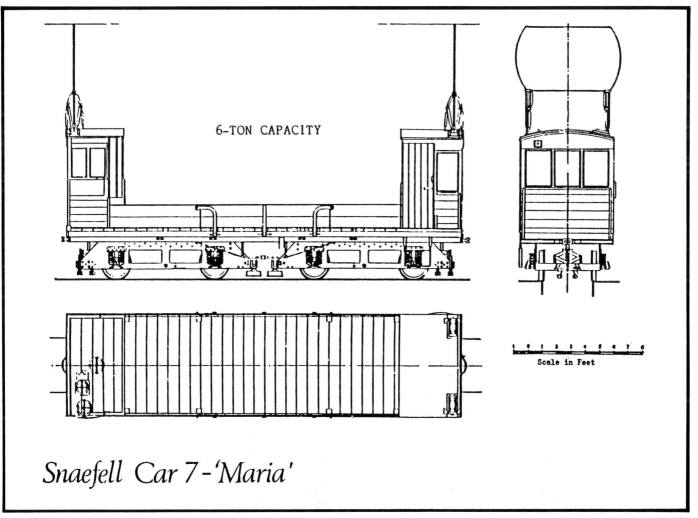

6-TON CAPACITY

Scale in Feet

Snaefell Car 7 - 'Maria'

THE DEMISE OF THE SNAEFELL MOUNTAIN RAILWAY ASSOCIATION

With the Mountain Tramway fully operational, the original syndicate responsible for its construction then sold the complete undertaking to the Isle of Man Tramways & Electric Power Co. Ltd. in December 1895. The Snaefell Association's assets were sold for no less than £72,500, whilst the costs of construction and equipment were later to be quoted in Court as amounting to a mere £40,000, and even this figure was contested as having been inflated. The Snaefell line's sale involved a cash settlement of £32,500 with the balance in an equal number of Ordinary and 6% Preference Shares in the Isle of Man Tramways & Electric Power Co. Ltd. The "Snaefell Association" was wound up in 1896 but the transactions involved in its demise were to be subjected to considerable scrutiny in the aftermath of the IoMT&EP

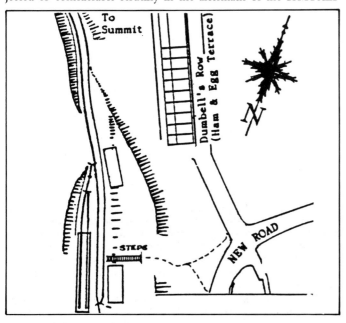

The Laxey Terminus in 1895.

Laxey Terminus 1897–8.

Right: An MER Co Argus 16-seat char-a-banc of 1907 at the entrance to Sulby Glen prior to 1914, when both vehicles were withdrawn.
Manx Electric Railway

Left: A 1900 view of the Snaefell Summit Station with Car No 4 arriving. The original Summit Hotel was some way to the left of the picture.
Frith & Co, courtesy Manx Museum

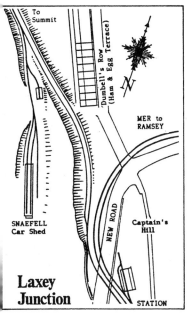

Layout at Laxey after 1898.

Right: The ex-Corkill 1933 Bedford WLB 20-seat coach with convertible bodywork (MN 8874) seen here at Tholt-y-Will in the immediate post-war period. Both of these Bedford coaches were withdrawn in 1953.
Manx Electric Railway

bankruptcy.

The arrangements for passengers in Laxey remained unsatisfactory, with a fairly long walk between the respective termini of the Snaefell Tramway and the Douglas and Laxey line, which since its original opening in 1894 had terminated just beyond the present Car sheds on the coastal tramway. By the spring of 1896 this terminus had been moved to a point some hundred yards or so beyond the Rencell Road underline bridge. By the end of February 1897 some additional land at Dumbell's Row ("Ham & Egg Terrace") had been acquired and the Snaefell line diverted and extended to a new terminal alongside New Road. This site was to remain until the final extension of the line in 1898 when a single line was laid across the road and right into the present Laxey Station.

To provide for passengers' requirements on the Snaefell Tramway, the line boasted a wooden station building at the Summit, with a single storey hotel building, some distance away and connected to the tram terminus by wooden duckboarding. The Summit Hotel was a considerable success and was extended in 1896 at the same time as a new additional hotel was built by the side of the crossing on the Mountain Road, where it superseded a structure known as the "Half-Way Hut" (which was little more than a shelter) and thereafter became known as "The Bungalow" hotel .

The bankruptcy of the Isle of Man Tramways & Electric Power Company in February 1900, and the subsequent inquiries not surprisingly questioned (amongst other things) the role of the Snaefell Association and the sale of this undertaking to the IoMT&EP Co. in particular. The Association had evidently consisted of just over twenty members but had never been registered in accordance with the Companies' Acts requirements, which insisted on the registration of "any company or

association comprising more than twenty members, associated for the purpose of gain or profit. . . . ." And gain there certainly had been, in addition to many other irregularities. In addition, with the exception of one individual, all of the IoMT&EP Directors were also members of the Snaefell Association as well. Since the Articles of Association of the IoMT&EP prohibited any director from voting on any matter in which he had a direct financial interest, it was therefore impossible for the IoMT&EP Board to have constitutionally voted for the purchase of a concern in which they (in person) were the beneficial owners. And not content with a substantial personal profit on the sale of the Snaefell line, it seemed that as soon as settlement had been made, a very large number of the shares then issued were placed on the market. Since in 1896 IoMT&EP Co. Ordinary Shares had been selling for £1 17s 6d and the Preference at £1 10s 0d and since the Snaefell purchase had involved the issue of 20,000 £1 fully paid Ordinary Shares and 20,000 6% preference shares to the vendors, the personal profit accrued by these people amounted to a sum adjacent to £100,000. There was a number of other problems too, since while the payments to the Common Lands Trustees for the right of way up the Mountain was fixed at £290 per annum (plus a royalty on income in excess of a certain amount), it transpired that the conveyance had not been made to the IoMT&EP Co. who had not paid any rent at all during 1899, and in April 1900 a Warrant was issued against the members of the former Snaefell Association.

F.K. Pearson's history of the MER relates that during the winding up of the Snaefell Association in 1896 Mr. Alexander Bruce was given "an Engraved Service of Silver Plate, a Gold Watch bearing his Family Crest, and jewellery for his wife and daughters . . ." In fact the value

Left: Snaefell Mountain Car No 7 "MARIA" dumped alongside the depot in May 1956 with the Tower Wagon and the Hurst Nelson wagon.   *Mike Goodwyn*

Right The first Air Ministry railcar was built by Wickhams in 1951, and carried staff to and from the Radar Station at the Summit if the normal service was not operating. This petrol-engined car is seen at the Depot in 1956.   *Mike Goodwyn*

Below: Snaefell No. 1 seen here near the old Mountain Power Station shortly after steam generation ceased here in 1924.
Ian L. Cormack

of this shareholders' gift was £472, and the items were seized and sold at auction on 30th August 1900 by the Auctioneer Mr. William Thompson, acting on the instructions of Mr. W.H. Walker, trustee of the bankrupt estate of the late Mr. Bruce. The sum of £229 13s 2d was realised.

THE MER TAKES OVER

The prolonged period of uncertainty and strife, sparked off by the collapse of Dumbell's Bank in 1900, ended with the sale of the Douglas–Ramsey and Snaefell electric lines to the new Manx Electric Railway Co. Ltd. on 18th August 1902. Under this concern a start was made on a comprehensive re equipment, for the undertaking had paid dearly for being a pioneer in the science of electric traction. The great and rapid strides in design and manufacture had made much of the original equipment obsolete or outmoded, in some cases almost as soon as it had been delivered. The MER Co. brought in Kincaid, Waller, Manville and Dawson as consultants and their subsequent recommendations were very comprehensive. Although nothing was done to replace the unusual traction motors of the Snaefell cars, with their extended poles and huge single field coils, the control gear was partly replaced and the line generally benefited from the massive improvement in the electrical generation and distribution revisions. During 1904 one of the original Mather & Platt sets was taken out of the Snaefell Power Station and replaced by a spare rotary converter from Ballaglass Power Station on the Ramsey line. This converter was fed from Laxey by means of a 7,000 V a.c. supply. The Snaefell Power Station was thereafter steamed as required.

The question of regenerative braking on the Mountain line was brought up again in 1904 when the practical difficulties of this system were discussed with Sir Philip Dawson. Regenerative braking had been in use experimentally in 1895 but Josua Shaw the line's gifted engineer at the time, (and who was to spend the greater part of his life in charge of that other "MER" – the Mersey Electric Railway), decided that it needed a consistent level of skill on the part of the motormen, and which could not always be guaranteed.

By the early years of the century, the Snaefell Mountain Tramway had settled down to a largely humdrum (if profitable) existence, opening each season just before the Whitsuntide weekend, and running until the latter part of September each year. Catering facilities at the Summit were overwhelmed by demand, and a most elaborate new stone building, complete with castellated towers and battlements was erected alongside the terminus of the line in the space of four months to supersede the original building. The new Summit Hotel was opened on 10th August 1906.

The relative tranquility of normal operations on the Snaefell line was very rudely shattered on 14th September 1905 by a major collision. Shuttle working was in operation on the lower section, owing to a motor car race along the Mountain Road, and the last of a convoy of three cars in the process of running down to Laxey, met a stalled car and failed to stop in time. Several of the passengers were injured and their compensation claims substantially marred the year's financial results particularly since additional expense was also being incurred by embankment improvements at Lhergy Veg and which included the construction of a new retaining wall and buttresses.

The original proposals to build a branch of the line from the Bungalow to Tholt-y-Will in Sulby Glen (where substantial tearooms and a hotel had been built) and which had been first mooted in 1896

and referred to in items of IoMT&EP Co. literature in 1897, were pursued no further and instead, in 1907, the Manx Electric Railway Co. became the Island's first operator of motor char-a-bancs running a service from the bungalow down to Tholt-y-Will. The two original vehicles consisted on a pair of Argus 2 litre petrol-engined chain-driven chassis, registered MN 67 and MN 68. Both vehicles were fitted with 16/18 seat open bodywork but as was the custom and practice of the period, their char-a-banc bodies were interchangeable with a flat-bed lorry body, so that the vehicles also be used as motor lorries during the winter. In spite of the severely-graded route, the vehicles appear to have given great satisfaction, and a third char-a-banc was added to the fleet in April 1914. This, registered MN 475 was a de Dion Bouton, and one contemporary account refers to this machine having left hand drive, although it would appear that the vehicle was actually built as right-hand drive, but there was a seat for a (small) passenger to the right of the driver's seat. This arrangement was not forbidden under construction and use regulations until very much later. The career of this vehicle was very short, since the MER Co. withdrew all of the vehicles in early August, with the outbreak of the First World War. For the same reason, the Snaefell Mountain Railway was closed down on 9th August. By the spring of 1915 all of the char-a-bancs had been sold, although the precise fates are not known.

THE INTER-WAR YEARS

The railway remained closed to all traffic until 10th June 1919, after a mammoth effort had been made to make up the arrears of deferred maintenance through the war years and it seems that the plant and machinery at the Snaefell Power Station had suffered to some extent during the prolonged period of disuse. Moreover, the general increases in costs and wages was substantial and the process of hauling coal halfway up the mountain was increasingly difficult.

However, the line resumed its usual tempo and the motor char-a-banc tours from the Bungalow down to Tholt-y-Will were duly introduced in either May or June 1920, when two grey-painted Caledons arrived to run the service. These were fitted with 27 seat open bodies, and registered MN 1053/4. Their lives on the mountain trek were not long, (although one was later to become a motor lorry for Messrs. Corlett Sons and Cowley Ltd.) and they were both replaced by three bright blue Model 'T' chassis in May or June 1926. These were fitted with 14 seat open char-a-banc bodies and the vehicles became almost legendary on account of their long lives; indeed they carried on the service

Below: The second Air Ministry car for Snaefell was much larger and had a 28 horsepower Ford diesel engine. In 1977 it was bought by the MER Board for works use and is seen here in 1979.
Mike Goodwyn

until the end of 1938 when two second hand Bedford coaches were bought for the season of 1939. In the later 1930s the Bungalow–Tholt-y-Will-Sulby service was also served by a route of the Isle of Man Road Services Ltd..

A mixed-gauge interchange siding was laid at Laxey Station during the winter of 1931–2 in order to ease the difficulties of transferring Snaefell cars from their 3' 6'' gauge for their journey from Laxey to Derby Castle Carworks in Douglas where overhauls and repaints were carried out. The Snaefell cars thenceforth ran onto the siding to be jacked up, the Snaefell trucks run out, 3' 0'' gauge trucks placed underneath, the carbody lowered, and the car towed away for its journey south.

The final surviving sector table at the Snaefell car depot was also replaced with orthodox switches about this time. Whilst normal points were installed at the Bungalow and in Laxey Station, the Summit head-shunt retained its single-tongue switchblade. The very unusual Snaefell Depot connection off the main line at Laxey remained. This was sited on a gradient of 1 in 12, and in order to continue the Fell centre rail through the switch, a design which consisted of four movable sections of track evolved. When set for the depot, the four sections roughly approximated to the curve radius through a series of kinks. At times it was the scene of shunting derailments. As rails expand and contract each day and tend to creep where it is laid on a severe gradient with no clips or anchors, these effects on the Snaefell line were focused at this point and frequent adjustments were needed. At one stage the switch would work only before the heat of the sun locked things solid and for many years it was the practice to empty the depot of all the cars needed for the day or capable of moving, before this happened. To some extent the expansion process was delayed by spraying the point with a hosepipe with water from a nearby mountain stream. The entire installation was superseded in 1984–5 with a standard switch which finally eliminated the recurring problems.

In 1934 the MER Co. reached agreement with the IoM Electricity Board to purchase current, thus bringing to an end generation of power by the Railway itself. The new "all island" supply fed power at 33,000 V 50 Hz a.c. to transformer-rectifiers sets at Ballaglass, Belle Vue and Laxey. The Snaefell Power Station was stripped of its rotary converters and re-equipped with a pair of Hackbridge-Hewittic transformer rectifiers, each with a capacity of 150 kW, and fed from a 6,600 V a.c. supply from the Sub-station at Laxey, using the 1904 a.c. feeder cable.

The only other somewhat later modifications to the power supply were to involve the installation of automatic switchgear by Bertram Thomas (Engineering) Ltd. during 1964, which eliminated the need for substation manning at Snaefell. Since then the mountain sub-station is switched in by the staff of the first car up in the morning, and shut down by the last car in the evening.

In 1939 the MER Co. withdrew the Ford char-a-bancs dating from 1926 and replaced them on the Bungalow–Tholt-y-Will service with two Bedford WTB-type 20-seat coaches one of which was acquired from G.C. Gale ("Gale's Western Motors") of Peel in May, whilst the other was purchased from Mr. R.H. Corkill of Onchan in June. Both vehicles were then only six years old. The ancient Fords were stored until April 1942. when they were scrapped. The MER Co.'s motor coach services were suspended on the outbreak of the Second World War, together with the Snaefell line itself, which closed to all traffic on 20th September 1939. Whilst the line did not officially re-open to passenger traffic until 2nd June 1946, the line did see some limited wartime traffic when the extensive peat bogs to the south and west of the Bungalow were extensively developed to assist in relieving the fuel shortages: the resulting traffic was carried mainly by Car No. 7 ("MARIA").

POST-WAR DECLINE

Immediate post-war traffic on the Snaefell Mountain line reached high levels as the Island enjoyed the Indian summer of Manx tourism. In line with the rise in prices, the return fare from Douglas to the Summit of Snaefell had also risen to 5s 0d. The Island's post-war boom promptly collapsed in 1950, but the Mountain line was kept very busy, even during the winter for the Air Ministry had decided to build a major radar station close to the summit of the Mountain, and for this project the railway was used to carry all of the men and building materials, as well as supplies and personnel once the radar station was commissioned. However, the relatively high winds and intense cold encountered on the upper reaches of the Mountain during the winter had hitherto demanded that all of the overhead wire beyond the Bungalow be taken down each autumn and tied to the track. Whilst the MER Co. required an indemnity against damage to the overhead line through trying to operate through the winter for the Ministry, they had no objection to the Air Ministry providing and running its own self-propelled rolling stock along the line in return for a modest charge. Accordingly in 1951 the Air Ministry had a Wickham railcar delivered, which was housed in a little depot building of its own at the north west end of the Snaefell depot yard at Laxey and connected by a siding. As delivered this 2½ ton railcar had Fell rail calliper brake gear as well as normal wheel brake equipment, and was propelled by a Ford V8 engine. In 1954–5 the railcar was also fitted with Fell rail guide wheels principally to alleviate the car's tendency to tip over under high crosswind conditions. A second Wickham railcar was delivered in 1957 and was fitted with a Ford 28 hp diesel engine and fully equipped with Fell gear. In order to demonstrate the Fell gear to Wickham's design staff, the late Mr. Alan McMullen, for many years the engineer in charge at the Snaefell sheds, made a scale model of a Snaefell car-truck in brass, featuring fully working wheel and rail brake equipment. Mr. McMullen was one of the Island's best known model engineers and built a large number of ¾'' and 1'' scale steam locos at his "Laxey Loco Works" on Ramsey Road, Laxey. Shortly after the commissioning of the second railcar, Wickham's submitted a letter of apprecia-

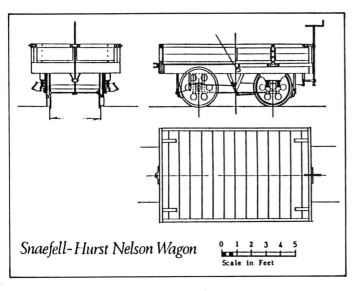

Snaefell-Hurst Nelson Wagon

0 1 2 3 4 5
Scale In Feet

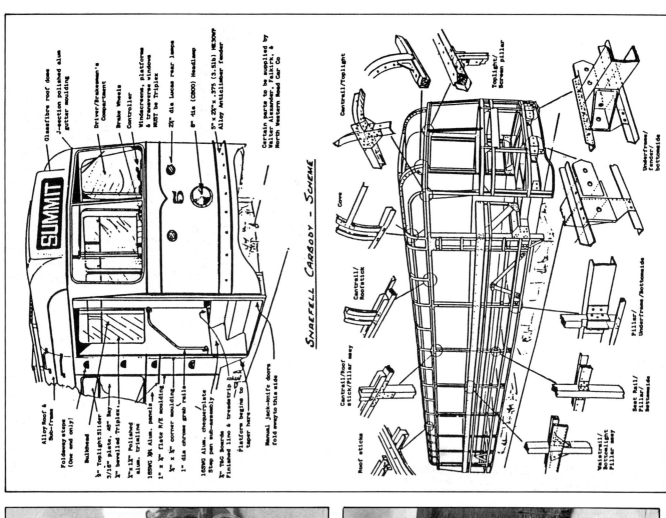

SNAEFELL CARBODY - SCHEME

Glassfibre roof dome
J-section polished alum gutter moulding
Driver/Brakeman's Compartment
Brake Wheels
Controller
Windscreen, platform & transverse windows MUST be Triplex
2½" dia Lucas rear lamps
8" dia (CIBIE) Headlamp
5" x 2⅝"x .375 (3.5lb) Hi30WP Alloy Anticlimber fender
Certain parts to be supplied by Walter Alexander, Falkirk, & North Western Road Car Co

Alloy Roof & Sub-frame
Foldaway steps (One end only)
Bulkhead
3" Toplight Slider
3/16" plate, 45° Bay
¼" bevelled Triplex.
2"x 1⅛" Polished alum. trialine
18SWG 3A Alum. panels
1" x ¾" flate R/I moulding
¾" x ¼" corner moulding
1" dia chrome grab rails
16SWG Alum. chequerplate Step pan sub-assembly
¼" T&G Boards Finished lino & treadstrip
Platform begins to taper here
Manual jack-knife doors fold away to this side

Cantrail/Toplight
Toplight/ Screen pillar
Underframe/ fender/ bottomside
Cove
Cantrail/ Roofstick
Pillar/ Underframe /Bottomside
Cantrail/Roof stick/Pillar assy
Seat Rail/ Pillar/ bottomside
Cantrail/Roof stick/Pillar assy
Waistrail/ Bottomlight Pillar assy
Roof sticks

Bungalow Hotel, Snaefell Mountain, I-O-M.

107

Bungalow Station and Hotel. Snaefell Mountain Railway

Two views of the Bungalow Hotel showing (top) the building and an Argus char-a-banc about 1907 – 8; (lower) the building about 1938.
Unfulfilled proposal for a home-built replacement for Snaefell No 5 in 1971. *Mike Goodwyn*
Collection: Ian L. Cormack

Above: The Snaefell Mountain Power Station in 1895.   *Mather & Platt, Courtesy Manx Museum Archives*

tion for the assistance that had been provided by the model.

The MER Company's motor coach service from the Bungalow had been reinstated in 1946 and enjoyed a good level of patronage until 1949. Traffic markedly declined in 1950, however, after which it continued to dwindle. The coaches were withdrawn altogether in 1953 and one of the Bedfords (MN 8874) was then converted into an MER lorry. The other coach was scrapped shortly after its withdrawal.

The downturn in the tourist trade was now being felt throughout the Island, and the stormclouds of trouble began to gather over the Manx Electric Railway Company. Despite an era of financial stringency the disruption caused to the Snaefell line by the closure of the Bungalow level crossing for road races, was at last eased by the insertion of a new crossover on the line just downhill from the level crossing. This made it possible to operate normally instead of running a single-line shuttle service. It was a long-overdue improvement.

At the end of the 1955 season, the MER Co. notified the Isle of Man Government that it would be unable to carry on after the end of the following season owing to its overwhelming financial predicament. As a result, agreement was eventually reached for the nationalisation of the Railway and which became effective on 1st June 1957.

The newly constituted Manx Electric Railway Board of Tynwald soon sought to improve their prospects, and under the chairmanship of the late Sir Ralph Stevenson a former British Ambassador to Egypt at the time up to the Suez Crisis, sought to reinstate the motor coach service from the Bungalow to Tholt-y-Will. Two ancient pre-war Leyland Cubs were purchased from Douglas Corporation Transport Department. These two KPZ1 buses, with 20 seat bodies by Park Royal (CMN 709 and DMN 585) of 1938 and 1939 respectively, were numbered "1" and "2" by the MER Board, and entered service on the old route. Few passengers took advantage of the facility. The following year the coach service was extended from Tholt-y-Will to the Isle of Man (steam) Railway station at Sulby Glen, where participants might catch a train on to Ramsey and then return to Douglas along the Manx Electric. This too was a facility that was not noticeably used by anybody, and it ceased at the end of the season when it was obvious to even the MER Board (by this time headed by another chairman, the late H.H. Radcliffe) that the coach service was an economic disaster. In addition to the lack of customers, the two vehicles were allegedly so often withdrawn for repairs, it was never very clear just when the tours

would be operating. In fact the buses appeared in public only once more, operating a shuttle service from Ramsey Plaza and the Royal Manx Agricultural Show ground on Lezayre Road on 7th August 1959. The gruesome twosome were then withdrawn.

Whilst the Summit Hotel was redecorated in 1958, the Bungalow, always a popular venue, was closed down and demolished by the MER Board early in the same year. In an attempt to project its vibrant image, it was also decided to adopt a new and lurid paint-scheme of green and white, and this was applied to Nos. 2 and 4 of the Snaefell fleet. In fact No. 4 proved to be the last car on the system to receive this unpleasant livery, in September 1963, and thereafter the cars were repainted and restored to their traditional colours.

INCREDIBLE DECISIONS

From the mid-1960s the overall condition of the Snaefell Mountain rolling stock and permanent way were showing increasingly serious signs of age, unreliability and corrosion. The Fell centre-rail was particularly affected and it seemed to be only a matter of time before it became unsafe. Rather than looking at the obvious technical alternatives available, the Board took a decision to relay the centre-rail. This was said to be "good news" by "MODERN TRAMWAY" at the time, but was technically indefensible. Sir Henry Sugden, the then chairman of the MER Board, sought and obtained Tynwald's approval for the supply and fitting of a new Fell rail. Since no steel rolling mill had produced rail of this sort for well over sixty years, the MER Board also had to pay to have rolls made, at considerable cost, so that the Fell pattern could be produced. The Workington steel mills would not run off a quantity of less than their standard minimum batch, but they were prepared to allow the MER Board to draw off from an agreed stock, and pay for each batch as it was delivered.

The first new Fell rail was produced at Workington at the end of 1967 and arrived at Ramsey aboard *BEN VARREY*. The stock was then piled up on the spare ground at the corner of Queen's Pier Road and Walpole Avenue Ramsey, whence it was taken down to Laxey as required. Relaying commenced on the worst affected lengths of track from the Summit to the Bungalow late in 1968. To bend the rail as it was laid, the Derby Castle Carworks produced a rail-bending jig or "jim-crow" from a surplus Brush type "D" truck side frame. This unbelievably heavy tool was, in the event, to be little used as it was

Left: Snaefell No 4 at Laxey Station in July 1962 in its somewhat repulsive (but short-lived) green and white livery.
Mike Goodwyn

Below: Snaefell No 1 climbing just east of the lower crossover near the Bungalow in the hazy heat of September 1957.
F. Deane

quickly found that despite its double-head the rail would bend quite easily as it was laid, drilled for chairs, and bolted down. A large number of new chairs was also needed, and produced by means of the antique hydraulic press in Derby Castle Carworks machine shop. The work on Snaefell Mountain was necessarily carried out when the line was closed for traffic in the winters, but the extreme and appalling weather conditions experienced on the Mountain's upper reaches, meant that work proceeded slowly. Nevertheless, by 1975, slightly over three-quarters of the downside road had been relayed.

Whilst this permanent way work was in progress, the condition of the line's rolling stock ought to have been giving cause for equal concern. Whilst the 1895 car bodies were in remarkably good condition, mainly through their limited seasonal use, good maintenance and the absence of harsh traction or braking demands, the electrical gear was only kept going by an enormous effort on a superhuman scale and at substantial costs in repairs and lost mileage. A number of possible solutions to these ongoing and increasingly serious problems were mooted over a lengthy period, and most of these were summarised in "Is This Any Way to Run A Railway?" published in 1976 by the Manx Electric Railway Society:

1958: Snaefell cars giving rise for concern and offer of five ex-Lille ERLT 200 class cars in perfect order at £5,700 each – *Rejected*.
1959: Snaefell situation getting worse: An offer of ideal Metrovick MV109 traction motors (new price £3,200 each) at £30 each plus spares – *Rejected*.
1961: Situation becoming desperate: New offer of modern control equipment and contractor switchgear – *Rejected*.
1965: Situation getting hopeless: Fell Rail relaying programme advocated by the MER Board and authorised by Tynwald.
1970: Situation frantic: Offer of modern trucks, motors and equipments from Valencia at bargain price lost because of procrastination. Ex-Toronto and ex-Brussels equipment offers – *Rejected*.
1971: Situation extremely serious: Offer of ex-Blackpool Maley & Taunton trucks and motors at £100 per car; complete package offered but eventually only one car set of trucks was purchased and conversion work bungled.
1973: Situation catastrophic: Offer of ex-Nagoya equipments – *Rejected*.
1975: Situation utterly beyond belief: MER Board calls in London Transport (!) as Consultants.

In considering the proposals of the Rapid Transit Technical Services Co. Ltd., it was noted by the government that this firm was opposed to the Fell Rail relay and had a comprehensive series of schemes to eliminate its need as soon as possible. As the same government had failed to respond to the other propositions of the RTTS Co. it was rather difficult to acquire the means or technical "know-how" to implement such a scheme. At the same time, members of the MER Board

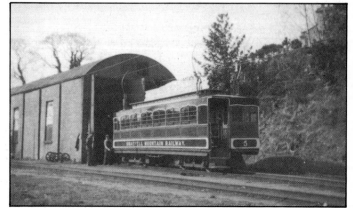

Above: Early morning sunlight on Snaefell No 5 outside the depot in 1956. This car was destroyed by an electrical fire at the Summit on August 16, 1970.
Mike Goodwyn

Left Snaefell No 6 at the entrance to the Depot yard at Laxey in July 1957.
G.C.J. Morris

Above: A side view of the original 1895 Milnes plate-frame truck for the Snaefell Mountain Railway.
Manx Electric Railway

Right: Fell Brake end of an original Snaefell car truck in 1895. Note the grooved rail on which the truck is standing. *Mather & Platt; Manx Museum Archives*

Below: The other end of one of the original Snaefell trucks showing the horizontal Fell-rail wheels in the foreground attached to the headstock and the massive single field coil. *Manx Electric Railway*

		Motor Failures	Miles per failure	Failures per 100,000 miles
1971-2	S.M.R.	25	696	146.6
1972-3	S.M.R.	32	543	183.9
1972	LT	86	2,560,000	0.039
1972	LT[2]	28	632,000	0.158
1972	LT[3]	0		-

2 LT—Worst Line, oldest stock
3 LT—Best line, newest stock

were trying to insist that the condition of their empire was nowhere near as dismal as the RTTS Co. inferred.

On the morning of 16th August 1970, Car No. 5 set off for its first trip of the day up to Snaefell Summit. Weather conditions were atrocious and the Island was being lashed by storm-force winds. The tramcar reached the Summit and unloaded, whilst the crew sought shelter inside the building until it was time to return. Somebody then noticed that the car had burst into flames and, aided by a Force 8 gale, made short work of the car's destruction. With good fortune, not a soul was hurt. The origin of the fire was a high-tension cable that had repeatedly rubbed on the underframe until the insulation was worn through and when the power shorted across to earth. A somewhat over-simplistic account of the episode was printed in the September 1979 edition of "MODERN TRAMWAY". In fact several significant details differed from the facts of the fire:

It had not been the practice to rewire the Snaefell cars at the normal intervals of around 28–30 years, and indeed some of the insulation consisted of vintage double cotton-covered material. As nobody in living memory had rewired a car, it was not known that the bus-line between the two current collectors on the roof did *not* travel along the roof, but was routed down each bulkhead, and included in the bundle that ran along the underframe. This in turn meant that as long as a bow collector was in contact with the overhead wire, there were live cables in the bundle, inside the car, irrespective of the position of the circuit breakers and switchgear.

By virtue of their design and construction, the Hopkinson Patent bow collectors could only be removed from contact with the overhead wire by a fitter armed with spanners or a man with an axe. A further discovery was that whilst the Douglas and Ramsey cars had been fitted with lightning arresters and choke coils (for protection) the mountain cars were not so fitted. The "MODERN TRAMWAY" correspondent, Mr. J.H. Price opined that the "fraying of the cables was thought to have been caused by the tram car rocking sideways in high winds" and which resulted in the immediate removal of the large advertisement boards previously mounted on top of the clerestory. However local opinion was much more inclined to consider the known history of this particular tramcar, especially when it was found that none of the others was suffering from frayed insulation to the same extent. For very many years Car No. 5 transferred both her trucks and equipment over to freight car No. 7 'MARIA' each winter and it thus was held to follow that No. 5's cables had been interfered with to a far greater extent than any of the others. The cables might very well not have been as tightly rigged as the others, simply to enable rapid de trucking whenever it was necessary to fish out the trucks for use under Car No. 7.

The remains of Car 5 consisted merely of the trucks, the underframe and part of one cab, together with an assortment of heat-treated metalwork. Although the MER Board was promptly supplied with both a drawing and specification for a suitable modern carbody, it was decided to have a replica of the 1895 body manufactured, in the event by H.D. Kinnin of Ramsey. This car lacked the clerestory and bulkhead panelwork of the original, but featured a set of modern aluminium-framed windows in the saloon. The car re-entered service on 8th July 1971.

Whilst the RTTS proposals of 1971 had specifically outlined a scheme to provide five (and not six) suitably equipped cars for Snaefell, involving modern trucks and motors and control gear fitted with fail safe provision for one man operation, and with rheostatic electric braking in place of the Fell rail, along with "the removal of this rail . . . ." the problem that now confronted the government and the Board was how to do it.

THE TRANSMARK REPORT

To help them, the Government had some what unwisely turned to a British Railways subsidiary, Transmark, for advice. Their infamous "Transmark Report" on the MER of 1973 had depended in turn for technical advice on Mr. G.H. Hafter, Divisional Engineer (Railways) of London Transport. It was Mr. Hafter who, after discounting the RTTS proposals had then preceded to recommend "his own proposals" which by some inexplicable coincidence proved to be almost identical to those of RTTS, item by item, even down to the use of the peculiar RTTS nomenclature – "An unparalleled plagiarism which appears to be relieved only by carelessness, ignorance or sheer stupidity . . . . ." For example, RTTS planned to use the Ohio Brass Co. carbon slipper trolley head on the coastal line, but Mr. Hafter recommended the use of "swivelling carbon slipper trolleyheads" – a technical difference that

MANX ELECTRIC RAILWAY
SNAEFELL MOUNTAIN SECTION - ROLLING STOCK

NO	BUILT	BUILDER	SEATS	TRUCKS	MOTORS
1	1895	G.F.Milnes	48	Milnes Special	Kiepe 4 x 50kW
2	1895	G.F.Milnes	48	Milnes Special	Kiepe 4 x 50kW
3	1895	G.F.Milnes	48	Milnes Special	Kiepe 4 x 50kW
4	1895	G.F.Milnes	48	Milnes Special	Kiepe 4 x 50kW
5	1971	H.D.Kinnin	48	Milnes Special	Kiepe 4 x 50kW
6	1895	G.F.Milnes	48	Milnes Special	Kiepe 4 x 50kW
7	1896	Underframe by			
Wagon	1895	Milnes; 6-ton Freight car			
Tower		Hurst Nelson 4-ton open wagon			
Wagon	1895	?	-		
Railcar 1	1951	Wickham	-		Orig. Ford V8 Petrol
Railcar 2	1957	Wickham	-		Ford 28hp diesel engine

MOTOR COACH FLEET

REG NO	BUILT	ACQD	CHASSIS	BODY	TYPE	WITHDRAWN
MN 67	1907	1907	Argus	?	Ch.16	-/14
MN 68	1907	1907	Argus	?	Ch.16	-/14
MN 475	1914	1914	De Dion Bouton	?	Ch.18	-/14
MN 1953	1920	1920	Caledon	?	Ch.27	6/26
MN 1054	1920	1920	Caledon	?	Ch.27	6/26 See Note A
MN 4416	1926	1926	Ford 'T'	?	Ch.14	9/39 Scrp 4/42
MN 4417	1926	1926	Ford 'T'	?	Ch.14	9/39 Scrp 4/42
MN 4418	1926	1926	Ford 'T'	?	Ch.14	9/39 Scrp 4/42
MN 8685	1933	1939	Bedford WLB	?	C20F	5/53
MN 8874	1933	1939	Bedford WLB	Duple	C20F	To motor lorry 6/53[2]
CMN 709	1938	1957	Leyland KPZ1 Cub	P.Royal	B20F	5/60
DMN 585	1939	1957	Leyland KPZ1 Cub	P.Royal	B20F	5/60

NOTE: A: Sold to Corlett Sons & Cowley as lorry.
2 — Withdrawn 6/57 and scrapped 6/62

Above: Car No 1 pushing the Hurst Nelson 4-wheel wagon (with water tank) to the Summit in 1979. The Hotel was destroyed by fire on the night of August 5/6 1982. *W.P. Cubbon*

Right: Vorsprung durch technik-Aachen No 1010 being unloaded from the LUNE FISHER at Douglas in 1976. The tramcar was used as a Mess-hut until broken up in 1985. *Mike Goodwyn*

Left Car No 6 in present condition on the west Snaefell Siding at Laxey in 1979, waiting for passengers from Douglas off MER Car 22. *W.P. Cubbon*

Left: Arrival of the first replica 1895 trucks from London Transport at Laxey in 1977. *Mike Goodwyn*

Ramsey section of the Manx Electric Railway, did so on 30th September 1975, against a chorus of condemnation and bitter criticism. The decision was ultimately to bring to an end the political careers if those who had served the interests of the Railway so very poorly. Nevertheless, no doubt eager to be seen in the aftermath of this closure to be doing something positive, the board retained London Transport (Railways) as their Consultants in October 1975 to advise and to implement a Snaefell Mountain Railway equipment scheme. It was scarcely a very propitious choice.

RE-EQUIPMENT

London Transport studied the problems of Snaefell in some detail, and suggested that new traction motors would be needed not only to propel the cars, but also to enable them to use dynamic braking. The existing 1895 equipment was considered to be "unsatisfactory for modernisation" and it was (rightly) claimed that "newly designed equipments for such a number would be too expensive." Nobody in their right minds would have suggested otherwise. In order to meet Snaefell's requirements, LT now proposed to do what everybody else had been proposing for years, namely to locate and procure suitable second-hand equipment. The LT experts considered that the likely cost of the programme would be somewhere "about £150,000" although quite what the Snaefell line would finish up with was by no means clear. To justify the outlay, LT was asked to quantify the savings that were to be expected. LT responded by citing the following "immediately realisable savings" as follows:

TRACTION MOTOR REPAIRS: Rewound armatures and field coils for the Mather & Platt motors of 1895 were said to be costing £600 per motor, but with modern traction motors, these costs would be totally eliminated.

would have meant rehanging most of the 34 miles of overhead wire to no advantage whatsoever. Similarly Mr. Hafter was the Transmark expert who noticed that "some (traction) poles suffer from a lack of verticality...." So they did but a closer inspection may have revealed a more important lack of metal as well. In the Transmark Report, Mr. Hafter produced a table showing a comparison of traction motor failures on Snaefell and on London transport's rolling stock (see table).

Quite what on earth this compilation was supposed to prove is not entirely clear, for there could hardly be any valid comparison between 1895 technology climbing a mountain in the middle of the Irish Sea and the LT environment and equipment. It was Hafter's impression that the Fell brake shoes had to be changed after every three trips during heavy traffic, at the Summit. He also believed that the Fell rail "had a function of keeping the vehicles on the track...."

The MER Board having decided to implement another of Transmark's recommendations to close down the entire Laxey and

"Which one goes first?"

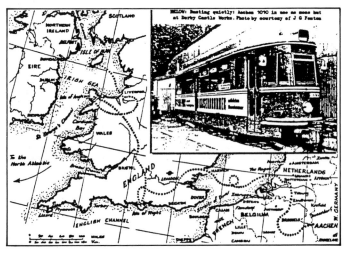

THE INCREDIBLE JOURNEY Cruel contemporary cartoons from "The UnOfficial Guide to IoM Railways" (1979)

AVAILABILITY: The 1895 motors were said to fail so often that it was rare for all the cars to be available for traffic "and resulted in passengers being turned away with consequent loss of earnings...." Such a scenario might well have been true on at most four days during 1975; three days in 1974 and perhaps two days in 1973. As it happened, it was exceedingly rare for all six cars to be simultaneously needed for traffic except perhaps when the line was coping with a series of special parties.

RUNNING TIME: Increased speeds and the use of modern motors would obviously reduce the overall journey time in fact the saving was quoted at "about one-sixth," and LT tried to make out that this "would allow extra trips to be run on busy days...with consequent extra earnings." This represented an unrealistic assessment of the potential. On the other hand it might have been an attempt to refute the contention of RTTS that all of the line's traffic could be carried in a total of five cars that actually worked all the time, with a spare or "float" set of cartrucks to be used for the instant replacement of any defective unit. LT's hypothesis was fundamentally flawed in these respects.

POWER CONSUMPTION: Modern motors were expected to reduce current consumption by "about 30% and might produce savings of £700 per year in power costs". Certainly major savings were theoretically possible, if applied to the motors alone but nobody had evidently noticed that track bonding for the return current was noticeably deficient on the Snaefell line (and others), and indeed, above the Bungalow was virtually absent altogether.

MAINTENANCE: Daily maintenance and the repair of defects were reasonably expected to be reduced "to the point where the labour cost would be substantially reduced" and while this was true in part, very few of the Snaefell staff would then be occupied full-time on Snaefell maintenance, and there was no other use to which they could be put.

Perhaps without looking too closely, the chairman, Mr. John Clucas MHK, and other members of the MER Board agreed to buy the LT proposals; the speed of resolution evidently surprised even London Transport, and Tynwald approval for the expenditure was readily forthcoming with remarkably little debate or discussion.

During this time, an increasingly fraught pursuit had been in progress by LT and its followers in search of some suitable second hand equipment. The quest was by no means as easy as they thought at first; how far the search extended is not known, but some pre-eminently suitable equipments were most certainly overlooked. By May 1976 LT had only managed to find a batch of surplus cars with fairly inappropriate equipments at Aachen in West Germany.

Owned by the ASEAG (Aachener Strassenbahn Elektrische AG), these metre-gauge Grossraumwagen-type cars were available at a price of DM 10,000 (about £2,000) per car on a batch of eleven. Built in 1956–7, by Waggonfabrik Talbot of Aachen, these modern all-metal tramcars were numbered 1001–11 in the fleet, and were fitted with traction motors and control equipment by Elektrotechnischer Fabrik Theodor Kiepe, and had compound-wound, regenerative 300 V motors driving equal-wheel pivotless bogie trucks via Secheron quill drive units. When introduced in 1956–7 the cars' motors were quoted as having a rating of 50 kW, but something serious must have evaporated later, for LT quoted a reduced rating of 46 kW or about 61 h.p. for the same units. The cars were fitted with Knorr air wheel and electro-magnetic track brakes. The Kiepe control gear used a master circuit at 24 V to operate sets of remote electro-pneumatic contactors, and fed from an air compressor, a motor-generator and banks of batteries.

The Master controllers featured no less than 21 power notches, with Nos. 1–9 being Series resistance steps, No. 10 as the full series running notch, and No. 11 as a full Series weak field shunt point. Notches Nos. 12–19 were parallel resistance points with No. 20 as the full parallel motoring point, whilst the last notch, No. 21, was a high speed full parallel weak field point. The complicated multiple electric braking system was controlled by 12 additional notches.

All in all, these fine 43' 0" long double ended cars represented a complicated and intricate design, which not surprisingly had been taken out of use sometime prior to the closure of the Aachen tramways in favour of less complex cars. Their unusual complexity rendered them unlikely candidates for resale and further use. By now, the Aachen cars were being offered at close to scrap price in order to clear the depot.

In June 1976 Mr. John Clucas and Mr. H. Gilmore, respectively Chairman and General Manager of the MER Board, travelled over to Aachen with two London Transport Engineers to view the cars on offer. The ASEAG wished to sell the whole batch as one lot, but finally agreed to sell the seven cars needed by LT for the Snaefell programme. The unsold remaining cars were destined for museums, although one was broken up for spare parts. LT's original scheme was to ship only the trucks, equipment and other bits and pieces required, and then leave the stripped carbodies in Aachen to local scrapmen. However the ASEAG needed to clear the depot immediately and killed the idea by quoting an outrageous price for the facilities required, and by refusing to negotiate further. As a result LT was obliged to ship the cars out and over to Lots Road Power Station in London, where by 12th November 1976 Cars Nos. 1003/4/5/9 and 1011 arrived for stripping and scrapping whilst Aachen 1010 made a lonesome journey all the way from Germany to Douglas, arriving on the *LUNE FISHER* on 12th November. The arrival of this sleek and graceful car at the MER's Derby Castle Carworks was destined to remain a major mystery for some time until it was discovered that LT's original intention had been to send all of the remaining Aachen spares loaded in one of the tramcars, direct to the Isle of Man. Only when Aachen 1010 got to Douglas and was found to be almost empty, that it was realised that the wrong tramcar had been sent, and the one loaded with the spares was now lying at Lots Road Power Station in London. At a later date, the MER Board was obliged to dispatch staff to retrieve the parts. All of the carbodies at Lots Road were stripped and scrapped. Car No. 1010 in Douglas was used for some time as a mess-hut in the Carworks Yard, but was scrapped in 1985 after a period of grotesque dereliction. By this time sufficient had been leaked or uncovered about the barely credible antics involved in LT's Snaefell re-equipment plan and with 16 tons of evidence now lying in Douglas as indisputable evidence, London Transport and its experts locally became the butt of cruel jokes and nasty cartoons.

Meanwhile, the trucks of Snaefell Car No. 1 had been shipped to London Transport's Acton Works, where it was rapidly found that the original proposition of fitting the ex-Aachen motors into the original trucks was completely impractical, as a result of the unusual mountings and Secheron drive arrangements involved. Unfortunately, this confirmed the increasingly vociferous and scathing criticisms of the local MER Society which had been somewhat less than enthusiastic about the MER Board's choice of consultants and were still less impressed when a weird and unbelievable contingency plan was uncovered,

Snaefell Railway

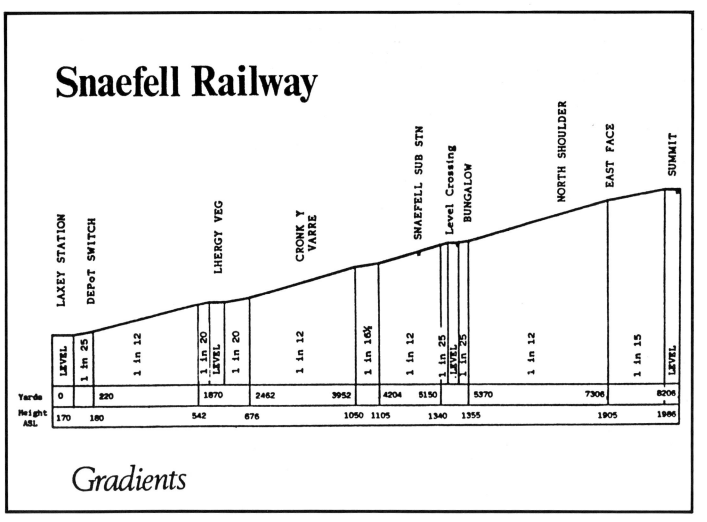

Gradients

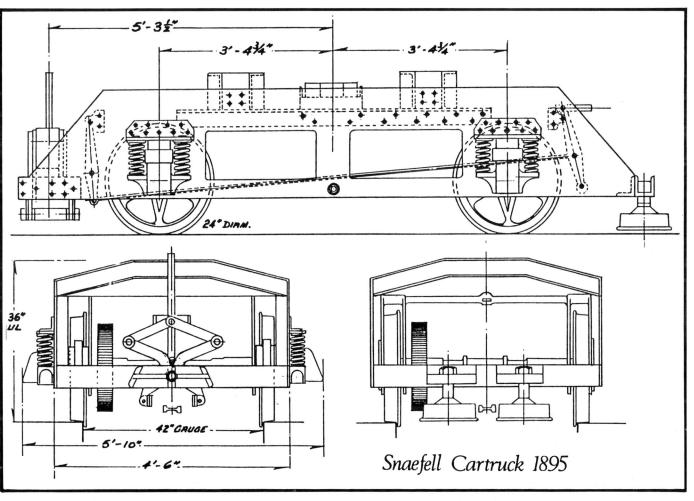

Snaefell Cartruck 1895

Outline of the original 1895 Snaefell equal-wheel bogie trucks built by G.F. Milnes & Co, Birkenhead.

Left: A fine view of Snaefell No 2 running downhill to the bungalow from the Summit in July 1987. The white tape on the pole denotes optimum controller settings for rheostatic braking.
Alex Townsend, IoM Dept of Tourism

whereby if everything else was found to be impossible, LT would then advocate a regauging of the tracks of the entire Snaefell line from 3' 6" down to metre gauge (3'3⅜"), which would thus enable the Aachen car trucks to be utilised virtually as they were bought. Things were not helped by the publication of a letter from a former German soldier, who had served on the Eastern Front during World War II and who had extensive experience in the rebuilding of the wide-gauge Russian railway tracks to the European standard gauge of 4' 8½" and who now thought that the LT contingency plan lay "well within the scope of one Panzer Pioneer Corps with quite small loss of life and equipment...." This alternative scheme was not heard of again.

London Transport's "consultancy" service was reorganised and formalised under the new name of 'London Transport International Services Ltd.' about this time, and this organisation took over the Snaefell project, although no changes in personnel seem to have been involved. London Transport's further study of the Snaefell brake problem had "conclusively concluded" that rheostatic electric brakes "would be feasible." So they should have been, baring in mind that this was now a science that had been established for at least three-quarters of a century. Mr. Josua Shaw, the IoMT&EP Co. Engineer had had a Snaefell car successfully working on re-generative electric brakes in 1895.

London Transport International Services Ltd. now claimed (as everyone else had done previously) that the use of electric braking would reduce (if not eliminate) the costs of the Fell rail braking system:

> "The Fell brake shoes are likely to last six times as long; the pads would not need changing on an average of about every five trips," (note how this figure had inexplicably risen from Mr. Hafter's "three trips") and no longer would a car need to be taken out of service for 20 minutes when the shoes needed relining...
> Although the Fell gear is to be retained as a final brake, (the rail's) renewal will no longer be regarded as urgent."

Quite what reasoning, if any, lay behind the decision to retain and rely on the old Fell gear is unclear. It was contended by one LT friend that it was somehow desirable to demonstrate that the Fell rail was not needed and not used and could therefore be removed later. This is a scenario that ought not to be discounted on the basis of sheer absurdity alone. Others claimed that the inferred retention of the Fell rail ("its renewal will no longer be urgent...") was an attempt by LT to disparage the work of RTTS who had first identified an alternative technology to supersede it altogether. It is important at this stage to appreciate the differences between normal rheostatic braking, where the car's traction motors are used as dynamos and feed their current against the car's rheostats or resistances where it is burned off as heat, and the variant known as regenerative braking as used in Aachen and for which the German motors were specially wound. Regenerative braking also involves using the car's motors as dynamos, but feeding the generated current back into the overhead line, where it can be used by other (climbing) cars on the same circuit. Such an arrangement, however, needs a series of sub-station safeguards, not least to counter the problems caused by the first car out in the morning and the last car in at night, and which will otherwise have nothing to feed their current against. There are often severe operational difficulties involved with pure regenerative braking and for a variety of technical reasons the system was never widely adopted in general tramway practice.

LT's Acton Works, having now given up all hope of ever getting the Aachen motors into the original Snaefell trucks also discovered (providentially) that when the old truck frames were cleaned right down to bare metal "there were signs of incipient cracking...." which might reasonably have been expected in any truck of this age or construction, but which ought not to have given much trouble. It was never clearly stated just where these cracks were, but LT admitted that "...they could probably have been repaired and the transmission altered but this would have cost more than designing and manufacturing entirely new trucks around the ex-Aachen components...." which by now evidently included everything except the Fell gear from the old trucks. Fortunately LT was very skilled in the design and manufacture of plate-framed trucks of the Victorian era, as any who are familiar with LT's own Underground ironmongery will be painfully aware, and Acton Works proceeded to produce a set of trucks for Snaefell that would have done credit to the technology of about 1900.

Happy in the knowledge that Mr. Hafter had believed that the Fell rail "also had a function of keeping the cars on the track" it was also most unwisely decided to re-use the Aachen wheels, which had the very much narrower tread and profile for street tramway work, as opposed to the generous quasi-railway profile of the Snaefell originals. By this time the MER Board had the services of a "consultant," Mr. W. Jackson, (later the Board's "chief executive") and who visited Acton Works more than once to view the work in progress. It would evidently have been of greater value to have had the work assessed by someone with a working knowledge of the subject.

The first brand new set of replica 1895 trucks designed around the Aachen components was built by Acton Works and sent over to Laxey just before Easter 1977. For some inexplicable reason they incorporated the original plain-bearing axleboxes, but subsequent trucks were delivered with roller bearings, and the original set (for Snaefell No. 1) were retroactively fitted.

Whilst the car trucks were being built at Acton, the body of Car No. 1 was stripped at Derby Castle Carworks prior to the installation of the ex-Aachen control gear and other equipment. The cars were not to be fitted with compressed air brakes, but the electro-pneumatic contractor control gear needed compressed air to work it, as well as a low-voltage supply. Instead of replacing the electro-pneumatic contactors with electro-magnetic ones (which did not need either a low-voltage supply or compressed air) LT used the ex-Aachen motor air compressor sets, automatic governors, switch gear, reservoirs and piping systems and so on, and added them to the Snaefell car and representing a completely unnecessary additional energy source aboard the car. The control gear also needed a 24 V d.c. supply, and rather than feeding the batteries via a resistor inserted in series with the compressor circuit, it was decided to fit the ex-Aachen motor-generator sets as well and which were accommodated under one of the seats. The batteries were likewise fitted in racks under the bulkhead seats. The electro-pneumatic contractor cabinet was mounted transversely in the motorman's compartment at the Laxey end. The Aachen resistors were also fitted onto the roof of the car, which was shielded by sheet metal and asbestos. Not surprisingly perhaps the carbody began to creak under the sheer weight of the equipment, much of which was quite superfluous. In the 'MODERN TRAMWAY' article Mr. J.H. Price opined that the ex-Aachen equipment "was rather more sophisticated than the Snaefell line required", whilst others insisted that it was more akin to opening an oyster with a nuclear explosion. As it was, there was nothing to have prevented an appropriate simplification of suitable componentry .

With all of the equipment fitted, circuit layout and cable-run diagrams were evidently prepared from the ad-hoc work carried out inside, underneath and on top of Car No. 1, which began to run a series of trials in May 1977, and which finally entered service the following month. By virtue of the various limitations now involved, the ex-Aachen control gear now utilised only the first eleven power notch positions on the controllers. Of these, Nos.1–9 were series resistance points – No. 10 was the full series motoring position and No. 11 was a full series weak field notch. It is clear that it was intended to restrict the cars to series-only notches on account of the limitations imposed by the power supply and partly by the massive over-capacity of the Aachen traction motors for the duty now required. As it was, the Laxey sub-station (which also feeds a good deal of the Douglas–Ramsey coastal section) has no more than two 200 kW output rectifiers and the Snaefell sub-station has two smaller sets rated at 150 kW. The testing programme for Snaefell No. 1, (usually run after the normal service had ceased and power was good) certainly included some uphill runs with the motors in parallel, providing climbing speed said to be "about 25 m.p.h." but which was timed on one occasion by an MER Society member at close to 38 m.p.h., partly because the wet and rainy evening provided low tractive resistance and an excellent return to the power. Line supply conditions on the mountain are not however consistent, and it was found useful to permit the use of parallel controller notches on the section above the Bungalow because of the voltage drop and the lack of track bonding.

The other Snaefell cars underwent similar treatment and were equipped with new replica trucks and motors, control gear, air compressors, motor-generators and racks of batteries, with Nos. 2–3 being done in 1977–8, and Nos. 4–6 in 1978–9 and having to use a mixture of rheostatic and Fell rail braking in service. It had been found by trial and error that the maximum permissible temperature (about white hot) of the resistances was reached after about 10 minutes of continual rheostatic braking and the roof mounted resistors provided the peculiar sight of an electric tramcar standing with clouds of steam drifting off the roof. By October 1977 London Transport had finally completed a specification for proper rheostats to cope with a continuous load,

and a contract was placed with Westinghouse Brake & Signal Co. Ltd., who duly provided heavy-duty Cor-ten units, two per car, and each weighing 125 lbs. The first set of these was fitted to Snaefell No. 6 in 1979, and the five other cars were subsequently fitted. For the work involved in producing a scheme for continual rheostatic braking. London Transport International was paid a further £15,000. The Snaefell cars were also fitted with the electric bells off the Aachen cars together with headlamps for evening operation.

Since the re-equipment scheme was finally completed, the Snaefell fleet has operated quite successfully in spite of the demerits introduced by it. There can be no doubt that the cars have more than ample power for from a set of four 25 h.p. motors to four 61 h.p. motors with a total rating of 244 h.p. is rather more than a quantum leap. Both in theory and in practice the series-only motor control contravenes universal traction practice and is indefensible. Many cogent arguments in favour of electromagnetic track brakes fell on deaf ears, and the Aachen units were scrapped. By far the most serious shortcoming, irrespective of any other provisions incorporated, was the retention of the Hopkinson bow collectors. The Aachen cars were equipped with modern pantographs and these could have been readily adapted. The decision to use the Aachen wheels with their very narrow treads had led to innumerable derailments and a vastly increased expenditure on track maintenance to ensure that the gauge is maintained to very close tolerances. Whilst there had been no derailments on the Snaefell main line between 1920 and 1977, thereafter it became by no means uncommon to have up to three assorted minor derailments in a single day. It is now planned to re-wheel the entire fleet. The disruption to services caused by the old equipment of 1895 has in part given way to those caused by the defects introduced by the LT programme. The Fell centre-rail, now understood by everyone not to be a means of preventing derailments, remains in situ in increasing dereliction. There has been no suggestion that power costs have in any way diminished.

There is no evidence that any advantage accrued from the re-equipment of all of the six cars, instead of the five proposed by RTTS; although Snaefell traffic has held up well in the face of a declining market, it must be remembered that seasonal tourists between the May

Snaefell Car No. 2 at the points leading to the depot. This photograph, taken c.1978 shows the five segment connection from the main line. The points are being controlled by the man on the left.

and September period of 1981 amounted to 456,643. In 1985 the figure was 351,240, and by 1986 had dropped to 339,284. On the question of whether London Transport managed to effect the scheme within overall fees of £165,000, and given the otherwise exorbitant costs of this undertaking, it would seem at best to be unlikely. At the time, some insisted that the cost over-run was met by the unfortunate ratepayers of the Greater London Council; a major critic of LT, Sir Horace Cutler, was said to have regarded the ill-fated LT involvement in the Snaefell line as "severely indicative."

THE SUMMIT HOTEL

For many years the Summit Hotel was very professionally managed by Mr. George Lawson of Laxey, who was responsible for the only trading profits produced anywhere within the aegis of the MER Board, but when his retirement loomed, efforts were made to lease off the hotel. As it happened this was averted by public ridicule, but in 1982 the Board again offered to lease the Hotel, which was taken over by Mr. K. Whipp of Douglas. On the night of 5th–6th August 1982 the hotel was gutted by a major fire which was discovered only when a member of the Civil Aviation Authority found smoke and flames belching from the building on his way to work. As a result the Mountain Railway service was suspended until 9th August. Despite the short time it took in 1906 to build the original hotel, the wrecked hotel stayed closed throughout the 1983 season and finally reopened in 1984. The freight traffic generated by this rebuilding was accommodated on a new siding, laid on the Summit side of the Bungalow crossing and by the insertion of a crossover a short distance from the Summit terminus, which enabled passenger cars to load or unload, clear of rebuilding operations. Two of the 1895 car trucks were given small wagon bodies for this work, though they were evidently not fitted with brakes. The Hotel has subsequently passed into other hands.

CONCLUSION

The Snaefell Mountain Tramway has now seen over 90 seasons and provides a valued service to the tourist as well as remaining the first and only such electric mountain railway in the British Isles. It remains to this day as a unique testament to the ingenuity and flair of the Victorian engineers who conceived and constructed it, and to those who have maintained and worked this most remarkable line ever since.

CORRECTION:

The caption for the back cover photograph printed opposite is incorrect. It should read:

Back Cover: A scene at Laxey on 30th May 1974. Passengers are having their tickets checked as they board Snaefell Mountain Railway car No. 5, whilst a Manx Electric Railway crossbench motor with trailer No. 62 has arrived from Douglas. Snaefell car No. 5 was burnt out on 16th August 1970 and is seen here in its rebuilt form with sliding ventilators on the windows.

Bernard Mettam

ABOUT THE AUTHOR

Mike Goodwyn has had a deep and personal interest in the MER since 1949 and has lived on the Island since 1973. He was elected to the committee of the local Manx Electric Railway Society (a registered charity) in 1976 and became chairman in 1978, a position he still holds. He has travelled extensively throughout the world in pursuit of the electric tramcar and its technology.

His prime interest in tramway and electric light railway technology relates to the study of trucks and their associated equipment; in 1978 he was the Gratwicke Memorial Lecturer at the Science Museum, London, and the TLRS's "Evolution of the British Electric Tramcar Truck" was the first definitive outline of the subject to be published in Britain. His other booklets include "Douglas Head Marine Drive and Tramway, 1978 (reprinted 1993), Manx Transport Kaleidoscope (1977), Snaefell Mountain Railway (1986) and others, usually published by the Manx Electric Railway Society.

Mike Goodwyn is employed as a Motorman on the MER.

THE MANX ELECTRIC RAILWAY SOCIETY

Originally formalised in 1973, the Manx Electric Railway Society is charged with the express purpose of protecting and promoting the retention and development of the MER and other Island tramways at reasonable cost. It successfully campaigned for the reinstatement and re-opening of the Laxey – Ramsey section of the MER in 1975 – 7. The Society became a Registered Charity in 1978. The Manx Electric Railway Society is the only Island-based organisation concerned with all aspects of Island transport, and pursues an active and direct interest through its comprehensive and fully-illustrated magazine, MANX TRANSPORT REVIEW, the Island's leading transportation journal which deals with road, rail, sea and air transport topics. It is scheduled for publication every fourth month and is distributed free to members. It includes major historical and technical articles and forms a vital forum for the exchange of views. It is of paramount importance to all who have an interest in the Island's fascinating panoply of transport, past and present.

If you wish to keep abreast of developments and informed of historical research into the many aspects of Manx tramways, railways, buses, coaches, shipping and aviation, MANX TRANSPORT REVIEW is the only publication that provides both comprehensive and objective coverage.

Members of the MER Society also qualify for special discounts on booklets and publications as they are introduced. Ordinary membership is currently £5.00 per annum, from 1st April of each year. For details of membership and a free sample copy of the magazine, and a list of publications and sales items, please write to:

The Manx Electric Railway Society, PO Box 117, Douglas, Isle of Man. IM99 1JS.